HORRIBLE
SCIENCE

Nick Arnold has been writing stories and books since he was a youngster, but never dreamt he'd find fame writing about Fatal Forces. His research involved falling off buildings, lying on a bed of nails and skiing uphill and and he enjoyed every minute of it.
When he's not delving into Horrible Science, he spends his spare time teaching adults in a college.

His hobbies include eating pizza, riding his bike and thinking up corny jokes (though not all at the same time).

Tony De Saulles picked up his crayons when he was still in nappies and has been doodling ever since. He takes Horrible Science very seriously and even agreed to test what happens when your parachute doesn't open. Fortunately, his injuries weren't too serious.
When he's not out with his sketchpad, Tony likes to write poetry and play squash, though he hasn't written any poetry about squash yet.

Fatal Forces

Text © Nick Arnold, 1997, 2014
Illustrations © Tony De Saulles, 1997, 2014
Index by Caroline Hamilton

First published in the UK by Scholastic Ltd, 1997
Korean translation © Willbook, 2025

This edition is published by arrangement with Scholastic UK Ltd through KidsMind Agency, Korea.

이 책의 한국어판 저작권은 키즈마인드 에이전시를 통해 Scholastic UK와 독점 계약한 윌북에 있습니다.
신 저작권법에 의해 한국 내에서 보호를 받는 저작물이므로 무단 전재와 복제를 금합니다.

처음 만나는 과학 영어 수업

HORRIBLE SCIENCE

닉 아놀드·지소철 글 | 토니 드 솔스 그림

FATAL FORCES
물리

이 힘은 치명적이라고!

월북 주니어

✦ 이 책의 사용법 ✦

1. 100% 영어로 쓰인 〈Horrible Science〉 원문을 한 챕터씩 읽는다.

2. 형광펜 표시가 된 단어와 밑줄 그은 문장을 눈여겨보며 읽는다. 기억해 두면 좋을 과학 용어와 과학적인 내용을 담은 문장이 표시되어 있다.

3 쉽게 풀어 쓴 해설을 읽으며 단어의 어원과 사용법, 문장의 구조와 해석문을 확인한다.

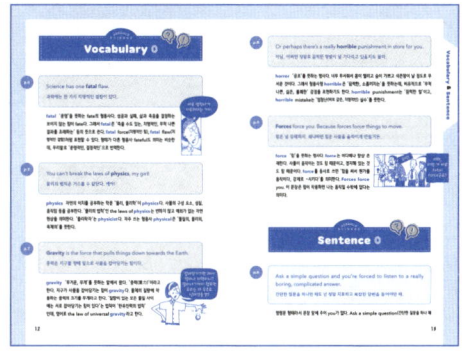

4 한층 더 똑똑해진 자신을 칭찬하며 다음 챕터로 넘어간다.

일러두기

- 이 책에 나오는 colour, centre, metre 등의 단어는 영국식 표기이고, 미국식으로는 color, center, meter라고 표기합니다. 이 책에서는 원서의 영국식 표기를 그대로 사용했습니다.

- 과학 용어 표기는 《2022 개정 교육과정에 따른 교과용도서 개발을 위한 편수자료 Ⅲ – 기초 과학, 정보 편》을 따랐습니다.

목차

이 책의 사용법	4
0. Introduction	8
1. Nasty Newton	15
2. Forceful facts	44
3. Smashing speed	63
4. Gruesome gravity	89
5. Under pressure	118
6. Facts about friction	138
7. Stretching and straining	163
8. Getting in a spin	180
9. Bouncing back	209

10. Mighty machines	226
11. Build or bust	243
12. May the forces be with you	266

Fatal Forces quiz	273
Index	283

CHAPTER 0 KEYWORDS

#force #physics #gravity

Introduction

Science has one fatal flaw. It can be seriously boring. Ask a simple question and you're forced to listen to a really boring, complicated answer.

And some answers have masses of mysterious mathematics ···

And don't try arguing with a scientist either⋯

Or you'll get a forceful reply⋯

See what I mean? It's enough to make you die of boredom. Now that would be fatal.

* English translations:

1. Gravity is the force that pulls things down towards the Earth. The same force pulls a smaller object towards a much larger object.
2. Gravity makes the ball speed up as it falls. This depends on the mass (amount of material) in the Earth and your distance from the Earth's centre.
3. You're asking too many questions. I'll try blinding you with science.

So what are these laws? And what happens if you break them? Do you get expelled? Or perhaps there's a really horrible punishment in store for you. Maybe you'll be forced to endure extra science lessons with megatons of homework? And who forces you to obey these horrible laws anyway? Teachers? No.

Forces force you. Because forces force things to move. And a force can be anything from you flicking a pea, to the awesome gravity of a giant star. So the effects of forces can be an inter-galactic explosion or the pea ending up in your teacher's ear-hole. (This might cause an explosion too!)

But forces can have fascinating fatal effects. Like crushing people, or making them sick, or pulling their heads off. (Getting forces wrong at school isn't usually quite as fatal – just a bit of en-forced detention from your teacher.)

So here's the real-life story of forces. It's a story involving fatal fortunes and horrible happenings. And it's all true. And who knows? Afterwards you might feel that forces have a fatal attraction for you, too. You might even force your teacher to take your science homework seriously. If you can just force yourself to read the next page now…

REVIEW

왜 공을 위로 아무리 세게 던져도 결국 밑으로 떨어질까? 왜 지구가 태양의 주위를 돈다고 할까? 왜 토끼는 빠르고 거북이는 느릴까? 왜 엄마는 버럭 화를 내실까?

모두 force, '힘' 때문이다. 힘은 뭐든 움직이고 변하게 만든다. 이런 힘을 공부하는 학문을 physics, '물리학'이라고 한다. 쪼금은 어렵고 무척 재미있다. 지금부터 우리가 사는 지구를 포함해 우주에 어떤 힘이 존재하는지 알아보자!

Vocabulary ❶

p.8

Science has one **fatal** flaw.
과학에는 한 가지 치명적인 결함이 있다.

fatal '운명'을 뜻하는 fate의 형용사다. 성공과 실패, 삶과 죽음을 결정하는 보이지 않는 힘이 **fate**다. 그래서 **fatal**은 '죽을 수도 있는, 치명적인, 무척 나쁜 결과를 초래하는' 등의 뜻으로 쓴다. **fatal** force(치명적인 힘), **fatal** flaw(치명적인 결함)처럼 표현할 수 있다. 형태가 다른 형용사 **fateful**도 비슷한 의미로, '운명적인, 결정적인'이라는 뜻이다.

p.9

You can't break the laws of **physics**, my girl!
물리의 법칙은 거스를 수 없단다, 얘야!

physics 자연의 이치를 공부하는 학문인 '물리, 물리학'이다. 사물의 구성 요소, 성질, 움직임 등을 공부한다. '물리의 법칙'인 the laws of **physics**는 변하지 않고 예외가 없는 자연 현상이다. '물리학자'는 **physicist**다. 자주 쓰는 형용사 **physical**은 '물질의, 물리의, 육체의'를 뜻한다.

p.9

Gravity is the force that pulls things down towards the Earth.
중력은 지구를 향해 밑으로 사물을 잡아당기는 힘이다.

gravity '무거운, 무게'를 뜻하는 말에서 왔다. '중력(重力)'이라고 한다. 지구가 사물을 잡아당기는 힘이 **gravity**다. 물체의 질량에 작용하는 중력의 크기를 무게라고 한다. '질량이 있는 모든 물질 사이에는 서로 잡아당기는 힘이 있다'는 법칙이 '만유인력의 법칙'인데, 영어로 the law of universal **gravity**라고 한다.

> Or perhaps there's a really **horrible** punishment in store for you.
> 아님, 어쩌면 정말로 끔찍한 형벌이 널 기다리고 있을지도 몰라.

horror '공포'를 뜻하는 명사다. 너무 무서워서 몸이 떨리고 숨이 가쁘고 식은땀이 날 정도로 무서운 것이다. 그래서 형용사형 **horrible**은 '끔찍한, 소름끼치는'이라는 뜻인데, 비유적으로 '무척 나쁜, 싫은, 불쾌한' 감정을 표현하기도 한다. **horrible** punishment는 '끔찍한 벌'이고, **horrible** mistake는 '엄청난(바보 같은, 치명적인) 실수'를 뜻한다.

> **Forces** force you. Because forces force things to move.
> 힘은 널 강제하지. 왜냐하면 힘은 사물을 움직이게 만들거든.

force '힘'을 뜻하는 명사다. **force**는 어디에나 항상 존재한다. 사물이 움직이는 것도 힘 때문이고, 정지해 있는 것도 힘 때문이다. **force**를 동사로 쓰면 '힘을 써서 뭔가를 움직이다, 강제로 ~시키다'라는 의미다. Forces force you. 이 문장은 힘이 작용하면 나는 움직일 수밖에 없다는 뜻이다.

Sentence 0

> Ask a simple question and you're forced to listen to a really boring, complicated answer.
> 간단한 질문을 하나만 해도 넌 정말 지루하고 복잡한 답변을 들어야만 해.

명령문 형태라서 문장 앞에 주어 you가 없다. Ask a simple question(간단한 질문을 하나 해

봐) 다음에 붙은 and는 '그러면'으로 해석한다. [명령문 A and 문장 B]는 'A하라, 그러면 B하게 된다'는 의미다.

p.9

Gravity makes the ball speed up as it falls.
중력은 공이 낙하할 때 속도를 증가시킨다.

[make A 동사]는 'A가 ~하게 만들다'란 표현이다. speed up은 '속도를 더하다, 더 빨라지다'를 뜻한다. as it falls는 '공이 떨어지면서, 공이 떨어질 때'를 뜻하는 부사절이다.

p.10

Getting forces wrong at school isn't usually quite as fatal - just a bit of enforced detention from your teacher.
학교에서 힘을 잘못 사용하는 것은 대개 그다지 치명적이지 않아. 선생님이 강제로 나머지 공부를 시키는 정도겠지.

문장의 주어인 Getting forces wrong at school은 '학교에서 힘을 잘못(나쁘게) 받는 것'을 뜻한다. fatal 다음에는 as you think 정도가 생략되었다고 보면 된다. as fatal (as you think)로, '(네가 생각하는 것만큼) 치명적인'을 뜻한다.
detention은 다른 곳에 가지 못하게 한곳에 가둬 둔다는 의미인데, 학교에서 쓰면 '방과 후 남아 있기' 처벌을 뜻한다.

CHAPTER 1 KEYWORDS

#Newton #Newton's law #Principia #Calculus

Nasty Newton

The prisoner was sick. In the madness of his fever he imagined the courtroom candles were fiery ghosts. Again and again he heard the sentence of the judges: "Death!" Then he fainted.

He awoke in darkness. Dragging himself upright he tried to explore the pitch black cell. His feet slithered on the slimy floor. Then he stumbled, his hands grabbing at empty air. He'd collapsed on the edge of a bottomless pit. One more step and he'd have dropped like a stone. Exhausted, the prisoner fell asleep. But when

he awoke he found himself strapped to a low bench. Helpless, he peered upwards and gasped in horror.

A giant statue towered over him. The grotesque figure had a huge pendulum swinging from its hands. The pendulum swung to and fro with an evil hiss. It ended in a razor-sharp blade and each slow sweep brought the blade a little lower. A little closer. Hiss… hiss… HISSSSSS! Scores of huge rats stared hungrily from the shadows, waiting to feast on the prisoner's butchered corpse. The deadly hissing blade skimmed his bare chest…

DON'T PANIC! It's only a story – The Pit and the Pendulum was written in 1849 by the American author Edgar Alan Poe. But for scientists Poe's story has a fatal fascination. The nasty forms of death – the pit and the pendulum – involve forces. Falling into the well under the influence of gravity; the pendulum's swing controlled by gravity and centripetal force (see page 181). (That's the

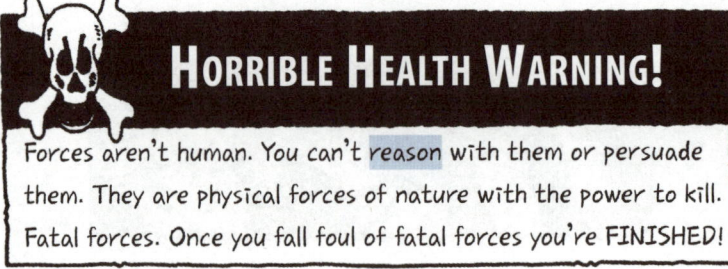

HORRIBLE HEALTH WARNING!

Forces aren't human. You can't reason with them or persuade them. They are physical forces of nature with the power to kill. Fatal forces. Once you fall foul of fatal forces you're FINISHED!

force on the pendulum shaft that stops the swinging weight pulling away from the rest of the machine.) These forces are fatal for the prisoner.

Postscript:

Oh – by the way you'll be pleased to know the prisoner escapes. How? By getting the rats to gnaw through his straps, of course. Bet you didn't think of that! Amazingly enough these forces had already been explained by a forceful scientific mega-star, the amazing Sir Isaac Newton.

 **Hall of fame:** Sir Isaac Newton (1642–1727)
Nationality: British

Isaac Newton was born on Christmas Day. The doctor thought baby Isaac wouldn't live because he was so weak and small.

But Isaac survived. He soon became interested in science but his teachers didn't think he was especially brainy. In fact, Isaac was too busy performing experiments at home to work hard at school. (Don't try this excuse.) When young Isaac was 16 his mum asked him to run the family farm. But he proved to be a useless farmer. He spent all his time experimenting and allowed the sheep to guzzle their way through a cornfield.

So Isaac went to Cambridge University instead. At University he read every maths book he could find. (Including the ones without pictures.) He wore scruffy clothes and was so absent-minded he often got lost on his way to supper. As far as Isaac was concerned supper was for wimps. Who needed supper when you could do lovely science calculations instead?

In 1665 a deadly plague struck London. Soon 7,000 people were dying every week and the authorities closed Cambridge University to stop the plague spreading. So Isaac went home. But instead of taking a holiday he  did extra homework. Very strange. But what homework! He invented calculus – a mathematical system still used today to plan rocket trips, and he also discovered that light contains colours.

These vital discoveries were to influence maths and physics for 300 years. Then Isaac made a really incredible breakthrough. It may have happened like this…

The apple and the moon

Woolsthorpe, England 1666

It was getting dark, but the skinny young man ran his fingers through his shoulder-length hair and carried on reading. Isaac Newton was sitting in the orchard trying to figure out how the moon went round the Earth. Suddenly a call rang out from the old farmhouse:

"Hmm," thought Isaac, "she always calls me half an hour before supper. It's a trick to get me in on time."

So he did nothing. If he had left the orchard when his mother called him the entire history of science would have been different. But just then something grabbed his attention.

It had been waiting for this moment. Waiting for months, silently. At first it was no larger than a tiny green bulge. But now it was bright red and the size of a man's fist. A living bubble of water and sugars with sweet juicy flesh and bitter seeds all wrapped in a waxy skin. An apple. The most famous apple in science.

"Isaac! Your supper's on the table and it's your favourite!"

"Coming, mother!"

Isaac shivered as a cool breeze rustled the trees. Then he sighed and reluctantly closed his book. There was a silent snap. The slender stalk holding the apple to the tree gave way. Wrenched by an unseen force the apple hurtled downward. It tumbled through the rustling leaves and bounced gently on Isaac's brainy bonce.

What would you have done? Perhaps you'd have eaten your supper and forgotten the apple. But Isaac wasn't like that. He rubbed his head and looked at the moon. It shone like a bright silver coin in the evening sky.

"So why doesn't the moon fall, too?" he asked himself, as he absent-mindedly munched the famous apple.

For some strange reason Isaac remembered his school and the dreaded "bucket game". He hated the other kids for making him play. He remembered having to whirl a bucket of water around his head on a rope. It was hard work and Isaac was a thin little boy. But amazingly all the water had stayed in the bucket as if trapped by an unseen force.

"Maybe that's what keeps the moon in place," he murmured.

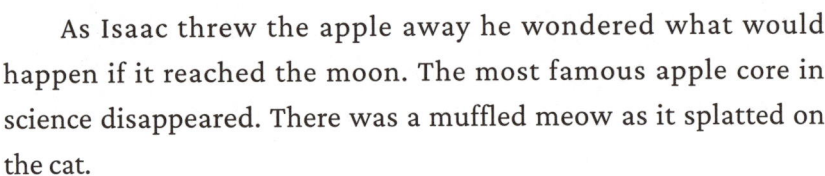

Then his mother shouted again: "Isaac, your supper's on the table and it's stone cold."

"I said I'm coming, mother!"

As Isaac threw the apple away he wondered what would happen if it reached the moon. The most famous apple core in science disappeared. There was a muffled meow as it splatted on the cat.

Isaac had forgotten his supper. He was calculating how strong gravity would need to be to stop the apple sailing into space. Then he thought about how fast the moon has to move to prevent it crashing down to Earth.

Later a very annoyed Mrs Newton stood in the doorway shielding her candle from the cold night air.

"Isaac!" she yelled. "I've fed your supper to the cat. And I'm going to feed your breakfast to the pigs!"

There was no answer from the orchard. But Isaac was still out there. And still thinking hard.

Test Your Teacher

How much does your teacher really know about this famous scientist?

1 As a child what was Isaac Newton's favourite toy?
a) A chemistry set.
b) A toy windmill powered by a mouse in a wheel.
c) He hated toys. He preferred tricky maths sums.

2 What did he buy on his first day at university?
a) A desk, ink and a notebook for extra homework.
b) New clothes and a ticket to the local fun fair.
c) A loaf of bread to eat.

3 How did Newton solve tricky scientific problems?
a) The answers came in a flash of inspiration when Newton was on the toilet.
b) By talking things over with scientific friends.
c) Worrying away at the problem day and night until he figured out the answer.

4 Newton became Professor of Mathematics at Cambridge but no one attended his bum-numbingly boring lectures. So what did he do?
a) He rounded up students and forced them to listen.
b) Carried on talking to an empty room.
c) Tried to make his lectures interesting with a few jokes and amusing stories.

5 Newton's dog, Diamond, knocked over a candle and years of hard work went up in flames. What did he do?
a) Drew his sword and killed the dog.
b) Re-wrote his work from memory.
c) He told the dog off and went on to study something new and experimental.

Answers:

1 b) He designed it himself. **2 a)**, **3 c)**, **4 b)** Does your teacher have this problem? **5 b)**.

What your teacher's score means.
1-2 Your teacher's guessing.
3-4 Your teacher knows a bit but doesn't know everything. (Much like any other teacher.)
5 Hard luck. Your teacher's read this book.

Newton's moving book

Newton didn't publish his discoveries for 20 years. He was too busy with his mathematical work. But then at last, fearful others might grab the glory, Newton wrote a book about his ideas. He shut himself away for 18 months and worked 20 hours a day.

Sometimes Newton's assistant reminded him that he'd missed supper.

"Have I?" Newton would murmur sleepily. Then he nibbled at the food and got back to work.

Newton's book was called The Philosophiae Naturalis Principia Mathematica and it was the most brilliant science book ever written. In it he explained the whole universe in a way that made sense. (Well – it would have made sense if the book hadn't been in Latin and filled with mystifying maths.) Newton described gravity and three crucial laws about forces and how things move. These laws show how squids squirt water backwards in order to move forwards. They explain what happens when distant stars blow up and why low-flying sparrow droppings splat on your head.

One way to imagine Newton's laws is to think of a really horrible morning. What d'you mean – every day's like that?

Newton's First Law

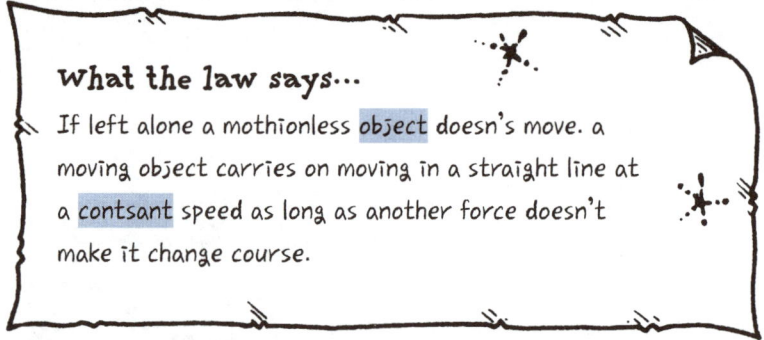

What the law says...
If left alone a mothionless object doesn's move. a moving object carries on moving in a straight line at a contsant speed as long as another force doesn't make it change course.

What the Law means...
You stare wearily at your breakfast. Your cornflakes are motionless and they're going to stay that way until you summon up the energy to eat them. You clumsily knock your spoon and half your breakfast goes flying. A cornflake falls on your dad's head. The

cornflake would have flown in the same direction for ever but the force of gravity pulled it down.

Newton's Second Law

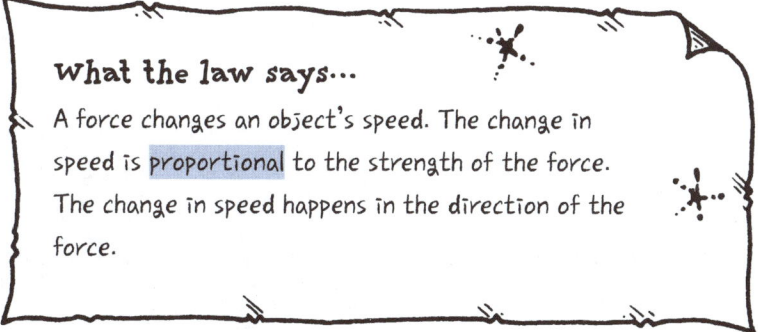

what the law says...
A force changes an object's speed. The change in speed is proportional to the strength of the force. The change in speed happens in the direction of the force.

What the Law means...
The harder you kick the ball, the faster it flies in that direction. It's a rotten result for the goalie!

Newton's Third Law

what the law says...
When an object exerts a force on another object the second object will push back just as hard.

What the Law means…
You're late and you're jogging to school. But you're still not properly awake. You slam into a lamppost. And the lamppost wallops you back! It's true – this really does happen.

Bet you never knew!

When Newton's apple hit the ground the Earth bumped against the apple. That's what Newton's Third Law says: things always push back with equal force. But the Earth moved such a tiny distance no one noticed. Oddly enough a unit of force was later named the "Newton" in the scientist's honour. And the weight produced by one Newton is roughly the same as… an apple. But Newton was no ordinary genius. He had a nasty side, too.

Newton's nasty nature

1. When Newton was three years old his mum remarried. Isaac hated his stepfather and often thought of killing him. He didn't of course, but he was pleased when the stepfather died.

2. At school Newton had no friends until he thumped the school bully with great force. Newton was smaller than his opponent but his courage helped win the fight. After this nasty incident Newton became popular.

3. Newton disliked women and never married. He hated his friend John Locke's attempts to introduce him to ladies. Later Newton wrote to Locke:

When a woman told me you were sickly and would not live, I answered t'were better you were dead.

THANKS A LOT!

1. Nasty Newton

But that didn't stop Newton generously allowing his niece Catherine to do his cooking and cleaning.

4) Newton was a miserable man. He had no hobbies apart from work. He rarely laughed and he called poetry:

5) In 1686 Newton fell out with scientist Robert Hooke (1635–1703). Hooke unjustly accused Newton of pinching his ideas on gravity. In a letter Newton called Hooke "a pretender and a grasper" and refused to talk to him.

6) After writing the Principia Newton had a nasty turn. He went mad for two years and did no scientific research. Some historians reckon Newton was a bit depressed but others say he was poisoned by the mercury he used for chemistry experiments.

7) When he got better Newton was appointed Warden of the Royal Mint and reformed Britain's coinage. It was said that nasty Newton enjoyed catching forgers and arranging especially nasty executions for them.

8 German Gottfried Leibniz (1646–1716) claimed he invented calculus. Newton accused Leibniz of pinching his idea. But in fact Leibniz had made the discovery independently at the same time as Newton. (And it was Leibniz who actually coined the word "calculus" – Newton called it "fluxions" – which sounds like the effects of a nasty tummy bug.)

9 Newton came to a horrible end. He moved to the country to improve his health. But a few weeks later he fell sick and died of a stone in his bladder. By then, however, he was a nasty-tempered old man of 84, but still a great genius.

Newton in his own words

Like many geniuses Newton was hard to understand. Here's what he said about himself:

Note: Newton didn't mean human pyramids. The giants he referred to were earlier scientists who inspired him.

He also said:

Note: Newton meant that he'd learnt enough to realize there was more to learn. He was right. He'd only scratched the surface. There are loads more fatally fascinating facts about forces. You'll find them in the next chapter.

REVIEW

영국의 수학자, 물리학자, 천문학자인 아이작 뉴턴은 중력과 만유인력의 법칙을 발견하고 증명한 위대한 인물이다. 뉴턴은 노력하는 천재 과학자였고, 다소 괴팍한 성격도 갖고 있었다. 1687년 근대 과학의 명저인 《자연철학의 수학적 원리 Philosophiae Naturalis Principia Mathematica》를 발표했는데, 흔히 "프린키피아"라고 부르는 이 책에는 가장 중요한 물리의 법칙들이 설명되어 있다. 그중에는 모두가 기억해야 할 세 가지 운동 원리가 있다.

- 뉴턴의 제1법칙 = 관성의 법칙
- 뉴턴의 제2법칙 = 가속도의 법칙
- 뉴턴의 제3법칙 = 작용/반작용의 법칙

Vocabulary 1

p.15

He'd **collapsed** on the edge of a bottomless pit.
그는 바닥이 없는 구덩이의 가장자리에 풀썩 쓰러졌다.

collapse '함께'를 뜻하는 col과 '떨어지다, 넘어지다'를 뜻하는 lapse가 합쳐진 말이다. '쓰러지다, 무너지다'란 의미인데, 살짝 넘어지거나 일부분이 무너지는 것이 아니라 '철퍼덕' 쓰러지거나 '와르르' 무너지는 모습을 표현하는 동사다.

p.16

The **grotesque** figure had a huge pendulum swinging from its hands.
괴기한 형상의 양손에는 흔들리는 커다란 추가 달려 있었다.

grotesque '동굴의(of cave)'를 뜻하는 말에서 왔다. 먼 옛날 사람들이 동굴에 그려 놓은 원시적인 그림이나 표식 등을 표현하는 말로 쓰기 시작했다. 수천 년 후 사람들의 눈에는 그런 것들이 이상하고 기괴하게 보일 수밖에 없다. 그래서 형용사 **grotesque**는 '괴상한, 기괴한'을 뜻한다.

p.16

The **pendulum** swung to and fro with an evil hiss.
그 진자는 쉭쉭 소름끼치는 소리를 내면서 앞뒤로 흔들렸다.

pendulum '매달려서 아래로 늘어진(hanging down)' 것을 표현하는 명사다. 이렇게 매달린 것은 바람이 불거나 힘을 가하면 앞뒤나 좌우로 움직이게 되는데, 가해진 힘이 다 사라질 때까지 계속 똑같이 움직인다. 이런 물건을 우리말로 '추, 진자'라고 부른다. 대표적으로 벽시계의 '추'가 있다.

p.16

You can't **reason** with them or persuade them.

당신은 그들과 논리적으로 따지거나 그들을 설득할 수가 없다.

reason '이유, 근거, 이성'을 뜻하는 명사로 자주 쓰는데, 여기서는 동사로 쓴 것이다. '생각하고 이해하다, 상식적으로 말이 통하다'라는 의미를 갖고 있다. them은 forces를 지칭한다.

p.17

In fact, Isaac was too busy performing **experiments** at home to work hard at school.

사실 아이작은 집에서 실험을 하느라 너무 바빠서 학교에서는 공부를 열심히 할 수 없었다.

experiment 호기심을 충족시키기 위해, 또는 어떤 사실이 맞는지 증명하기 위해 새로운 것을 해 보는 '실험'이 experiment다. 학생들이나 과학자들이 실험실에서 하는 '과학 실험'을 표현할 때 자주 쓴다. 형용사형 '실험의, 실험적인'은 **experimental**이다.

p.18

These vital discoveries were to **influence** maths and physics for 300 years.

이 중요한 발견들은 300년 동안 수학과 물리학에 영향을 미치게 되었다.

influence in은 '안으로'를, fluence는 '흐르다(flow)'를 뜻한다. 안으로 흘러들어 온다는 의미다. 마른 화초에 물이 흘러들면 생기를 띠게 되고, 연못으로 폐수가 흘러들면 오염된다. 어떤 식으로든 영향을 미치는 것이다. 그래서 **influence**는 주로 '영향, 영향력'을 뜻하는 명사로 쓰는데, 이 문장에서는 '영향을 주다(미치다)'를 뜻하는 동사로 썼다.

p.19

A living bubble of water and sugars with sweet juicy flesh and bitter seeds all **wrapped** in a waxy skin.

즙이 가득하고 달콤한 과육과 쓴 씨앗들이 전부 왁스 같은 껍질에 싸여 있는, 물과 당분으로 이루어진 생생한 구체.

wrap 종이나 천으로 어떤 물건을 둘러싸는 동작이다. '포장하다, 둘러싸다'를 뜻한다. **wrap**을 명사로 쓰면 '포장지'를 의미한다. 슈퍼마켓의 포장된 식재료, 식당에서 배달되는 포장 음식 등을 싸는 '비닐 랩'이 바로 이 **wrap**이다.

p.19

Wrenched by an unseen force the apple hurtled downward.

보이지 않는 힘에 비틀리고 끌려서 사과가 밑으로 떨어졌다.

wrench 세게 비틀거나 잡아당겨서 떼어 내는 동작을 표현하는 말이다. 나무에 달린 사과나 감, 배 등을 잡아당기거나 비틀어서 딸 때 아주 유용하게 쓸 수 있는 동사다. **wrench**를 명사로 쓰면 볼트나 나사 등을 비틀어 고정시키거나 열 때 사용하는 공구 '렌치'를 뜻한다.

p.20

"Maybe that's what keeps the moon in place," he **murmured**.

그가 중얼거렸다. "어쩌면 그것이 달을 제자리에 고정시키는 것일 수 있어."

murmur 우리말에 '구시렁거리다'란 표현이 있다. 남이 알아듣든 말든 혼잣말처럼 중얼거린다는 의미다. 이런 말을 표현하는 영어 동사 중 하나가 **murmur**다. '뭐라뭐라' 한다는 뉘앙스와 느낌이 통한다. '중얼거리다, 속삭이다'로 해석한다. '중얼거림, 속삭임'을 뜻하는 명사로도 쓸 수 있다.

1. Nasty Newton

p.20

He was **calculating** how strong gravity would need to be to stop the apple sailing into space.

아이작은 사과가 우주로 날아가는 것을 막으려면 얼마나 강한 중력이 필요한지 계산하고 있었다.

calculate calc는 흰색 가루가 나오는 '석회석'이다. 먼 옛날에 손가락 발가락을 십분 활용해 셈을 하다가 계산이 조금 복잡해지면 어딘가에 써서 계산을 해야 했는데, 대개 벽이나 나무판에 '백묵, 분필'로 써서 계산을 했다. 그래서 **calculate**는 '(조금 복잡한) 계산을 하다, 셈을 하다'를 뜻하는 말이 되었다. **calculator**는 '계산기'다.

p.21

The answers came in a flash of **inspiration** when Newton was on the toilet.

뉴턴이 변기에 앉아 있을 때 번쩍하는 영감과 함께 답이 떠올랐다.

inspire '안으로(in) 숨을 불어넣다(spire)'란 의미를 가진 동사다. '숨'은 생기와 활력을 의미한다. 내 안에서 생각과 감정이 부풀어 올라 새로운 아이디어와 의지와 꿈이 생기게 하는 것이 **inspire**다. '영감을 주다, (감정, 욕구 등을) 부추기다, 격려하다'로 해석한다. 명사형 **inspiration**은 '영감, 격려, 고취'를 뜻한다.

p.23

He was too busy with his **mathematical** work.

뉴턴은 수학 연구로 너무 바빴다.

이래봬도 중요한 발견 중이라고.

mathematics '배우다(learn), 배운 지식'을 뜻하는 말에서 왔다. 배운다는 것은 우주의 진리를 탐구해 세상을 이해하는 것이었고, 그 기초가 수학이었다. **mathematics**는 흔히 줄여서 **math**로 표현한다. '수학 선생님'이 **math** teacher다. **mathematical**은 형용사로 '수학의, 수학적'을 뜻하고, '수학자'는 **mathematician**이라고 한다.

p.24

Newton described gravity and three **crucial** laws about forces and how things move.

뉴턴은 중력, 힘에 관한 세 가지 중요한 법칙, 사물의 운동 방식에 대해 설명했다.

crucial '교차, 십자가'를 뜻하는 crux에서 온 말이다. 갈림길, 교차로에는 항상 십자가 모양의 표지판이 서 있다. 예를 들어 고속도로에도 왼쪽에는 '서울', 오른쪽에는 '부산'으로 갈림길이 표시된 푯말이 있는데, 반대 방향으로 가면 낭패다. 대단히 중요한 선택, 결정, 운명 같은 뜻을 갖고 있기 때문에, 형용사 **crucial**은 '중대한, 결정적인'이라는 뜻이 된다.

p.24

If left alone a motionless **object** doesn't move.

움직이지 않는 물체를 그대로 두면 움직이지 않는다.

object ob는 '앞'을, ject는 '던지다'를 뜻한다. 앞에 뭔가를 던져서 막거나, 앞에 놓아둔 물건을 뜻하는 말이다. 그래서 명사 **object**는 앞에 있어서 보거나 만질 수 있는 '물건, 사물'을 뜻한다. 물건을 앞에 두어 전진하지 못하게 막는다는 의미에서 '반대, 항의'를 뜻하기도 한다. a motionless **object**는 '움직이지 않는 물건'이다.

p.24

A moving object carries on moving in a straight line at a **constant** speed as long as another force doesn't make it change course.

움직이는 물체는 다른 힘이 진로를 바꾸지 않는 한 일정한 속도로 계속해서 직선으로 움직인다.

constant '함께'를 뜻하는 con과 '서 있다, 같은 자리에 있다'를 뜻하는 stant가 합쳐진 말로 함께 있거나 붙어 다니는 모습을 표현하는 말이다. 그래서 항상 내 곁에 붙어 있는 친구가 a **constant** friend다. 변함없이 그 자리에 있고 어디에나 붙어 다니기 때문에 **constant**는 '계속되는, 변함없는'을 뜻하는 형용사로 쓴다. '계속, 항상'이라는 뜻의 부사형은 **constantly**다.

p.25

The change in speed is **proportional** to the strength of the force.

속도의 변화는 힘의 세기에 비례한다.

proportion port는 '나누다(part)'를 뜻하고, 앞에 붙은 pro-는 '미리, 우선'을 뜻한다. 어떻게 나눌지 미리 정하거나, 그렇게 정해서 나눠진 부분을 뜻하는 말로 쓴다. '비율, 부분'이다. 형용사형인 **proportional**은 '비례하는, ~비율의'라는 뜻인데, 대개 [A is **proportional** to B](A는 B에 비례한다)의 형태로 쓴다.

p.26

When an object **exerts** a force on another object the second object will push back just as hard.

한 물체가 다른 물체에 힘을 가하면, 두 번째(힘을 받은) 물체는 그만큼의 힘으로 밀어 낸다.

exert '밖으로 밀다, 앞으로 뻗다'란 의미를 갖고 있다. 뭔가를 밀거나 잡기 위해서 힘을 쓰는 것이다. 에너지, 힘, 능력 등을 '발휘하다' 또는 '열심히 노력하다, 애쓰다'라는 뜻이다. 명사형은 '노력, 수고, 발휘'를 뜻하는 **exertion**이다.

p.27

But Newton was no **ordinary** genius.

그러나 뉴턴은 결코 평범한 천재가 아니었다.

ordinary ordin은 '질서(order)'를 뜻한다. 처음에 **ordinary**는 '질서 있는'을 뜻하는 말이었다. 차들이 정해진 속도와 차선을 맞춰 달리면 사고가 나지 않는다. 학생들이 말을 잘 들으면 선생님이 화낼 일이 없다. 질서가 잡히면 이렇게 세상이 사건·사고 없이 조용하고 평범하게 돌아가는 것이다. 그래서 **ordinary**는 질서 있는 상태가 계속되는 '일상적인, 평범한, 보통의'를 뜻하는 형용사로 쓴다.

p.28

He rarely laughed and he called poetry: A kind of **ingenious** nonsense.

그는 거의 웃지 않았고, 시를 '일종의 기발한 난센스'라고 불렀다.

ingenious in-은 '안에, 안으로'를, gen은 '물려받은, 타고난'을 의미한다. 부모에게서 물려받거나 자연적으로 생성되어 내 안에 있는 '지적인 능력, 재능'을 뜻한다. 그래서 형용사형인 **ingenious**는 '독창적인, 생각이 기발한'을 뜻하는 말로, an **ingenious** idea(기발한 생각), an **ingenious** inventor(독창적인 발명가)처럼 쓸 수 있다. 명사형 **ingenuity**는 '독창성, 기발한 생각이나 재주'를 뜻한다.

p.28

Some historians **reckon** Newton was a bit depressed but others say he was poisoned by the mercury he used for chemistry experiments.

몇몇 역사가들은 뉴턴이 약간 우울증을 겪었다고 판단하지만, 또 다른 이들은 그가 화학 실험에 사용한 수은에 중독되었다고 말한다.

reckon '곧은, 똑바로(straight)'란 의미가 담겨 있다. 이성적으로 생각해서 말하고, 실수 없이 똑바로 계산하고, 상식에 맞게 판단하는 것이 **reckon**이다. 그래서 근거와 법칙에 따라 '~라고 생각하다, 판단하다, 예상하다'를 뜻하는 동사로 쓴다. 명사형은 **reckoning**이다.

p.28

It was said that nasty Newton enjoyed catching forgers and arranging especially nasty **executions** for them.

성미 고약한 뉴턴은 화폐 위조범들을 잡아서 특별히 더 끔찍한 처형을 하는 것을 즐겼다고 한다.

execute '끝까지 따르다'란 뜻이 담겨 있다. 법과 명령에 따라 끝까지 일을 완수한다는 의미다. 그래서 동사 **execute**는 '실행하다, 수행하다'란 뜻으로 쓴다. 또한 중죄인을 법에 따라 끝까지 처벌한다는 의미에서 '사형을 집행하다, 처형하다'란 뜻으로도 쓴다. 명사형인 **execution**은 '실행, 수행, 사형 집행, 처형'을 뜻한다.

p.30

He'd only **scratched** the surface.

그는 겨우 표면만 긁은 셈이었다.

scratch '긁다, 할퀴다'를 뜻하는 동사다. surface는 '표면, 겉면, 지면, 수면' 등을 뜻하는 명사다. 그래서 **scratch** the surface는 '표면을 긁다, 겉을 긁어내다'란 뜻을 갖고 있는데, 부정적인 의미에서 근본적인 문제를 해결하지 않고 임시방편으로 대처할 때 쓰는 표현이다. 우리말 표현 중 '수박 겉핥기, 변죽만 울리기'에 해당한다.

Sentence 1

p.15

Dragging himself upright he tried to explore the pitch black cell.

그는 몸을 질질 끌듯이 힘겹게 일어서며 깜깜한 감방 안을 탐색하려 했다.

주어 he는 두 가지 동작을 동시에 하고 있다. 문장의 본동사에 해당하는 tried to explore는 '더듬어서 알아내려고 했다'라는 뜻이고, 그와 동시에 하는 행동은 dragging himself upright

(몸을 질질 끌듯이 힘겹게 일어서며)다. 이렇게 동사에 ing를 붙여서 동시에 하는 행동을 표현할 수 있다.

p.16

> Scores of huge rats stared hungrily from the shadows, waiting to feast on the prisoner's butchered corpse.
> 수십 마리의 커다란 시궁쥐들이 그림자 속에서 굶주린 눈으로 지켜보며 죄수의 도살된 시체를 맘껏 먹기를 기다리고 있었다.

이 문장에서 score는 '약 20개'를 뜻하는 말이다. 그래서 scores of huge rats는 정확히 셀 수는 없지만 '적어도 40마리가 넘는 커다란 시궁쥐들'을 뜻한다.
waiting 이하는 동시에 일어나는 일을 표현한 것으로, '그 죄수의 잘린 사체를 마음껏 먹을 수 있길 기다리며'로 해석할 수 있다. 즉 본동사인 stare(뚫어져라 지켜보다)와 wait(기다리다)는 동시 상황이다.

p.17

> Amazingly enough these forces had already been explained by a forceful scientific mega-star, the amazing Sir Isaac Newton.
> 대단히 놀랍게도 이런 힘은 이미 강력한 영향력을 행사하는 과학계의 슈퍼스타, 경이로운 아이작 뉴턴 경에 의해 설명되었다.

앞에 붙은 Amazingly enough는 '몹시 놀랍게도'라는 뜻의 부사구로, 문장 전체를 꾸며준다. a forceful scientific mega-star(강력한 과학계의 초대형 스타)와 the amazing Sir Isaac Newton(경이로운 아이작 뉴턴 경)은 같은 존재를 의미하는 '동격' 표현이다.

p.18

> As far as Isaac was concerned supper was for wimps.
> 아이작에게 있어 저녁 식사란 약골들을 위한 것이었다.

[as far as A be동사 concerned]는 'A의 입장에서는, A로서는' 등을 뜻하는 표현이다. 동사 concern은 '영향을 미치다, 관련짓다'를 뜻한다.
wimp는 심신이 미약한 '약골, 겁쟁이'다. supper was for wimps는 '저녁 식사는 약골들을 위한 것이었다'는 의미다.

1. Nasty Newton

p.19

If he had left the orchard when his mother called him the entire history of science would have been different.

만약 어머니가 불렀을 때 그가 과수원을 떠났더라면, 과학의 역사 전체가 달라졌을 것이다.

'과거에 이랬다면, 지금은 어땠을까'를 표현하는 가정법 문장이다. if he had left the orchard는 [had+left(leave의 완료형)]를 써서 '그가 과수원을 떠났다면'이라는 가정이고, when his mother called him은 바로 앞 문장을 보충해 주는 말이다. the entire history of science would have been different는 [would(should) have+been(동사의 완료형)]을 써서 '그랬다면 현재 과학의 역사는 달라졌을 것'이라는 뜻이다.

사과가 아니라 바나나가 떨어졌어도 나는 만유인력을 발견했을걸?

p.20

But amazingly all the water had stayed in the bucket as if trapped by an unseen force.

그런데 놀랍게도 물은 전부 마치 보이지 않는 힘에 갇힌 듯 양동이 안에 그대로 남아 있었다.

as if(though)가 이끄는 부사절은 '마치 ~인 듯이'로 해석한다. 이 문장에서 as if 다음에는 주어와 동사 all the water was가 생략되어 있다. 없어도 충분히 이해할 수 있기 때문에 생략한 것이다. '마치 보이지 않는 힘에 갇힌 것처럼'으로 해석한다.

p.23

But then at last, fearful others might grab the glory, Newton wrote a book about his ideas.

하지만 그러다 마침내 뉴턴은 다른 사람들이 그 영광을 가로챌까 두려워서 자신의 아이디어에 관한 책을 썼다.

But then은 '그러나 바로 ~할 때'를, at last는 '마침내, 드디어'를 뜻한다.
fearful others might grab the glory는 '나쁜 다른 사람들이 그 영광을 낚아챌 수도 있겠지만'으로 해석하면 된다.

p.24

They explain what happens when distant stars blow up and why low-flying sparrow droppings splat on your head.

그 법칙들은 멀리 있는 별들이 폭발할 때 무슨 일이 일어나는지, 그리고 낮게 날아다니는 참새 똥이 왜 네 머리에 떨어지는지 설명해 준다.

They explain이 주어와 동사다. 목적어는 두 개의 절이다. 첫 번째 목적절 what happens ~ blow up과 두 번째 목적절 why low-flying ~ your head가 and로 연결되어 있다. 설명하는(explain) 내용이 두 가지인 것이다.

p.25

Cornflake would travel in a straight line for ever if it wasn't for the force of gravity (and the ceiling).

중력의 힘(그리고 천장)이 없다면 콘플레이크는 영원히 직선으로 이동할 거야.

in a straight line은 '직선으로, 곧게'를 뜻하고, for ever(forever)는 '영원히'를 뜻한다. [if it wasn't for A]는 실제로는 일어나지 않은 상황을 가정하는 가정법 과거형 문장의 조건을 나타내는 절이다. 'A가 없다면, A가 아니라면'이라고 해석한다.

p.25

The harder you kick the ball, the faster it flies in that direction.

공을 더 세게 찰수록, 공은 더 빠르게 그 방향으로 날아간다.

'the 비교급(형용사/부사) 문장, the 비교급(형용사/부사) 문장'은 '더 ~할수록, 더 ~하다'라는 표현이다.

p.27

That's what Newton's Third Law says: things always push back with equal force.

뉴턴의 제3 법칙이 말하는 게 바로 그거다. 모든 물체는 항상 동일한 힘으로 밀어낸다.

주절인 That's ~ says는 '그것이 바로 뉴턴의 세 번째 법칙이 말하는 것이다'로 이해하면 된다.

'콜론(:)' 다음에 나오는 문장은 세 번째 법칙의 내용이다. 콜론은 구체적인 내용을 열거하거나 설명을 덧붙일 때 주로 사용한다.

p.27

At school Newton had no friends until he thumped the school bully with great force.

뉴턴은 학교 불량배를 흠씬 때려 주기 전까지는 학교에 친구가 하나도 없었다.

until은 '~ (할) 때까지'를 뜻하는 말로, 명사 앞에서 전치사로 쓰거나 이 문장에서처럼 부사절 앞에 접속사로 쓴다. until 이하는 '뉴턴이 엄청난 힘으로 학교 깡패를 때려눕혔을 때까지'로 해석할 수 있다.

p.29

And it was Leibniz who actually coined the word "calculus" - Newton called it "fluxions" - which sounds like the effects of a nasty tummy bug.

그리고 실제로 "미적분학"이라는 말을 만들어 낸 사람은 라이프니츠였다. 뉴턴은 이를 "플룩션스"라고 불렀는데, 이 용어는 끔찍한 장염 증상과 소리가 비슷하게 들린다.

[It is A who(that) ~]는 '~한 것은 A이다'란 의미로, A를 강조하기 위해 사용한다. calculus(미적분)란 말을 만든 것은 바로 Leibniz(라이프니츠)였다고 밝히는 내용이다.

which 이하는 fluxions를 묘사하는 내용이다. tummy bug은 '장염', sounds like는 '~ 같은 소리가 난다'는 말이다. 마치 고약한 장염 증상 같은 (설사 터지는) 소리로 들린다는 의미다.

p.29

> The giants he referred to were earlier scientists who inspired him.
>
> 뉴턴이 언급한 거인들은 그에게 영감을 준 과거의 과학자들이었다.

이 문장의 주어는 The giants he referred to(그가 언급한 거인들)다. were가 동사다. refer to는 '~을 언급하다, ~에 대해 말하다'를 뜻하는 표현이다.

p.30

> I seem to have been only a boy playing on the seashore… whilst the great ocean of truth lay all undiscovered before me.
>
> 저는 진실이라는 해변에서 놀고 있는 소년에 불과했던 것 같습니다…. 거대한 진리의 대양은 아직 내 앞에서 모습을 드러내지 않은 채 있고요.

seem to be는 '~인 듯하다'를 뜻하는 표현이므로, I seem to have been only a boy는 '난 그저 소년이었던 것 같습니다'로 해석할 수 있다. whilst는 '~동안, ~하는 사이'를 뜻하는 말로 while로 바꿔 쓸 수 있다.

> **CHAPTER 2 KEYWORDS**
> #gravity #universal gravitation #friction
> #centrifugal·centripetal

Forceful Facts

Forces are everywhere. You can't do much without bumping into them. But hopefully not with a fatal CRUNCH. Oddly enough, though, before Newton, people knew very little about how forces worked.

Mixed-up motion theories

A scientist will tell you that a force is something that affects the movement or shape of an object or person. Sounds fairly vague. But before Newton, scientific theories were even more mixed–up. One of the first people to write about forces was a Greek genius called Aristotle.

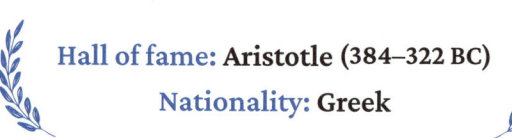

Hall of fame: **Aristotle (384–322 BC)**
Nationality: **Greek**

Aristotle was a doctor's son. His parents died when he was a child and as a young man he blew their money on wild parties. But when he was 17 years old Aristotle had a sudden change of heart and sent himself back to school.

He went to study under the brainy philosopher called Plato in the Academy at Athens. Aristotle liked it there so much that he stayed for the next 20 years as a pupil and then as a teacher.

Aristotle travelled for four years and eventually moved to Macedonia where his old mate Philip happened to be king. Phil asked Aristotle to teach his boy, Alexander. Aristotle must have done a good job because young Alexander became Alexander the Great and conquered a great chunk of Asia. By the time Aristotle died (of acute indigestion) he had written about everything from politics to how grasshoppers chirp. And he even had a few things to say about forces.

Mystery motions

Here's how Aristotle explained forces:

Wrong, wrong and wrong again. But for 2,000 years everyone thought Aristotle's wacko ideas were RIGHT. Eventually Newton used maths to prove Aristotle WRONG. So nowadays we've got forces sussed. As a scientist might say, "Learning about forces is as easy as riding a bike." Oh, yeah? Riding a bike is LOADS harder and just to prove it we've asked a scientist to try.

Lesson 1: Wobbly balance

Remember learning to ride a bike? Tough, wasn't it? Inside the scientist's ears are fluid–filled spaces, called semi–circular canals. (Teachers have a larger air–filled space where their brains should be. Ha ha.) These canals help her balance on two wheels. As the liquid sloshes around, sensors tell her brain whether she's still upright.

Her brilliant brain also notices the force of gravity, her speed, the slope and wind direction. Yep – all at the same time.

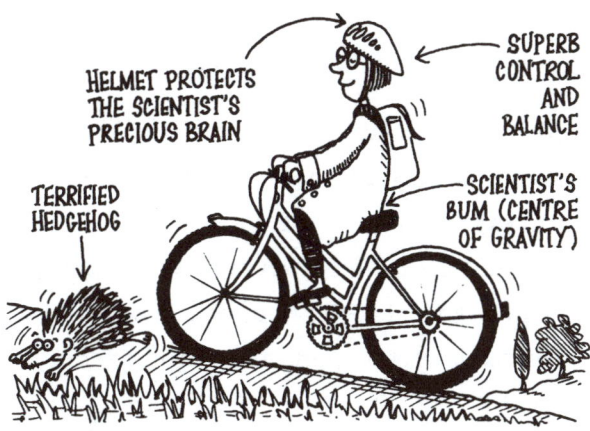

It helps her balance if her science books, sandwiches, etc. aren't draped over one handlebar. Ideally her bum is the centre of gravity – the point around which everything else is sensibly balanced.

Lesson 2: Effortless inertia

When she stands still inertia keeps her there. She overcomes inertia to get moving. Once she's moving, inertia keeps her going in a straight line. Mind you, she needs more pedal power to get up hills! Larger objects have more inertia. That's why it's hard to stop a

charging elephant. And if you're daft enough to try you might feel a bit flat afterwards!

Lesson 3: Mass-ive momentum

Momentum is a measure of the scientist's ability to keep going. And her momentum depends on her mass. If your reaction to this statement is to say "yer wot?", you'd better read the next bit. Mass means how much there is of the scientist – everything in her body, her clothes and even what she had for breakfast. Her mass, her bike's mass and her speed combine to produce her momentum. Wheee!

Lesson 4: Mixed-up momentum

Oops! She knocks the school bully flying. Scientists would say she's "transferred momentum" to the bully and call this "conserving momentum". The posh scientific word for speed in one direction is "velocity". So she'd better pedal at quite a velocity in order to conserve her life!

Oo–er the bully's heading towards her on a skateboard. THEY'RE GOING TO CRASH! As they crash the two momentums cancel each other. So they both grind to a halt. Result = TROUBLE!!!

Lesson 5: Galloping gravity

Velocity is greater when cycling downhill. Gravity tries to pull the scientist to the centre of the Earth. And the bottom of the slope is a bit nearer the centre of the planet than the top. This explains why, if she loses her balance, it's easier to fall off her bike than stay on. By the way, if she did make it right through to the Earth's centre, there would be no gravity and she would float around being roasted in the fiery heat. Not nice! Tired yet? Our scientist is. She's run out of kinetic energy. That's the posh scientific name for the energy she uses when moving. Oh well – we'll give her a few minutes to recover and then we'll put her back to work.

2. Forceful Facts   **49**

Lesson 6: Awkward acceleration and drag

For the scientist the word "acceleration" means changing speed or direction. So even when she slows down, she calls it "acceleration". But when she accelerates down a hill she feels the wind whistling up her nostrils (and everywhere else), and trying to slow her. This force is called "drag". If it's particularly windy it'll "drag" her off her bike – the result could be fatal.

Lesson 7: Curious cornering

As the scientist rounds the corner, centripetal (sen–tre–pee–tal) force pulls her bike into the corner. But her inertia opposes the change in course. It tries to keep her moving in a straight line – (remember Newton's First Law?) The scientist feels as if a force is pushing her outwards. As a scientist she knows this isn't a real force – it's all in her imagination!

Lesson 8: Grinding gears

The gears on the scientist's bike help her cycle uphill. The gears allow her to pedal quicker but with less force. This means she can cycle up the slope without getting puffed out. Yep – gears are great. As a scientist would say, "They're a great way of transferring forces."

Lesson 9: Furious friction

The force of friction slows moving objects. It happens when a moving object touches another object. The scientist's rubber tyres grip the road and provide this force. This helps her control the bike and avoid fatal collisions. Lack of friction makes cycling on ice a slippery experience. And performing wheelies on the local skating rink is definitely out.

When she wants to slow down, or stop the rubber brakes grip her wheels. Friction stops her bike. Hopefully. If she brakes too hard, her momentum throws her forward. And she performs spectacular but possibly fatal handlebar acrobatics.

Lesson 10: Vicious vibrations

When the scientist rides her bike along a bumpy path she may feel a few vibrations. These are shock waves carrying the force of impact from the tyres. Her tyres and saddle springs are designed to soak up some vibrations. But that doesn't stop her body vibrating, her muscles twitching and her eyeballs bouncing slightly in their sockets.

Freaky physicists

Scientists who study forces are called physicists (fizzy–sists). They also explore motion, probe what things are made of, and try to figure out how the universe works. A typical physicist is slightly scruffy and enjoys tinkering with things. A physics lab is rather untidy and full of interesting bits and pieces that have been salvaged in order to build a freaky machine.

Fatal expressions

Is this dangerous?

Answers:
Just a bit. It means that when the roller–coaster goes to the top of a slope it's built up a lot of potential energy that will allow it to rush down the other side.

Bet you never knew!
Physicists use two strange words in connection with forces – "energy" and "work". Well hopefully, they don't sound too strange to you. But we're not talking about summoning up the energy to do homework or wash the dishes here. No way.

Physicists say "work" when they want to explain what happens when a force causes an object to move a distance. According to them writing your maths homework is "work" but reckoning up the answers in your head isn't. Energy is the ability to do work. Sounds sensible – after all you need energy to work. Don't you?

Just thinking about energy and work is pretty exhausting isn't it, so why don't you take a little rest? Yeah – put your feet up. Get your breath back for the next chapter. You'll need it. 'Cos it's about speed and crashes!!! Fasten your safety belt.

REVIEW

에너지는 힘을 만들고, 힘은 사물을 움직이게 만든다. 움직임과 변화가 있는 곳이라면 어디에나 힘이 있다. 질량을 가지고 있는 모든 물체가 서로 잡아당기는 힘, 만유인력 universal gravitation. 지구가 중심으로 당기는 힘, 중력 gravity. 가해지는 힘에 대해 반발하는 힘, 반발력 repulsive force. 운동을 방해하는 마찰력 friction. 원운동으로 발생해 서로 반대 방향으로 작용하는 힘, 원심력 centrifugal force과 구심력 centripetal force 등등. 그런데 물리학에서 벗어난 아주 중요한 힘이 하나 있다. 모두를 반하게 하는 강력한 힘, 바로 나의 치명적인 매력!

2. Forceful Facts

Vocabulary 2

p.44

Sounds fairly **vague**.

상당히 모호한 얘기처럼 들린다.

vague '비어 있는(empty)'을 뜻하는 라틴어 vagus에서 왔다. 처음 보는 그릇이 비어 있으면 그것이 밥그릇인지 국그릇인지 요강인지 판단하기 힘들다. 눈에 분명하게 들어오지 않는 상태, 머리에 정확하게 실체가 그려지지 않는 상태를 표현하는 말이 **vague**다. '애매한, 모호한, 희미한, 어렴풋한' 등을 뜻하는 형용사다.

p.45

Aristotle liked it there so much that he stayed for the next 20 years as a **pupil** and then as a teacher.

아리스토텔레스는 그곳을 무척 좋아해서 학생으로, 그 후에는 교사로 20년 동안 그곳에 머물렀다.

pupil 보살핌과 가르침을 받는 '아이(child)'를 부르는 말이었다. 옛날에는 질병, 재해, 전쟁 등으로 인해 부모를 잃는 아이들이 무척 많았다. 이런 아이들을 고아원 같은 보육 기관이나 교육 기관에서 보살피며 기본적인 지식을 가르쳤고, **pupil**이 점차 '교육을 받는 어린 학생'을 뜻하는 말로 변했다.

p.46

> But for 2,000 years everyone thought Aristotle's **wacko** ideas were RIGHT.
> 그러나 2000년 동안 모두 아리스토텔레스의 이상한 생각이 옳다고 생각했다.

wacko '강하게 부딪히다, 때리다'를 뜻하는 whack과 같은 뿌리에서 나왔다. 머리를 맞아서 뇌를 다쳤다는 의미에서, '미친, 제정신이 아닌, 분별없는'을 뜻하는 형용사로 쓴다. **wacko**를 명사로 쓰면 '미친 사람'을 지칭하는 속어가 되는데, 친한 사람들끼리는 '4차원'을 뜻하는 말로 쓸 수 있다. 형용사 **wacky**는 '괴짜의, 이상한, 엉뚱한'을 뜻한다.

p.46

> As the **liquid** sloshes around, sensors tell her brain whether she's still upright.
> 액체가 출렁거리면서 감각 신경이 그녀가 여전히 똑바로 서 있는지 아닌지를 그녀의 뇌에 알려준다.

liquid '흐르다(flow), 흐르는 것'을 뜻하는 라틴어 liguere에서 왔다. 물, 우유, 주스, 기름처럼 용기에 담지 않으면 흐르는 '액체'가 **liquid**다. 학교의 과학 시간, 과학책에서 자주 만나는 단어다. '기체'는 gas, '고체'는 solid라고 한다.

p.47

> When she stands still **inertia** keeps her there.
> 그녀가 가만히 서 있을 때 관성이 그 자리에 머물러 있게 한다.

처음 움직이는 게 힘들지 한 번 움직이기 시작하면 다음부터는 조금 수월해. 이것도 관성 때문!

inert '부정(not, without)'을 뜻하는 in-과 '능력, 솜씨(skill)'을 뜻하는 ert가 합쳐진 형용사다. 능력이나 솜씨가 없다는 의미인데, 이런 상태에 있는 사람은 일이나 활동을 할 수가 없다. 그래서 **inert**는 '힘(능력)이 없는, 움직이지 않는'을 뜻한다. 힘이 없고 의욕이 없어 움직이지 않는 '무기력, 비활성 상태'를 표현하는 말로도 쓸 수 있다. 명사 **inertia**는 물리학에서 '관성'을 뜻하는 말로, '지금 상태를 유지하고 바뀌지 않으려는 성질'을 의미한다.

2. Forceful Facts

> **p.48**
>
> **Momentum** is a measure of the scientist's ability to keep going.
> 운동량은 계속 갈 수 있는지 그 과학자의 능력을 재는 척도다.

momentum '순간, 잠깐, 한때'를 뜻하는 moment란 단어를 알 것이다. 그런데 moment는 '움직임, 운동'을 뜻하는 말에서 왔다. 모여서 시간의 흐름을 만들어 내는 짧은 움직임이 '순간, 잠깐'이다. **momentum** 역시 운동과 변화를 일으키는 힘을 의미한다. 달리는 자동차의 속도가 줄 때 가속 페달을 밟으면 자동차의 속도가 다시 빨라진다. 이렇게 가속 페달의 작용으로 생기는 '운동량'이 **momentum**이다.

> **p.48**
>
> The posh scientific word for speed in one direction is **"velocity"**.
> 한 방향의 속력을 나타내는 세련된 과학 용어는 "속도"다.

velocity '빠르다, 민첩하다'를 뜻하는 말에서 왔다. 눈에 띌 만큼 빠르게 이동하는 것에 대해서는 얼마나 빠른지 표현하고 싶어진다. 이럴 때 생기는 개념이 speed와 **velocity**인데, 물리학에서는 이 둘을 구분한다. speed는 '속력'이다. '물체가 빠르게 이동하는 정도'로 방향은 고려하지 않는다. **velocity**는 '속도'다. '물체가 어느 방향으로 얼마나 빨리 움직이는지'를 나타낸다.

> **p.49**
>
> She's run out of **kinetic** energy.
> 그녀는 운동 에너지를 다 써 버렸다.

kinetic kine가 '움직이다(move), 동작(motion)'을 의미하기 때문에 형용사인 **kinetic**은 '운동의, 운동으로 생기는'을 뜻하는 말로 쓴다. 명사형 **kinesis**는 '운동, 움직임(movement)'을 뜻한다. 물리학에서, 운동하고 있는 물체가 가진 에너지인 '운동 에너지'를 **kinetic** energy 라고 한다.

> **p.50**
>
> For the scientist the word "**acceleration**" means changing speed or direction.
>
> 과학자에게 있어 "가속"이란 단어는 속도나 방향을 바꾸는 것을 의미한다.

accelerate 기본 의미는 '빠르게 움직이게 만들다'라는 뜻이다. '속도를 증가시키다, 빨라지게 하다'란 뜻의 타동사, '가속화하다, 빨라지다'를 뜻하는 자동사로 쓴다. 명사형 **acceleration**은 '가속, 가속도, 가속화'를 뜻한다. 자동차의 가속을 위해 밟는 '가속 페달'을 뜻하는 영어 단어는 **accelerator**다.

> **p.50**
>
> As the scientist rounds the corner, **centripetal** (sen-tre-pee-tal) force pulls her bike into the corner.
>
> 그 과학자가 코너를 돌 때 구심력이 그녀의 자전거를 모퉁이 쪽으로 끌어당긴다.

centripetal centr는 '가운데, 중심'을 뜻하고 pet는 '빠르게 이동하다'를 뜻한다. '중심으로 빠르게 움직이는, 구심력의'를 뜻하는 형용사다. 원 운동하는 물체가 원의 중심을 향해 나아가려는 힘, '구심력'을 **centripetal** force라고 한다. 구심력이 커질수록 원 운동의 속도는 빨라진다. 반대 개념인 '원심력'은 centrifugal force다.

> **p.51**
>
> The force of **friction** slows moving objects.
>
> 마찰력은 움직이는 물체를 느려지게 한다.

friction '문지르다(rub)'를 뜻하는 라틴어에서 왔다. 행주로 식탁을 문지르면 먼지와 얼룩이 없어지는데, 문지르는 동작 때문에 행주와 식탁 사이에 '마찰'이 일어나기 때문이다. 그래서 명사 **friction**은 물리학에서 '마찰, 마찰 저항'을 뜻하는 말로 쓴다. 일상생활에서는 사람 사이의 '갈등, 다툼'을 뜻하기도 한다.

2. Forceful Facts

p.51

When the scientist rides her bike along a bumpy path she may feel a few **vibrations**.

울퉁불퉁한 길로 자전거를 타고 가면 그 과학자는 약간의 진동을 느낄 수도 있다.

vibration 앞뒤나 양옆으로 가볍고 빠르게 흔들리는 움직임을 표현하는 동사가 **vibrate**다. '진동하다, 떨다, 빠르게 흔들다' 등을 뜻한다. **vibrate**보다 진동 폭이 큰 움직임은 shake, 그보다 더 큰 흔들림은 rock으로 표현한다. 명사형인 **vibration**은 '진동, 떨림'을 뜻한다. 음악에서 악기 소리의 울림에 진동을 주는 연주 기법을 '**vibrato**(비브라토)'라고 한다. 음을 상하로 가늘게 떨어 더 멋진 소리를 내는 것이다.

p.53

Just thinking about energy and work is pretty **exhausting** isn't it, so why don't you take a little rest?

에너지와 일에 대해 생각하는 것만으로도 상당히 피곤하지 않나? 그럼 잠깐 휴식을 취하는 게 어떨까?

exhaust '다 빨아 당기다, 다 끄집어내다'를 의미한다. 연못에서 물이 다 증발하면 메마르고, 사람도 에너지와 힘을 다 쓰면 기진맥진해서 움직이기 힘들어진다. 이런 의미에서 동사 **exhaust**는 '완전히 지치게 만들다, 고갈시키다'라는 뜻이다. 형용사 **exhausting**은 '완전히 지치게 만드는, 무척 힘들게 하는'을 뜻하고, **exhausted**는 '기진맥진한, 탈진한, 고갈된'을 뜻한다. 명사형은 **exhaustion**이다.

Sentence 2

p.44

A scientist will tell you that a force is something that affects the movement or shape of an object or person.

과학자라면 힘이란 물체나 사람의 움직임이나 형태에 영향을 미치는 거라고 말해 줄 것이다.

'누구에게 무엇을 (해)주다'란 의미를 전달하는 4형식 문장이다. tell이 동사, you가 간접 목적어, that 이하 문장이 직접 목적어다.
something 이하의 that은 something의 정체를 설명하는 말이다. '사물 또는 사람의 움직임이나 형태에 영향을 주는 것'이 바로 force라는 의미다.

p.45

By the time Aristotle died (of acute indigestion) he had written about everything from politics to how grasshoppers chirp.

(급체로) 사망할 때까지 아리스토텔레스는 정치부터 메뚜기의 울음소리에 이르기까지 모든 것에 관해 글을 썼다.

[by the time + 문장]은 '~할 때까지는, ~할 때쯤에는'으로 해석한다. [die of 질병]은 '~병 때문에 사망하다'란 의미다.
[everything from A to B]는 'A부터 B까지 모든 것'을 뜻한다.

p.45

Things move as long as they're in contact with whatever is moving them.

사물은 그것을 움직이는 것과 접촉하는 한 계속 움직이지.

이 문장에서 as long as는 '~하는 한, ~하는 동안'을 의미한다. long이 '시간의 길이'를 표현하고 있다.

2. Forceful Facts

전치사 with의 목적어 whatever is moving them은 '그 사물을 움직이고 있는 모든 것' 또는 '그 사물을 움직이는 것 무엇이든지'로 이해하면 된다.

p.46

> Inside the scientist's ears are fluid-filled spaces, called semi-circular canals.
> 그 과학자의 귓속에는 반고리관이라고 부르는, 체액으로 가득 찬 공간이 있다.

[부사구 + 동사 + 주어] 어순으로 도치된 문장이다. 주어는 fluid-filled spaces(액체로 채워진 공간)이고, 동사는 are이다.
콤마(,) 뒤의 called semi-circular canals(반고리관이라고 부르는)는 주어 fluid-filled spaces를 부르는 명칭을 덧붙인 것이다.

p.49

> By the way, if she did make it right through to the Earth's centre, there would be no gravity and she would float around being roasted in the fiery heat.
> 그런데, 만약 그녀가 지구 중심까지 곧장 도달한다면, 그곳에서 중력은 사라지고 그녀는 뜨거운 열기 속에서 구워지면서 떠다니게 될 것이다.

문장 앞 By the way는 '그런데, 그건 그렇고'의 의미로, 화제를 바꿀 때 쓰는 부사구다.
did make it는 '성공하다'란 의미인데, 강조하기 위해 made를 did make로 표현했다.
지구의 핵(core) 온도는 5000도가 넘는다. 그래서 being roasted(구워지며)란 표현을 쓴 것이다.

p.50

Wind blows against the scientist and causes "drag" which slows her down.
바람이 과학자를 향해 불면 "저항"을 일으켜서 그녀의 속도를 늦춘다.

이 문장에서 drag는 '끄는 힘'을 뜻하는데, 물리학에서는 '저항'을 뜻하는 용어다.
which slows her down은 drag를 꾸며 주는 말로, '그녀의 속도를 늦추는'을 뜻한다.

p.51

Lack of friction makes cycling on ice a slippery experience.
마찰력 부족은 얼음 위에서 자전거를 타는 것을 미끄러운 경험으로 만든다.

이 문장은 'A가 B를 C로 만들다'란 의미의 [A make B C] 형태다.
주어(A), 목적어(B), 목적 보어(C) 모두 명사구다. 주어 Lack of friction은 '저항의 부족', 목적어 cycling on ice는 '얼음 위에서 도는 것', 목적 보어 a slippery experience는 '미끄러지는 경험'을 뜻한다.

p.51

But that doesn't stop her body vibrating, her muscles twitching and her eyeballs bouncing slightly in their sockets.
그러나 그렇다 해도 그녀의 몸이 떨리고, 근육이 경련을 일으키고, 눈알이 눈구멍에서 위아래로 흔들리는 것을 멈추지는 못한다.

[stop A (from) 동사ing]는 'A가 ~하는 것을 막다, A가 ~을 못하게 하다'를 뜻한다.
her body vibrating(그녀의 몸이 진동하는 것), her muscles twitching(근육이 경련을 일으키는 것), her eyeballs bouncing(안구가 위아래로 튀는 것)이 모두 stop의 목적어다.

2. Forceful Facts

> Physicists say "work" when they want to explain what happens when a force causes an object to move a distance.
>
> 물리학자들은 힘이 작용해 물체가 일정한 거리를 이동할 때 발생하는 것을 설명하고자 할 때 "일"이라고 말한다.

"work" 다음에 나오는 when 이하의 문장은 '시간, 때, 경우, 상황'을 표현하는 부사절이다. explain의 목적어로 나온 what happens ~ a distance는 '힘이 물체를 일정 거리 이동시킬 때 무슨 일이 일어나는지'로 해석할 수 있다.

CHAPTER 3 KEYWORDS

#speed #velocity #momentum #inertia

Smashing Speed

Some people think speed is smashing. Others don't. Early railways scared some people because they reckoned no human could go faster than 32 km per hour (20 mph) and live. Well, they can, of course. But one thing's certain – the faster you go the more likely you are to meet up with some fatal forces. Gulp!

Test your teacher

Is your teacher quick-witted? Smile sweetly and ask:

(Note the subtle wording – your teacher probably thinks you're talking about pedalling – but she'd be wrong.)

Your teacher will probably say something like, "50 km per hour" (31

mph) – hopelessly wrong. At this point you can say, "No, I think you're wrong. In 1899 Mr C M Murphy smashed the record. He tied his bike to the back of a train and travelled 1.6 km in a minute." Don't try this at home.

Quick quiz

1 Super speedy
See if you can put these three objects in order of speed, starting with the fastest.
a) A bullet from a high-powered rifle.
b) The planet Mercury moving through space.
c) Three astronauts aboard the Apollo 10 spacecraft in 1969.

2 Fairly speedy
Which of these three objects do you think is the fastest?
a) A chameleon's tongue as it grabs a juicy fly.
b) A message sent along one of your nerves.
c) A person falling from the top of a 99.4-metre-high building.

3 Slow and sluggish
Can you put these three objects in order of speed starting with the fastest?

a) Your fingernails growing.
b) Bamboo plants growing.
c) The Atlantic Ocean getting wider.

Answers:

1 b) 172,248 km per hour (107,030 mph) When it comes to orbiting the sun, Mercury is the speediest planet in the solar system. c) 39,897 km per hour (24,791 mph) Feeling a teensy bit space sick? a) 3,302 km per hour (2,052 mph). That's too fast to see. The bullet travels faster than sound so a person could be shot before they heard the gun firing. Doesn't sound fair somehow.

2 b) 483 km per hour (300 mph). c) 141 km per hour (80 mph). This was the speed achieved by stuntman Dan Koko in 1984 as he leapt off the Las Vegas World Hotel. Lucky for Dan he smashed into an air cushion rather than the pavement. a) 80.5 km per hour (50 mph). Then it's bye-bye fly.

3 b) 3 cm (1.2 inches) an hour. If your fingernails grew any faster than this, you'd have problems. c) 0.0006 cm (0.0002 inch) an hour. The Atlantic Ocean is getting wider due to the movements of enormous slabs of rock deep beneath the Earth's surface. a) 0.00028 cm (0.0001 inch) an hour. Any faster than this and it could be fatal.

Bet you never knew!

You'd move faster if your shape allowed the air to flow round you rather than bumping into you. This kind of shape is called "aerodynamic" and it cuts down on drag. A bullet with its pointed head is an aerodynamic shape but a human head isn't. If it was we'd all have pointy heads. Record-smashing speed cyclists wear pointed helmets instead. And more speed means more momentum. Smashing!

Fatal forces fact file

NAME: Momentum

THE BASIC FACTS: Momentum keeps you moving. That way you don't smash Newton's First Law. (That's the one about going in a straight line unless something stops you.)

THE HORRIBLE DETAILS: Momentum makes your stomach jump when you go over the top on a roller coaster.

ARGHHHH!

The momentum of your half-digested food carries on up. If it comes up too far it could be fatally embarrassing!

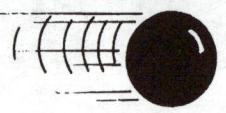

Murderous momentum facts

1 In 1871 showman John Holtum tried to catch a flying cannon–ball with his bare hands. It wasn't fired from a real cannon, of course. Holtum used a specially built gun that fired a slow–moving ball. But even so he nearly lost a finger. The stunt proved very popular and John bravely practised until he'd perfected the trick. He should have changed his name to "Halt–em".

2 In nineteenth–century America railways were rarely fenced off and brainless buffalo often blundered onto the tracks. To tackle this menace, by the 1860s

trains were fitted with wedge-shaped "cow catchers". The idea was that the train's momentum would scoop the buffalo out of harm's way.

3 In Finland, elk (otherwise known as moose) cause fatal road accidents. When hit by a car, the momentum of the car flips the moose over. So the loose moose lands on the car roof. Its weight crushes both the car and its driver. Perhaps the cars should be fitted with "moose catchers".

Idle inertia

Physicists use the word inertia to describe how things stay the same. Motionless things stay idle and moving things carry on until another force gets in the way. That's Newton's First Law again.

Dare you discover... the inertia of an egg?

You will need:

A plate

A raw egg

A hard-boiled egg

What you do:

1. Gently spin the raw egg on the plate.
2. To stop the egg touch it with your finger.
3. Gently lift your finger up.
4. Now repeat steps 1-3 with the hard-boiled egg.

What do you notice?

a) When you lift your finger the hard-boiled egg continues to spin.

b) When you lift your finger the raw egg continues to spin.

c) When you lift your finger the raw egg spins and the hard-boiled egg rocks from end-to-end.

Answers:

b) When you stop the raw egg, inertia keeps the egg white inside spinning. And this starts the entire egg spinning again when you lift your finger. The inside of the hard-boiled egg is hard, of course, so the white doesn't have its own inertia.

> Important note: The egg should spin on the plate. Not spin through the air and smash on the floor. If this happens you'll be force-fed omelette. And talking about smashing things ...

A smashing test

Car designers spend fortunes building new cars. And then they smash them up. This may sound stupid, but they need to test the car's structural design and materials under crash conditions and also find the best ways to ensure that the driver and passengers are as well protected as possible. These days most smashes happen on a computer screen. The engineers peer at a simulation of crashes at various speeds. They can even slow down the movement to one image every two milliseconds – that's far slower than a TV action replay.

But afterwards the engineers need real-life tests to check their findings. And this is when the poor old dummies get wheeled in to show the effects of the crash on real people. Of course, dummies don't have brains – that's why they're dummies. But they do have a smashing time.

11.02 am The engineers crouch behind steel barriers to protect themselves from the impact of the crash, and it turns out they *deliberately* forgot about the safety belts. Steel cables at the front of the car catapult it forward at speed. CRAACK! the car hits the wall. The dummies crash through the windscreen. The front of the car is completely smashed in.

12.00 noon The dummies are cut free from the wreckage. They're a little bit battered but they've survived to crash another day. They're pretty tough dummies.

1.00 pm The engineers stop for a sandwich. The dummies aren't all that hungry.

2.00pm Telly time! The dummies have become movie stars, but they don't even know it. As the dummies are wheeled away the engineers settle themselves in front of a screen to watch an action replay of the crash on video.

You can see how Newton's First Law affects the dummies. That's the law about things continuing to move in a straight line. When the car stops, the inertia of the dummies forces

them to carry on moving – straight through the windscreen. So the force of the wall hitting the car is transferred to the poor old dummies. You can see why seat belts are lifesavers. You'd be a real dummy not to wear one.

5.00pm The engineers set up tomorrow's test. This time the dummies will be trapped in a car as it rolls over in a crash. But that's just another smashing day in the life of the crash test dummies.
A dummy's life is full of hard knocks.

Safety first

As a result of this testing, engineers have come up with a few ingenious devices to help reduce the impact of a car crash on passengers:

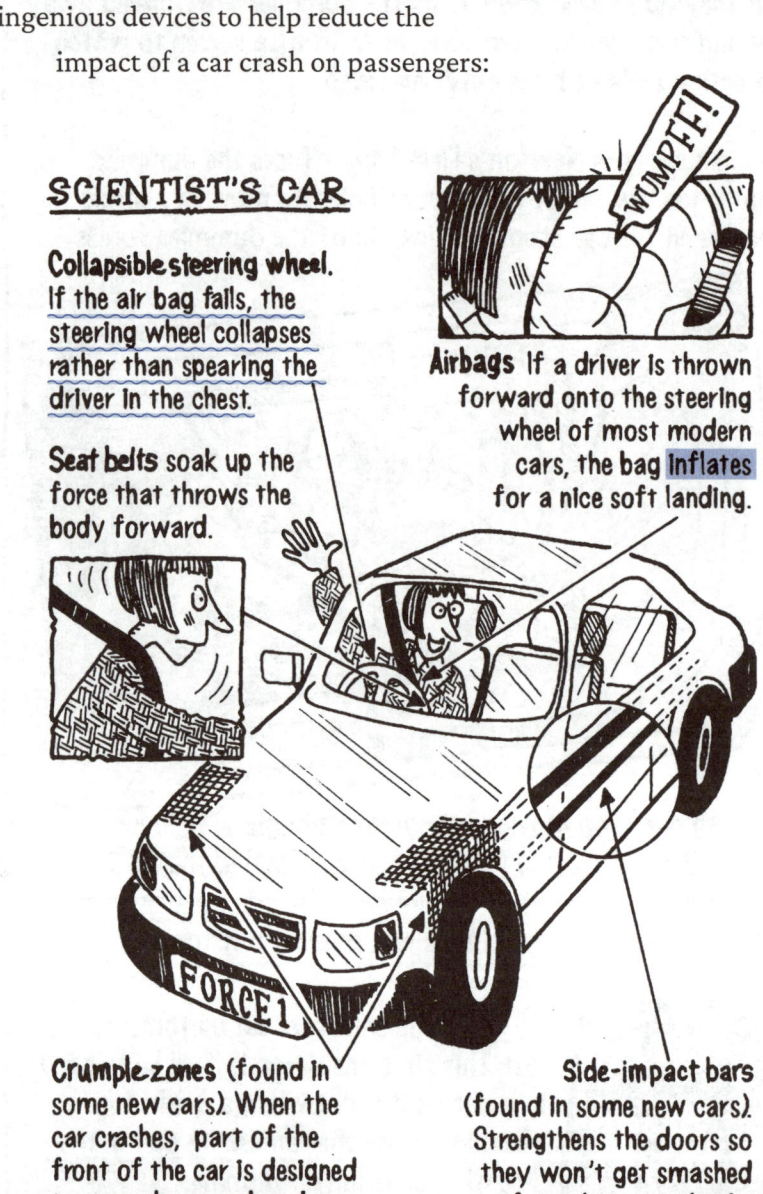

SCIENTIST'S CAR

Collapsible steering wheel. If the air bag fails, the steering wheel collapses rather than spearing the driver in the chest.

Seat belts soak up the force that throws the body forward.

Airbags If a driver is thrown forward onto the steering wheel of most modern cars, the bag inflates for a nice soft landing.

Crumple zones (found in some new cars). When the car crashes, part of the front of the car is designed to crumple up and soak up some of the shock.

Side-impact bars (found in some new cars). Strengthens the doors so they won't get smashed in if another car whacks into them.

Smashing sound speeds

Fatal though they often are, the forces in a car crash are nothing compared to those in really high-speed accidents like an air crash. Or the horrible effects of falling out of an aeroplane at high speed. The  effects of high speeds were studied by Austrian physicist Ernst Mach (1838–1916). Mach found that it's hard to travel faster than the speed of sound – 1,220 km per hour (760 mph). (By the way, the speed of sound is the speed sounds travel through the air.)

Here's why it's so difficult. All aircraft push air in front of them. But a plane flying at the speed of sound smashes into this air before it can escape. This makes for a violently bumpy ride that can shake the plane to pieces (not to mention your insides). In the 1940s several pilots died trying to smash the sound barrier. But in 1947 American pilot Charles E Yeager broke the barrier in a rocket-powered plane. It was known to be dangerous to fly really, really fast, but at this time no one knew what hitting the air at these speeds would do to an unprotected body. Could it be fatal?

Fly for your life

26 February 1955, California, USA

At 9.30 am precisely, ace test pilot George Franklin Smith picked up his washing. He turned left out of the launderette and walked slap bang into the worst day of his life.

He should have known better. How many people volunteer to work on a Saturday? But he had nothing better to do than finish a report. And of course when he got to work someone offered him a test flight in a gleaming brand new Super-sabre jet. This was a new type of jet plane capable of flying faster than sound.

George grinned. He loved test flying the powerful planes. In his laid-back way he replied:

It wasn't worth putting on a protective suit.

As George took off he noticed the controls were a bit stiff. But there seemed nothing to worry about – the pre-flight checks had been just fine. He chatted happily to a pilot friend over the intercom.

Minutes later he broke the sound barrier. Then the plane nosed down and the controls jammed. The jet was diving to destruction at supersonic speed.

As his speed increased George yelled: "Controls locked – I'm going straight down!"

His friend's voice exploded in the headphones. "Bale out, George! Get out of there!" He had seconds to escape or die.

About 2,100 metres below the blue sea glittered in the sunshine.

George wrenched the armrest and jettisoned the jet's perspex canopy. A tearing gale filled the cockpit. At this speed the violent force of the air pinned him down. He painfully stretched out his hand. His fingertips brushed the ejector seat handle. There was no time. No time to think of the danger. Every pilot who had baled out at supersonic speeds had been killed.

George's straining fingers clutched the handle. KERBAAAM! A powerful explosion tore him from the cockpit. He hit a wall of air. The world and the sky tumbled crazily. In a few seconds his shoes and socks, his watch and helmet

were torn away. He was bleeding fast and very, very scared.

His falling body felt like a feather. "A falling body" he thought vaguely, "has no weight – it's… something to do with gravity." There was a crack and a sharp jerk as the parachute opened, its canopy trapping and slowing the air as it rushed past. Then George felt himself slip into darkness. He felt no pain as his body slammed into the sea and began to sink.

"Hey, give me a hand!" shouted the fisherman to his friend as he hauled the heavy body from the water.

The other man looked doubtful. "There's no point – I think the pilot's dead."

But George Smith was still alive. Just…

The Air Force took a month to scoop up all the mangled pieces of George's plane from the sea bed 1.6 km from the shore. The wreckage filled 50 barrels and still no one knew what had caused the crash.

But scientists now had a chance to study the effect of extreme forces… on poor George's half-dead body.

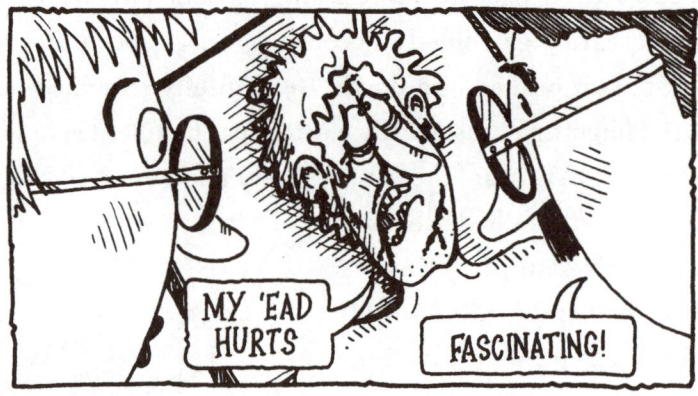

Here's what they found out:

① As George ejected from the plane his speed boosted the effects of gravity. What we call "weight" depends on the strength of the gravity affecting our bodies. So every part of the pilot's body became 40 times heavier. You may have felt this yourself. It's that weird feeling of being stuck to your seat as you climb a roller-coaster. Only George was moving much faster so this effect was almost fatal.

② Even his blood became heavier for a few moments. Heavy blood squirted from his heavy blood vessels. This caused a mass of bruises to appear on his body. He was so bruised that his head swelled up like a purple football.

3 George's eyelids bled after fluttering violently in the howling wind as he fell at speed.

In all George spent seven months in hospital. But he made a full recovery and went back to flying. He was the luckiest pilot in the world. Of course, every pilot's worst nightmare is to fall out of the sky. Because falling – under the influence of gravity – can be fatal. So if you want to survive the next chapter you'd better hang on tight. And DON'T FORGET YOUR PARACHUTE!

REVIEW

힘은 움직임을 만든다. 그리고 움직이는 모든 것은 저마다의 속도를 가진다. 멈추는 힘이 제대로 작동하지 않으면 끔찍한 충돌이 발생하기도 한다. 낙하와 회전을 반복하는 롤러코스터가 무서운 것은 멈추지 못하고 떨어질 수도 있다는 상상 때문일 것이다. 자동차에 브레이크, 범퍼, 에어백이 있는 이유가 뭘까? 찢어진 낙하산을 메고 비행기에서 떨어진 파일럿은 중력 가속도로 인해 1초에 9.8미터씩 빨라지는 낙하 속도를 어떻게 느낄까? 아찔한 속도와 충돌, 추락의 공포를 느껴 보자.

Vocabulary 3

p.63

Some people think speed is **smashing**.
어떤 사람들은 스피드가 멋지다고 생각한다.

smash '세게 때리거나 부딪혀 부수다'라는 의미로 '박살나다, 박살내다'라는 뜻이다. 라켓을 휘두르는 스포츠 종목인 테니스와 탁구에서 공을 아주 세게 쳐서 공격하는 동작을 **smashing**이라고 한다. 이런 공격이 성공하면 관중들이 환호하며 박수를 친다. 멋지기도 하고 뭔가 쾌감을 주기 때문이다. 그래서 형용사 **smashing**은 주로 영국 영어에서 '무척 멋진, 기분 좋은'을 뜻하는 말로도 사용한다.

p.63

What was the fastest speed **attained** on a bicycle during the nineteenth century?
19세기에 자전거로 달성한 가장 빠른 속도는 얼마였을까?

attain 여기서 at은 '방향(to)'을 의미하고 tain은 '닿다, 만지다'를 뜻한다. 손을 뻗어 뭔가를 잡거나, 몸을 움직여 원하는 곳에 간다는 의미다. 그래서 '(노력을 통해) 이루다, 획득하다'를 뜻하는 동사로 주로 쓴다. 또한 '특정한 나이, 수준, 자격에 이르다'란 뜻으로도 쓸 수 있다.

p.64

Can you put these three objects in **order** of speed starting with the fastest?
이 세 물체들을 가장 빠른 것부터 시작해서 속도 순으로 배열할 수 있는가?

order 기본 의미는 '자리(position), 위치'다. 있어야 할 자리를 의미한다. 수를 셀 때 1 다음 '자리'에는 2가 나온다. 그게 '순서'다. 순서가 맞으면 '질서'가 잡힌다. '명령'하는 지위와 명령에 따

대서양(Atlantic Ocean) 해저에는 중앙해령이라는 해저 산맥이 있어서 1년에 3cm 정도씩 넓어지고 있단다.

르는 위치는 정해져 있다. **order**는 내가 음식을 시킬 권한이 있으니 그 음식을 내어놓으라 지시한다는 의미에서 '주문하다'란 뜻도 갖고 있다. **order**를 보면 '순서, 질서, 명령, 주문'을 떠올려 보자.

p.66

A bullet with its pointed head is an **aerodynamic** shape but a human head isn't.

탄두가 뾰족한 총알은 공기 역학적 형태지만, 사람의 머리는 그렇지 않다.

aerodynamic '공기의 힘과 관련된, 공기 역학의'라는 뜻의 형용사다. aero는 '공기(air), 대기, 기체'를 뜻하고, dynamic은 '힘(power)'을 뜻한다. 대기권과 우주 개발과 관련된 '항공우주'가 aerospace, 모든 것을 날려버리는 힘을 가진 폭탄 '다이너마이트'가 dynamite 다. **aerodynamic**에 -s를 붙인 **aerodynamics**는 '공기 역학'이란 학문이다.

p.66

That's the one about going in a straight line **unless** something stops you.

그것은 어떤 것이 널 막지 않는 한 직선으로 간다는 내용의 법칙이다.

unless 'not on less than(~보다 적은 상태가 아니라면)'을 짧게 줄여서 한 단어로 표현한 말이다. '~하지 않는 한, ~한 경우를 제외하면'을 뜻하는데, 최소한의 상태나 조건을 표현하는 문장이 **unless** 뒤에 나온다. 그래서 **unless** something stops you는 '뭔가가 당신을 멈추지 않는다면'으로 해석할 수 있다.

p.67

To tackle this **menace**, by the 1860s trains were fitted with wedge-shaped "cow catchers".

이런 위험에 대처하기 위해 1860년대에 이르러 기차에 쐐기 모양의 "소잡이"가 장착되었다.

menace 위협을 느낄 만한 어떤 상황, 위협을 가하는 상대를 표현한 명사다. '위협하거나 협박하는 행동, 위험한 상황, 위협하는 존재' 등을 두루 포함한다. To tackle this **menace**는 '이

3. Smashing Speed

위험에 대처하기 위해'로 해석할 수 있다. **menace**를 동사로 쓰면 '위협하다, 위험할 수 있다'를 뜻한다.

이게 바로 소잡이! 장애물을 치운다고 해서 배장기라고도 해.

p.67

Physicists use the word inertia to **describe** how things stay the same.
물리학자들은 사물이 동일한 상태로 유지되는 방식을 설명하기 위해 관성이라는 단어를 사용한다.

describe '밑에(down)'를 뜻하는 de-와 '쓰다(write)'를 뜻하는 scribe가 합쳐진 말이다. 필기구로 종이에 글을 쓴다는 의미도 있고, 어떤 그림이나 글 밑에 설명하는 내용을 쓴다는 의미도 있다. 그래서 **describe**는 글이나 말로 '상세하게 묘사하다, 자세히 설명하다'란 뜻으로 쓴다. 명사형은 **description**이다.

p.69

The engineers peer at a **simulation** of crashes at various speeds.
엔지니어들은 다양한 속도에서의 충돌 시뮬레이션을 살펴본다.

simulate sim은 '하나, 비슷한, 닮은'의 뜻을 갖고 있다. 쌍둥이마냥 비슷하고 닮았다는 의미다. 그래서 동사 **simulate**는 '~와 같게(비슷하게) 만들다, ~인 척하다, 실제와 비슷하게 모의실험하다'라는 뜻으로 쓴다. 명사 **simulation**은 과학 분야나 산업 현장에서 증명과 확인을 위해 실시하는 '모의실험, 시뮬레이션'을 의미한다.

p.69

And this is when the poor old **dummies** get wheeled in to show the effects of the crash on real people.

그리고 이때 충돌이 진짜 사람들에게 미치는 영향을 보여 주기 위해 불쌍한 낡은 더미들이 바퀴 달린 의자에 앉혀진다.

dummy 원래 '말을 못하는 사람'을 뜻하는 dumb에서 온 말이다. '인형'은 말을 못한다. 그래서 '인체 모형, 실제 크기로 만든 사람 인형'을 뜻하는 말로 발전했다. 옷가게에서 옷을 입혀 놓는 인형인 마네킹(mannequin)도 같은 말이다. **dummy**는 가짜로 만든 물건을 뜻하는 '모조품'이란 의미도 있다. 또한 생김새는 사람 같은데 말과 행동을 못하기 때문에 '바보, 멍청이'를 뜻하는 말로도 쓴다.

p.70

The dummies are cut free from the **wreckage**.

그 더미들은 잘려진 채 잔해에서 빠져나온다.

wreckage 명사로 '온전한 형태가 아닌, 망가진 탈 것이나 건물, 잔해'를 뜻한다. wreck에 '상태, 과정'을 뜻하는 명사형 어미 age가 붙은 형태다. **wreck**은 '파괴하다, 망가뜨리다'를 뜻하는 동사, 또는 사고나 재난으로 부서진 '난파선, 자동차나 비행기 잔해'를 뜻하는 명사로 쓴다.

p.71

So the force of the wall hitting the car is **transferred** to the poor old dummies.

그래서 차에 부딪히는 벽의 힘은 불쌍한 낡은 더미들에게 전달된다.

벽에 부딪히면 차는 멈추지만 안전 벨트를 안 한 우리 더미들은 관성 때문에 앞으로 튕겨 나가. 그러니 안전 벨트를 꼭 매도록!

transfer trans는 '건너가다, 넘어가다'란 의미로 '이동, 변화'를 뜻하고, fer는 '옮기다(carry)'를 뜻한다. 여기에서 저기로 옮긴다는 의미에서 '이동하다, 옮기다, 전학가다' 등을 뜻하는 말로 쓰는데, 대개 뒤에 '방향'을 의미하는 전치사 to를 붙이고 이동 장소나 변화된 상태를 구체적으로 밝힌다. '이동, 이전'을 뜻하는 명사로도 쓸 수 있다.

3. Smashing Speed

p.72

If a driver is thrown forward onto the steering wheel of most modern cars, the bag **inflates** for a nice soft landing.

현대의 자동차들 대부분에서는 운전자가 전방의 운전대 위로 던져지면, 부드럽게 안착할 수 있게 에어백이 부풀어 오른다.

inflate '부풀다, 부풀리다'라는 뜻의 동사다. in은 '안, 속'을, flate는 '바람을 불다(blow)'를 의미한다. 어떤 물체 안에 바람을 불어넣으면 바람이 차면서 부풀어 오른다. 상품의 가격이 오르면 그 상품을 사기 위해 필요한 돈이 많아진다. 지갑이 부풀어 오른다. 그래서 경제학에서 물가 상승 현상을 '**inflation**(인플레이션)'이라고 부른다.

p.73

In the 1940s several pilots died trying to smash the sound **barrier**.

1940년대에 몇몇 조종사가 음속 장벽을 돌파하려다 사망했다.

barrier '장벽, 장애물'을 뜻한다. 여기서 bar는 기다란 '막대, 봉'인데, 옛날엔 이걸 출입하지 못하게 막는 막대기인 빗장으로 썼다. 어떤 행동이나 진행, 발전 등을 '가로막는 문제·상황·규칙' 등도 **barrier**를 써서 표현할 수 있다.

p.73

You wouldn't want to **mess up** your new book, would you?

새 책을 엉망으로 만들고 싶지는 않겠지, 그렇지?

mess up '심하게 더럽히다, 완전히 망치다'란 의미다. **mess**는 원래 여럿이 먹는 '식사, 음식' 또는 '식사 자리'를 뜻하는 말이었다. 지금도 군대나 공장 등 단체로 급식을 먹는 식당을 **mess** hall이라고 부른다. 급식실을 생각해 보면 알겠지만, 이런 식사 자리는 나중에 엄청 지저분해진다. 그래서 동사 **mess**는 '더럽히다, 지저분하게 어지르다'를 뜻하는 말로 사용한다. 명사 **mess**는 '지저분하거나 엉망인 상태'를 뜻한다.

p.74

> The jet was diving to **destruction** at supersonic speed.
> 제트기는 초음속으로 파멸을 향해 급강하하고 있었다.

destruction '파괴, 파멸'을 뜻하는 명사다. 동사 **destroy**는 '반대, 거꾸로'를 뜻하는 de와 '짓다'를 뜻하는 stroy가 합쳐진 말이다. '짓다'의 반대, 즉 '파괴하다, 부수다'란 의미다. 형용사형은 '파괴적인, 해로운'이라는 뜻의 **destructive**다. 공들여서 만든 것, 중요한 것을 파괴하고 망가뜨릴 때 **destroy**를 쓴다.

p.75

> There was a crack and a sharp jerk as the **parachute** opened, its canopy trapping and slowing the air as it rushed past.
> 낙하산이 펴지며 철썩하는 소리와 함께 휙 뒤로 당겨지더니 캐노피가 공기를 가두고 속도가 느려지면서 빠르게 떠밀려 갔다.

parachute 그냥 밑으로 떨어져서 중력 가속도에 희생되지 않게 막는 장치인 '낙하산'이다. 패러슈트라고 읽는다. para는 '막다, 보호하다'를 뜻하고, chute는 '떨어지다(fall), 낙하하다'를 뜻한다. '낙하산을 매고 비행기에서 뛰어내리다'란 뜻의 동사로도 쓸 수 있다.

p.77

> George's eyelids bled after **fluttering** violently in the howling wind as he fell at speed.
> 급속도로 떨어지면서 윙윙거리는 바람 속에서 조지의 눈꺼풀이 격렬하게 떨리다가 피가 흘렀다.

flutter 원래 새가 날개를 퍼덕이며 나는 모습을 표현하는 말이다. 새, 나비 등이 '날개를 파닥이다, 훨훨 날다'라는 뜻으로 쓸 수 있고, 그런 날갯짓처럼 '빠르고 가볍게 흔들다, 펄럭이다'는 뜻으로도 쓸 수 있다. 명사 **flutter**는 '연속적인 흔들림, 떨림, 두근거림'을 뜻한다.

3. Smashing Speed

Sentence 3

p.63

But one thing's certain - the faster you go the more likely you are to meet up with some fatal forces.

그러나 하나만은 확실하다. 빨리 갈수록 치명적인 힘에 맞닥뜨릴 가능성이 더 커진다.

certain(분명한) 뒤의 옆줄(-) 다음에, 주어 one thing에 해당하는 내용이 나온다. 옆줄 다음의 문장은 '~할수록 더 ~하다'란 의미를 표현하는 [the 비교급, the 비교급] 형태의 문장이다. the faster you go는 '당신이 빨리 갈수록', the more likely~fatal forces는 '어떤 치명적인 힘에 직면할 가능성이 더 커진다'는 의미다.

p.66

You'd move faster if your shape allowed the air to flow round you rather than bumping into you.

당신의 생김새가 공기가 몸에 부딪히지 않고 주위로 흐르도록 한다면, 당신은 더 빨리 이동할 것이다.

You'd는 You would의 줄임말이다. [A rather than B]는 'B하기보다는 A, B보다는 차라리 A'라는 뜻의 표현이다.

p.66

If it comes up too far it could be fatally embarrassing!

너무 멀리까지 올라오면 치명적으로 당혹스러울 수 있다!

앞에 나오는 it은 직전 문장의 half-digested food(반쯤 소화된 음식)의 대명사다. too far는 '(식도를 타고) 너무 멀리'라는 의미다.

뒤에 나오는 it은 위 안에 있는 음식이 식도를 타고 입 밖으로 나오는 '상황'을 가리킨다.
embarrassing은 '수치스러운, 창피한'을 뜻하는 형용사다.

p.67

> When hit by a car, the momentum of the car flips the moose over.
>
> 차에 치이면 자동차의 추진력 때문에 무스가 뒤집힌다.

시간을 표현하는 부사절(when hit by a car)에는 주어와 동사가 생략되어 있다. When a moose is hit by a car(큰사슴이 차에 치이면)를 줄여서 표현한 것이다.
[flip A over]는 'A를 확 뒤집다'란 표현이다.

p.68

> The inside of the hard-boiled egg is hard, of course, so the white doesn't have its own inertia.
>
> 물론 삶은 달걀의 내부는 단단하기 때문에 흰자 자체에는 관성이 없다.

중간의 of course는 '당연히'를 뜻하는 부사구로, '단단하게 완전히 익힌 달걀' hard-boiled egg를 hard하다고 표현하는 게 당연하다는 의미다.
white는 달걀의 '흰자'다. 달걀의 '노른자'는 yolk라고 부른다.

p.69

> This may sound stupid, but they need to test the car's structural design and materials under crash conditions and also find the best ways to ensure that the driver and passengers are as well protected as possible.
>
> 멍청하게 들릴지 모르지만, 그들은 충돌 조건에서 자동차의 구조적 설계와 재료를 테스트해야 하며, 운전자와 승객이 최대한 보호받을 수 있는 최선의 방법을 찾아야 한다.

앞 문장의 주어 This는 '자동차를 새로 만든 다음 박살내는 행동'을 의미하고, but 다음의 they는 car designers를 의미한다. 모두 앞에서 이미 나온 내용이다.
are as well protected as possible은 '가능한 한 잘 보호받다'라는 뜻이다.

3. Smashing Speed

p.71

You'd be a real dummy not to wear one.
안전벨트를 하지 않으면 당신은 정말 더미일 것이다.

가정법 형태의 문장이다. not to wear one은 '안전벨트를 하지 않는다면'처럼 가정의 의미로 해석해야 한다.
You'd는 You would의 줄임말이다.

p.72

If the air bag fails, the steering wheel collapses rather than spearing the driver in the chest.
에어백이 작동하지 않으면, 운전대가 운전자의 가슴을 찌르는 대신에 내려앉는다.

fails는 '작동하지 않다'라는 뜻이다. steering wheel은 '방향을 조종하는(steering) 둥근 모양의 바퀴(wheel)' 즉 '운전대, 자동차 핸들'이다.
[A rather than B]는 'B하지 않고 A하는, B라기보다는 A인'을 뜻하는 표현이다.

p.73

Fatal though they often are, the forces in a car crash are nothing compared to those in really high-speed accidents like an air crash.
치명적인 경우도 많지만, 자동차 충돌 사고에서 발생하는 힘은 항공기 충돌과 같은 정말로 속도가 빠른 사고에서 발생하는 힘에 비하면 아무것도 아니다.

앞의 부사절은 Though they often are fatal에서 '치명적'이라는 의미를 강조하기 위해 fatal을 맨 앞으로 보낸 도치형 문장이다.
[compared to]는 '~와 비교하면'을 뜻하고, 뒤의 those는 the forces의 대명사다.

p.74

He should have known better.
그는 더 잘 알았어야 했다.

과거의 행동이나 사건에 대해 후회하면서 '~했어야 했다, ~였다면 좋았을 걸'이라고 표현할 때 [should have + 동사 완료형(pp)]의 형태를 사용한다. '그는 더 잘 알았어야 했다.'로 해석할 수 있는데, '그때는 미련했다, 현명하지 못했다, 생각이 짧았다'는 의미다.

p.75

"A falling body" he thought vaguely, "has no weight – it's… something to do with gravity."
그는 막연하게 생각했다. "떨어지는 물체는 무게가 없다. 그것은… 중력과 관련이 있다."

he thought vaguely를 직접 인용문 사이에 삽입한 형태의 문장이다. A falling body has no weight(추락하는 물체는 무게가 없다)로 붙여서 이해하면 된다.
[something to do with A]는 'A와 관련이 있는 것'을 뜻하는 표현이다. 'A와 아무 관련이 없는 것'이라 표현할 땐 something 대신에 nothing을 쓴다.

> 자유 낙하를 할 때는 땅이 나를 밀어내는 반작용이 없어서 무게가 없는 것처럼 느껴져!

p.76

It's that weird feeling of being stuck to your seat as you climb a roller-coaster.
롤러코스터를 타고 위로 올라갈 때 좌석에 붙어 있는 것 같은 그런 이상한 느낌이다.

주어 it은 앞에서 언급된 내용을 표현한 지시 대명사다. that weird feeling은 '그 이상한 느낌'이다.
as you climb a roller-coaster는 부사절로, '롤러코스터를 타고 위로 올라갈 때'로 해석한다.

3. Smashing Speed

p77

> So if you want to survive the next chapter you'd better hang on tight.
>
> 그러니 다음 장에서 살아남고 싶다면 꼭 붙잡고 있는 게 좋을 것이다.

문장 앞에 쓰는 접속사 so는 '그러니까, 그러므로'를 뜻한다. 앞에 나온 내용이 원인, so 뒤의 내용이 결과가 된다. survive는 '~에서 살아남다, ~을 극복하고 생존하다'라는 뜻이다.
you'd better는 you had better의 줄임말로 '당장 ~하는 게 좋다, ~해야 한다'를 뜻하는 표현이다.

> **CHAPTER 4 KEYWORDS**
>
> #gravity #terminal velocity #weight #Galileo Galilei

Gruesome Gravity

What goes up must come down. This old saying is true as long as you're not in outer space where things float around all the time and don't "come down". Why? Because there's no gravity in space to bring you down to Earth. So what is this unearthly force? Read on for the full and gruesome details.

Fatal forces fact file

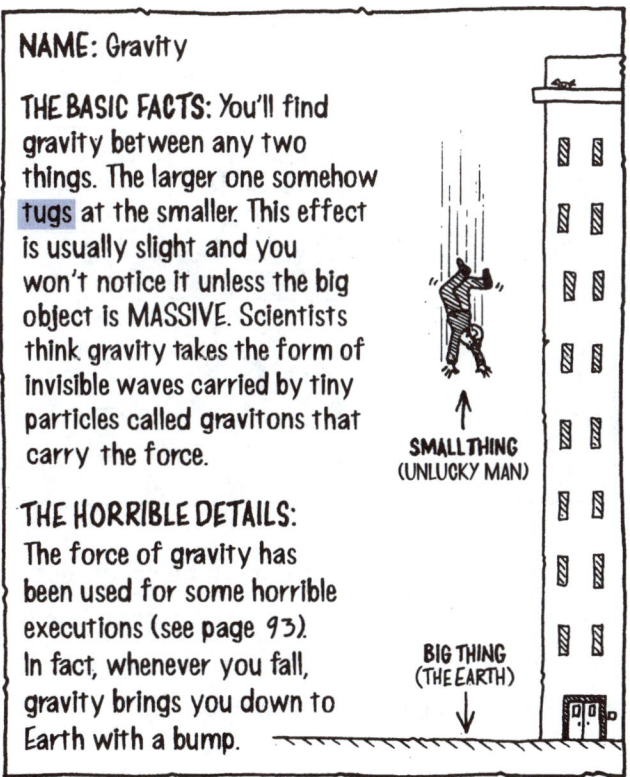

NAME: Gravity

THE BASIC FACTS: You'll find gravity between any two things. The larger one somehow tugs at the smaller. This effect is usually slight and you won't notice it unless the big object is MASSIVE. Scientists think gravity takes the form of invisible waves carried by tiny particles called gravitons that carry the force.

SMALL THING (UNLUCKY MAN)

THE HORRIBLE DETAILS: The force of gravity has been used for some horrible executions (see page 93). In fact, whenever you fall, gravity brings you down to Earth with a bump.

BIG THING (THE EARTH)

Terminal velocity

How's this for a thrill? You go for a flight in a plane up to, say, 6,100 metres and then you jump out. And you don't use a parachute. Well – not until you've fallen half-way to the  ground under the influence of gravity. Is this completely crazy? No, it's a popular sport called freefall parachuting. If you don't mind heights and enjoy a bit of danger you'll love this. If not, you'd better put on a blindfold before you read this next bit.

How to be a freefall parachutist in one quick lesson

1. Try not to look at the ground. Jump out of the plane.
2. Check your parachute is strapped securely to your back. (Come to think of it, that should have been Step One.)

3. Start tumbling. That's not something you've got to do – it's something that will happen to you anyway. You'll find your sense of balance can't help you stay upright. You'll feel sick. Try not to panic at this stage.

4) For 15 seconds you fall faster and faster. Every second you fall 9.8 metres faster until you hit – 50 metres a second (100–150 mph). That's the maximum speed you can fall. It's called terminal velocity. Gulp! It's  horrible feeling there's nothing under you except empty air, but some people can't get enough of it.

5) Good news. You won't fall any faster because the air slows you down – this force is known as drag.

6) Here's your chance to practise your freefall parachuting technique. Try to fall face downwards. Spread your arms and legs and stick your stomach out. You'll find your body curves forwards and your arms and legs are pushed backwards.

This makes a larger area for the drag to act upon. So you don't fall quite so fast. Flying squirrels and sky-diving cats do this in mid-air.

7) One minute later. Had fun? Good. You're going to hit the ground in 25 seconds. Better pull your parachute rip cord now or you'll really fall foul of gravity. And make a rather deep hole in the ground.

4. Gruesome Gravity

8. As you land make sure you drop down to a squatting position. Bending your knees soaks up some force as you hit the ground. Enjoyed it? Great – you'll be falling over yourself to make another jump.

Bet you never knew!

If you don't happen to have a parachute things can get a teensy bit more difficult. In 1944 Flight-Sergeant Nicholas Alkemade was in desperate danger 5,500 metres above Germany. His plane was on fire and his parachute was burnt to a cinder. He jumped and fully expected to die. But he was lucky. He fell on top of a tree and then onto a deep bank of snow and as a result much of the force of his fall was soaked up. Alkemade survived to tell his remarkable story and he didn't even break any bones!

More gruesome gravity

In the past gravity was used to make executions more efficient. During a hanging the victim dropped through a trapdoor and gravity acting on the rope broke the victim's neck. If the drop was too far the force yanked their head off too. Gruesome!

Another gruesome method of execution was the guillotine. This featured a 30.4 kg weight attached to a sharp blade. The force powering the gruesome blade as it fell was gravity. In the 1790s working model guillotines were popular children's toys. Their parents must have been off their heads.

In England in the seventeenth century criminals who refused to plead guilty or not guilty at their trials were crushed to death under heavy weights. Once again it was gravity doing the damage. You may be interested to know that a louse can withstand a force of 500,000 times its own weight. Unfortunately for the criminals, humans scrunch more easily.

Now for something a bit less fatal. Hopefully. You'd think that lying on a bed of nails would turn you into a gruesome human pin cushion. Surely gravity pins you to those nasty nails? Not necessarily. You can press down with a force of 450 g on a nail without harm. (Don't try proving this at home – nails are usually crawling with disgusting germs.) So 400 nails can support a huge 182 kg man for a comfortable night's sleep. Bet that's a weight off your mind.

Fatal expressions

Answers:

No. He's got a weight problem. Scientists say "mass" instead of weight because weight is just a measure of how strongly gravity is pulling you towards the Earth. Also scientists measure mass in a unit called the "slug". The overweight scientist in the picture weighs ten slugs (320 lbs). He should cut out chocolate and sticky puddings, or move to the moon. The moon's gravity is weaker than Earth's, so a human only weighs 1/6 as much there.

Test your teacher

Your teacher's bound to fall down on this really tricky question. Smile sweetly and say:

Answers:

Yes – but you'd have to be in a lift with a set of scales to prove it. If one day the lift cable snaps, quickly leap on the scales. In the few seconds you take to hurtle to the ground you're weightless! Weight is just a measure of gravity's pull. But when you fall you're not resisting gravity and you're weightless! You can blame Galileo for all this, he was the first person to discover how the force works.

Hall of fame: Galileo Galilei (1564–1642)
Nationality: Italian

Young Galileo wanted to study maths (strange boy), but his dad forced him to learn medicine instead. Doctors got more pay than mathematicians. But sneaky Galileo secretly studied sums until his dad gave up on him. When he was 25, Galileo became a maths professor at Pisa University. Then he got interested in gravity and performed amazing experiments to measure the force. Here's what his notebooks may have looked like.

> **GALILEO's BOOK of EXPERIMENTS**
>
> People laugh at me when I say that light and heavy things fall at the same speed. They say "Of course heavy things fall quicker - 'cos they're heavier." Grrr! I'll show them. 
>
> **Experiment 1**
> 1 Climb leaning Tower of Pisa with two balls of the same size. One ball is wooden and one is metal. Make sure the metal one is much heavier.
> 2 Reach top of tower. It's really slippery and there's no hand-rail. Careful now!
> 3 Chuck the two balls off the tower. Try not to chuck self off at same time.
> 4 Oh - nearly forgot. Check no one's underneath.
> 5 Note how balls land. If I'm right they'll both land at the same time.

 ME

People still don't believe me. Huh - this'll teach them a lesson.

Experiment 2

1 Get a wooden board with a little wooden gully on it. Line it with some nice shiny parchment made from animal skin with the fat scraped off.

USE SKIN FROM CAT KILLED IN EXPERIMENT 1

2 Raise the gully on a slope and roll a bronze ball down it. (If you don't have a bronze ball any other metal will do.)

3 Be sure to precisely measure the time taken for the ball to roll to the bottom of the slope. OOPS - silly me, I was about to forget, no one's invented an accurate clock yet. Better use pulse to time ball's speed. Mustn't get too excited, or my pulse will be racing. Better repeat the test a few times to make sure.

4 I believe gravity makes things accelerate at the same speed. If I'm right balls of different weights will roll at the same speed too.

Notes:

1 Galileo was proved right in both experiments.

2 It should be pointed out that boring old historians reckon there's no proof Galileo performed the first experiment.

Galileo's genius

There's no doubt Galileo was a genius. He invented the thermometer, a pendulum driven clock and an amazing compass that you could use to work out the purity of metals. He even discovered that cannonballs fall in a curved path. They move forwards at a constant speed and downwards at an increasing speed under the influence of gravity. This fatal discovery helped gunners fire more accurately and kill more people.

Could you think like Galileo? Now's your chance to find out.

Burning ambition quiz

1 You are Galileo. You look through the newly invented telescope and see planets orbiting the sun. (As Newton later proved, gravity stops them wandering off into space.) But there's one teeny little problem. Important people in the Church claim planets go round the Earth. They're all-powerful in Italy. And they don't want a smarty-pants scientist proving

them wrong. You realize you'd be wise to get the backing of these people. What do you do?
a) Start a reasoned debate.
b) Get them to look through your telescope.
c) Shout at them until they admit you're right.

2 You reckon the Church's experts that you talked to are friendly. They aren't. Your enemies falsely accuse you of being anti-Church. What do you do?
a) Go into hiding.
b) Write a book making fun of your enemies.
c) Set the record straight in a public statement.

3 In 1623 you have a stroke of luck. An old pal of yours is elected Pope. You drop in for a chat. He allows you to write a book so long as it doesn't support your views. What's in the book?
a) Support for your views and amusing abuse of your enemies.
b) A balanced survey of the different opinions which doesn't come to any conclusion.

c) A cleverly written argument which seems to back the traditional view whilst actually making it look stupid.

4 Your book is a best-seller but the Pope is chewing the carpet. You're accused of heresy and put on trial before the dreaded Inquisition. Your enemies forge a letter that claims the Church had banned you from teaching your views. If you're found guilty you could be tied to a stake and burnt alive. What do you do?
a) Proudly insist you were right.
b) Quietly remind the Pope that you're his friend.
c) Crack a joke about liking your "stake" well done.

5 In a bid to scare you, the Inquisition show you the torture chamber that is used to extract confessions. You see the rack, the thumbscrews and the red hot pincers. What do you say?
a) OK, where's the confession - I'll sign anything… Oh dear, I can't sign that, it's not grovelling enough.
b) The truth is the truth. I scorn your puny instruments of torture and laugh in the face of danger.

c) Can I have 20 years to think about it, please?

Answers:

1 b) Galileo talked to leading Church astronomers. They looked through the telescope and saw he was right. But they refused to admit it.

2 b) This was silly, because Galileo had been ordered not to talk about his views.

3 c) Galileo's book is a chat between three people. The person who backs his view is smart but the person who backs the Church's view is called "Simplicius". Can you guess why?

4 a) Of course, Galileo was right, but the Church wouldn't admit it until 1922. Galileo would have been 100 per cent delighted if he hadn't been 100 per cent dead by then. Fortunately, even in Galileo's own century, scientists in other countries, such as Isaac Newton, read his books. The scientists used Galileo's discoveries as a starting point to find out more about gravity and how the planets moved.

5 a) OK, Galileo didn't say this, but he did confess to the Inquisition that he was wrong. Don't blame him. Galileo spent the rest of his life at home under arrest. He continued to study forces but he never touched a telescope again. It was too dangerous. And now for something even more dangerous ...

4. Gruesome Gravity

Wobbly balance

Everything has a centre of gravity. Imagine a tightrope walker.

Her centre of balance is the point inside her body where gravity is pulling most strongly. If this crucial point is supported underneath and the performer's weight is evenly balanced around it she's OK. If not there'll be a gloopy mess on the pavement. Yet some balancing acts seem impossible.

Wobbly balancing quiz

See if you can guess which of these incredible balancing acts are true and which are false.

1 In 1553 a Dutch acrobat balanced on one foot on the weathervane of St Paul's Cathedral, London waving a 4.6-metre streamer. And he didn't fall off.
TRUE / FALSE

2 In 1859 French tightrope walker Jean Blondin (1824-1897) walked across the raging Niagara Falls 50 metres in the air. And he was wearing a blindfold.
TRUE / FALSE

3 In 1773 Dutch acrobat Leopold van Trump juggled ten tomatoes whilst balancing on a tightrope 30 metres in the air. If he had fallen he might have invented tomato ketchup.
TRUE / FALSE

4 In 1842 a Miss Cooke wowed London circus goers when she sat at a table and drank a glass of wine. Boring? Not really. Everything was balanced on a high wire.
TRUE / FALSE

5 In 1995 Aleksandr Bendikov of Belarus balanced a pyramid made of 880 coins. The coin pyramid was upside down and balanced on top of the edge of a single coin. Luckily, no one needed change for the bus.
TRUE / FALSE

6 In 1996 American Bryan Berg built a house of cards 100 storeys high – that's 5.85 metres.
TRUE / FALSE

7 In 1990 Brazilian Leandro Henrique Basseto cycled on one wheel of his bicycle for 100 minutes.
TRUE / FALSE

Answers:

1. **TRUE.** Some people will do anything to get attention.
2. **TRUE.** Blondin also went across on stilts. By then he was just showing off.
3. **FALSE**
4. **TRUE**
5. **TRUE**
6. **TRUE.** He built the record house of cards in Copenhagen, Denmark. Couldn't he find anything more exciting to do?
7. **FALSE.** In fact he cycled for an incredible 640 minutes.

Yes, it's amazing what incredible death-defying, gravity-defying, balancing acts people can do just as long as the force of gravity is exactly balanced. But getting it right on the high-wire certainly puts you under pressure. And oddly enough, the next chapter is about pressure too. The kind of pressure that can fatally crush a human being. Ouch!

REVIEW

질량이 있는 모든 사물 사이에는 서로 잡아당기는 힘이 작용한다. 바로 만유인력의 법칙이다. 가장 쉽게 경험할 수 있는 끄는 힘은 바로 지구가 당기는 힘, 중력이다. 중력은 잔인하다. 높은 곳에서 추락해 목숨을 잃은 사람은 셀 수 없이 많고, 교수형이나 기요틴을 이용한 참수형은 중력을 활용한 처형 방법이었다. 약 400년 전에 이탈리아의 과학자 갈릴레오 갈릴레이는 중력과 만유인력을 연구하다가 그런 식으로 처형될 뻔했다. '지구가 태양의 주위를 돈다'고 주장해서 교회 성직자들의 분노 호르몬을 돌게 만들었기 때문이다. 과연 중력은 어떻게 작용하는 걸까?

4. Gruesome Gravity

Vocabulary 4

p.89

The larger one somehow **tugs** at the smaller.

더 큰 것이 어떤 식으로든 더 작은 것을 잡아당긴다.

tug '세게 잡아당기다'를 뜻하는 동사다. 힘을 주어 여러 번 당기는 것이다. 강아지가 좋아하는 수건이나 장난감을 물고 있을 때 잡아당기며 노는 것을 '**tug**(터그) 놀이'라고 하고, 긴 줄 양쪽에 여럿이 서서 계속 줄을 당겨 승부를 정하는 게임인 '줄다리기'를 영어로 **tug** of war라고 한다.

p.90

If you don't mind **heights** and enjoy a bit of danger you'll love this.

높은 곳을 꺼리지 않고 약간의 위험을 즐긴다면, 당신은 이 게임을 좋아할 것이다.

height '수직 방향으로의 길이'를 뜻한다. 산이나 빌딩의 '높이', 비행기의 '고도', 사람의 '키' 등을 모두 **height**로 표현할 수 있다. '높은'이라는 뜻의 형용사는 **high**다. What is its **height**?나 How **high** is it? 같은 의문문으로 높이가 얼마나 되는지 물어볼 수 있다.

p.91

It's called **terminal** velocity.

그걸 종단 속도라고 부른다.

terminal '끝의, 최종의, 말기의'를 뜻하는 형용사다. term은 '끝(end), 한계(limit)'를 의미한다. 고속버스가 멈춰 서서 승객을 태우고 내려야 하는 여정의 '끝'이 '**terminal**(터미널)'이다.

p.92

In 1944 Flight-Sergeant Nicholas Alkemade was in **desperate** danger 5,500 metres above Germany.

1944년 공군 상사 니콜라스 알케메이드는 독일 상공 5500미터에서 절망적인 위험에 처해 있었다.

desperate de-는 '~로부터 멀어진'을 뜻하고, sperate는 '희망(hope)'을 뜻한다. 희망으로부터 멀어지고 희망이 보이지 않는 상황을 표현한 말이다. 이런 상황에서는 마음이 다급해지고 간절해진다. '절망적인, 필사적인, 간절한, 다급한'이라는 뜻이다.

p.93

During a hanging the victim dropped through a trapdoor and gravity acting on the rope broke the **victim's** neck.

교수형 도중 희생자가 함정문을 통해 떨어지면, 밧줄에 작용하는 중력으로 인해 그의 목이 부러졌다.

victim '생명을 잃는 사람'을 의미하는데, 원래 종교 의식에서 제물로 바쳐지는 사람을 부르는 말로 썼다. 지금은 전쟁이나 범죄, 불의의 사고나 재난 때문에 피해를 보거나 목숨을 잃은 '피해자, 희생자'를 뜻하는 말로 쓴다.

4. Gruesome Gravity

p.93

In England in the seventeenth century criminals who refused to plead guilty or not **guilty** at their trials were crushed to death under heavy weights.

17세기 영국에서는 재판에서 유죄나 무죄를 인정하지 않는 범죄자들이 무거운 무게에 짓눌려 죽었다.

guilty '유죄의, 잘못이 있는, 죄책감을 느끼는'을 뜻하는 형용사다. **guilt**는 비도덕적인 행동, 불법 행위를 저지른 사실, 또는 그로 인한 양심의 가책을 표현하는 말로, '유죄, 책임, 죄책감'을 뜻한다. 법정에서 판사, 변호사, 검사가 가장 많이 하는 말 중 하나가 'He/She is (not) **guilty**!'다.

p.94

So 400 nails can **support** a huge 182kg man for a comfortable night's sleep.

따라서 400개의 못이라면 182kg 거구의 남자가 편안하게 밤잠을 자도록 지탱할 수 있다.

support '떠받치다, 지탱하다'라는 뜻이다. sup는 '밑에서 위로'를 뜻하고 port는 '나르다, 전하다'를 뜻한다. 밑에서 위로 힘을 전달해야 위에 있는 것들이 무너지지 않는다. 기둥과 벽이 지붕을 지탱하는 모습이 바로 **support**의 개념이다. 또한 의식주를 책임지며 누군가를 돌보는 것도 **support**로 표현한다. '먹여 살리다, 지원하다, 지지하다'라는 뜻이다. 특정 스포츠 팀이나 연예인, 정당 등을 응원하고 지원하는 사람들을 '**supporters**(서포터스)'라고 부른다.

p.95

Weight is just a **measure** of gravity's pull.

무게는 단지 중력이 당기는 힘의 수치일 뿐이다.

measure 눈금을 읽어 수치를 확인하는 것이 **measure**다. '수치를 재다, 평가하다'라는 뜻의 동사로 자주 쓴다. me는 '수치, 눈금'을 의미하고, asure는 '확인하다'를 의미한다. 예문에서처럼 **measure**를 명사로 쓰면 '양, 정도'를 뜻하거나, '측정 단위, 기준'을 뜻하는 말이 된다. 명사형 **measurement**는 '측정, 측량, 치수' 등을 뜻한다.

> The **overweight** scientist **weighs** about ten slugs - 145kg.
> 그 과체중 과학자의 몸무게는 약 10슬러그, 즉 145kg이다.

weight '무게, 중량'을 뜻하는 명사다. 무거운 것을 들어서 근육을 만드는 운동을 **weight** training이라고 한다. **weigh**가 동사로 사용되면 두 가지 의미다. 'I **weigh** 60 kilograms.' (난 체중이 60킬로야.)처럼 '무게가 ~이다'는 뜻과 Let's **weigh** the potatoes.(감자 무게를 재보자.)처럼 '무게를 달다, 체중을 재다'라는 뜻으로 쓴다.

> **Chuck** the two balls off the tower.
> 공 두 개를 탑에서 떨어뜨린다.

chuck 기본 의미는 '던지다(throw)'이다. 던지는 동작도 여러 가지다. 받기 좋게 가볍게 던지는 건 toss, 야구공을 세게 던지는 건 pitch, 거칠게 막 던지는 건 hurl을 써서 표현한다. **chuck**은 어딘가를 정확히 조준하고서 물건을 던지는 게 아니라, 아무 생각 없이 대충 무심코 던지는 동작을 표현하는 동사다.

> It should be pointed out that boring old historians reckon there's no **proof** Galileo performed the first experiment.
> 고리타분한 나이 든 역사가들은 갈릴레오가 최초의 실험을 했다는 증거가 없다고 생각한다는 점을 지적해야 한다.

proof 첫 번째 뜻은 '증명, 입증'이다. 어떤 사건이나 진술이 사실인지 밝히는 행동이나 과정을 말한다. 두 번째 뜻은 '증거, 증거물, 증명서'다. 사실을 뒷받침해 주는 정보, 사물, 문서를 말한다. '~을 증명(입증)하다, ~로 판명되다'를 뜻하는 동사는 **prove**다. **proof**와 **prove**는 '자세히 조사하다, 탐사하다'를 뜻하는 **probe**와 어원이 같다.

4. Gruesome Gravity 109

p.98

> He invented the **thermometer**, a pendulum driven clock and an amazing compass that you could use to work out the purity of metals.
>
> 갈릴레오는 온도계, 진자시계, 금속의 순도를 측정하는 데 사용할 수 있는 놀라운 나침반을 발명했다.

thermometer 공기, 물, 기계, 몸의 온도를 재는 도구인 온도계를 말한다. thermo는 '뜨거운(hot), 열(heat)'을 뜻하고, meter는 '측정, 계량기'를 뜻한다. 얼마나 뜨거운지, 열에너지가 얼마나 있는지 측정하는 도구인 '온도계'가 바로 **thermometer**다.

p.98

> You look through the newly invented telescope and see planets **orbiting** the sun.
>
> 당신은 새로 발명한 망원경을 통해 태양을 공전하는 행성들을 관찰하고 있다.

orbit 행성이 '궤도를 따라 돌다'를 뜻하는 동사다. **orbit**을 명사로 쓰면 원운동을 하며 이동하는 행성의 '궤도, 경로'를 뜻한다. 태양계 행성인 수성, 금성, 화성, 지구는 각자의 궤도로 태양의 둘레를 돈다.

p.100

> You're accused of heresy and put on trial before the dreaded **Inquisition**.
>
> 당신은 이단으로 고발되어 끔찍한 종교 재판에 회부된다.

inquisition 진지한 '질문, 심문'을 뜻한다. 대답을 제대로 안 하면 처벌을 할 거라고 위협을 하며 질문을 하는 것이다. 그런데 첫 글자를 대문자로 쓴 **Inquisition**은 더 심각한 질문이다. 기독교 하나님을 믿는지, 이교도인지, 마녀인지 묻는 '종교 재판'이다. 그 과정에서 고문과 협박이 가해졌다. 동사 **inquire**(enquire)는 '묻다, 질문하다'를 뜻한다. 어떤 중요한 정보를 알아내거나 사실인지 확인하기 위해 진지하게 물을 때 쓴다.

p.100

In a bid to scare you, the Inquisition show you the **torture** chamber that is used to extract confessions.

당신을 겁주기 위해, 종교 재판소는 자백을 끌어내는 데에 사용되는 고문실을 보여준다.

torture '비틀다(twist)'란 뜻을 가진 tort가 들어 있다. 상대의 손을 가만히 잡으면 인사하는 '악수'지만, 손을 잡고 '비틀어' 버리면 '폭력'이 된다. 목도 비틀고, 팔다리도 비틀고, 코도 비틀면서 체벌을 해 '원하는 정보'를 말하게 강요하는 행동이 **torture**다. 명사로 '고문, 고문 같은 괴롭힘'을 뜻하고, 동사로 '고문하다, 고문하듯 괴롭히다'를 뜻한다.

p.101

OK, Galileo didn't say this, but he did **confess** to the Inquisition that he was wrong.

그래. 갈릴레오는 이런 말을 하지 않았지. 하지만 그가 종교 재판소에 자신이 틀렸다고 자백한 건 맞아.

confess '자백하다, 고백하다, 시인하다'를 뜻한다. con은 '모두, 함께(together)'를 뜻하고, fess는 '말하다'를 뜻한다. 모두에게 전부 말한다는 의미로 이해할 수 있다. 다 말하면 더 이상 숨기는 것도, 비밀도 없다. 그래서 동사 **confess**는 잘못을 자백하거나 부끄러운 비밀을 털어놓을 때 쓴다. 명사형은 **confession**이다.

p.102

See if you can guess which of these **incredible** balancing acts are true and which are false.

이 놀라운 균형 잡기 중 어느 것이 진실이고 어느 것이 거짓인지 맞혀 보자.

incredible '믿을 수 없는, 믿기지 않는'이라는 뜻이다. 볼을 꼬집어 볼 만큼 '믿기지 않을' 정도로 좋을 때에도 '너무 좋은, 엄청난'의 뜻으로 자주 쓴다. '믿을 수 있는, 신뢰할 수 있는'을 뜻하는 형용사 credible 앞에 '부정(not)'을 뜻하는 in이 붙은 형태다. 어근 credi는 '믿다, 신뢰하다'를 뜻한다. 카드 결제는 나중에 돈을 내는 일종의 외상 거래로, 사용자에 대한 '믿음, 신뢰'가 있어야 한다. 그래서 신용 카드를 영어로 'credit card(크레딧 카드)'라고 부른다.

4. Gruesome Gravity

p.104

In 1990 Brazilian Leandro Henrique Basseto **cycled** on one wheel of his bicycle for 100 minutes.

1990년 브라질의 레안드로 엔히크 바세토는 자전거 한쪽 바퀴로 100분 동안 자전거를 탔다.

cycle 여기에는 '원, 바퀴, 회전, 돌다'라는 의미가 포함되어 있다. '동그라미, 빙빙 돌다'를 뜻하는 circle과 어원이 같다. 18세기 말에 자전거가 발명되어 보급되면서 두발자전거(**bicycle**), 세발자전거(**tricycle**)를 부르는 이름에 **cycle**을 붙였고, 오토바이도 **motorcycle**로 부르게 되었다. 지금은 '두 바퀴로 움직이는 탈것'을 부르는 이름으로 쓰는데, 대개 '**cycle**' 하면 '자전거'를 떠올리면 된다.

Sentence 4

p.89

This old saying is true as long as you're not in outer space where things float around all the time and don't "come down".

이 옛 속담은 당신이 우주에 있지 않는 한 진실이다. 우주에서는 물체가 항상 떠다니며 "내려오지" 않는다.

old saying은 옛날부터 내려오는 속담이나 격언을 말한다. as log as는 '~하는 한, ~하는 동안에는'을 뜻하는 표현이다.
where 이하는 중력이 작용하지 않아 "내려갈" 일이 없는 '지구 밖 우주' outer space를 설명하는 내용이다.

p.90

> Come to think of it, that should have been Step One.
> 생각해 보니, 그게 첫 단계가 되어야 했네.

문장 앞에는 Now I가 생략되어 있다. come to think of it은 '(지금)생각해 보니'로 해석한다. [should have 동사 완료형]은 '~했어야 했다'란 의미로, 과거의 일을 떠올리며 후회할 때 쓰는 표현이다.

p.90

> That's not something you've got to do - it's something that will happen to you anyway.
> 그건 꼭 해야 하는 일은 아니지만, 어쨌든 당신에게 일어날 일이다.

you've는 you have의 줄임말이다. [have got to]는 '~해야 한다'라는 의미로 have to, must와 같은 말이다.
이 문장에서 it ~ that 구문은 something을 강조하기 위해 썼다. 부사 anyway는 '어쨌든, 어떻게든'을 뜻한다.

p.91

> Better pull your parachute rip cord now or you'll really fall foul of gravity.
> 지금 낙하산 립 코드를 당기는 게 좋다. 안 그러면 정말로 중력에 희생될 테니까.

문장 앞에 You had가 생략되어 있다. had better 는 '꼭 ~해야 한다, ~해야 좋다'라는 표현이다. rip cord는 낙하산을 펼치기 위해 잡아당기는 줄이다.
두 문장을 연결하는 or는 '~하지 않으면'을 뜻한다. [fall foul of]는 '~을 어겨서 해를 입다, ~와 문제가 생기다'라는 표현이다.

4. Gruesome Gravity

p.92

He fell on top of a tree and then onto a deep bank of snow and as a result much of the force of his fall was soaked up.

그는 나무우듬지에 떨어졌다가, 그다음에는 깊은 눈 더미 위로 떨어졌는데, 그 결과 그의 낙하의 힘은 상당 부분 흡수되었다.

and then은 '그런 다음'을 뜻한다. 시간이나 순서상 '다음'에 일어나는 일 앞에 쓴다.
as a result는 '결과적으로, 그렇기 때문에'를 뜻하는 부사구다.

p.93

The force powering the gruesome blade as it fell was gravity.

그 무시무시한 칼날이 떨어질 때 힘을 갖게 한 것은 중력이었다.

The force ~ as it fell이 주어 구문으로, 주어가 길다. was는 동사, gravity가 보어다.
as it fell은 '그것(blade)이 떨어질 때'란 뜻으로 부사절이다.

p.94

Bet that's a weight off your mind.

그러면 분명 마음의 무게도 덜어질 것이다.

Bet 앞에는 화자인 주어 I가 생략되어 있다.
이 문장에서 weight는 '걱정, 근심, 부담감' 같은 마음의 무게를 의미한다. off는 '떨어져 나간다'라는 의미다. 그래서 a weight off your mind는 '마음의 부담(걱정, 두려움)을 덜다'를 뜻하는 표현이다.

p.95

> Your teacher's bound to fall down on this really tricky question.
> 당신의 선생님은 정말 까다로운 이 문제에서 틀림없이 실패할 것이다.

[be bound to 동사]는 '반드시 ~하다, ~하지 않을 수 없다'를 뜻하는 표현이다. 분명히 그렇게 행동한다는 의미다.
[fall down on A]는 A 위에서 (넘지 못하고) 걸려 넘어진다는 의미로 'A를 잘 못하다, A에서 실패하다'를 뜻하는 표현이다.

p.96

> Make sure the metal one is much heavier.
> 금속 공이 훨씬 더 무거워야 한다.

[make sure (that) 문장]은 '반드시 ~하게 하다, ~인지 분명히 확인하다, 꼭 ~이어야 한다'를 뜻하는 표현이다.
heavier는 '무거운'을 뜻하는 형용사 heavy의 비교급으로 '더 무거운'을 뜻한다. '훨씬 더 무거운'으로 강조하려면 부사 역할을 하는 much를 앞에 붙여 much heavier로 쓰면 된다.

p.97

> Be sure to precisely measure the time taken for the ball to roll to the bottom of the slope.
> 공이 경사면 하단까지 굴러가는 데 걸리는 시간을 정확하게 측정해야 한다.

[be sure to 동사]도 '반드시 ~하다, ~하는 것을 꼭 확인하다'를 의미한다.

4. Gruesome Gravity

measure의 목적어인 the time 뒤에 어떤 '시간'인지 설명하는 내용이 분사 구문 형태로 연결되어 있다. 공이(for the ball) 경사로의 바닥까지(to the bottom of the slope) 구르는(to roll) 데에 걸리는(taken) 시간이다.

p.98

> As Newton later proved, gravity stops them wandering off into space.
> 뉴턴이 나중에 증명했듯이, 중력은 행성들이 우주로 떨어져 나가는 것을 막는다.

As Newton later proved는 '나중에 뉴턴이 증명했듯이'로 해석한다.
[stop A (from) 동사ing]는 'A가 ~하지 못하게 막다, A가 ~하는 것을 멈추게 하다'를 뜻한다. wander off는 '벗어나다, 떨어져 나가다'를 뜻하는 표현이다.

p.99

> You reckon the Church's experts that you talked to are friendly.
> 당신은 함께 이야기를 나눈 교회의 전문가들이 친절하다고 생각한다.

reckon은 어떤 근거를 갖고서 생각하고 평가한다는 의미로, '기대하다, 판단하다, 믿다'를 뜻하는 동사다.
reckon의 목적어는 the Church ~ friendly 문장이다. 그리고 목적절의 주어는 the Church's experts인데, that you talked to(당신이 대화한)가 수식하고 있다. 여기에서 that은 who로 바꿔 쓸 수 있다.

p.100

> If you're found guilty you could be tied to a stake and burnt alive.
> 유죄로 판명되면 당신은 말뚝에 묶여 산 채로 불태워질 수도 있다.

[be found 형용사]는 '~인 상태로 발견되다, ~임이 드러나다'라는 의미다. 그래서 If you're found guilty는 '당신이 유죄로 드러난다면'으로 해석할 수 있다.
be tied to a stake(말뚝에 묶여서) and burnt alive(산 채로 불태워지다)는 중세 유럽에서 행해졌던 화형을 묘사한 것이다.

p.101

The scientists used Galileo's discoveries as a starting point to find out more about gravity and how the planets moved.

과학자들은 갈릴레오의 발견을 출발점으로 삼아 중력과 행성의 움직임에 대해 더 많은 것을 알아냈다.

find out은 '알아내다, 밝혀내다'를 뜻하는 표현이다. 목적어는 두 개다. more about gravity (중력에 관해 더 많은 것들)와 how the planets moved(행성들이 어떻게 움직이는지).

p.102

If this crucial point is supported underneath and the performer's weight is evenly balanced around it she's OK.

이 중요한 점이 아래에서 지지되어 있고 그 곡예사의 무게가 주위로 고르게 분산된다면 그녀는 무사하다.

이 문장의 주절인 she's OK.는 '그녀는 괜찮다(무사하다)'는 뜻이다. 공중에 달린 로프에서 떨어지지 않는다는 의미다.

If this ~ around it이 부사절이다. 부사절에서 중요한 역할을 하고 있는 underneath는 '밑에서, 아래에서'를 뜻하고, evenly는 '고르게, 균등하게'를 뜻한다.

p.105

Yes, it's amazing what incredible death-defying, gravity-defying, balancing acts people can do just as long as the force of gravity is exactly balanced.

그렇다. 중력이 정확히 균형을 이루는 한, 사람들이 죽음을 무릅쓰고 중력을 거스르고 균형 잡는 행위를 얼마나 믿을 수 없을 정도로 해내는지 놀랍다.

what 이하의 문장이 진짜 주어인데, 너무 길기 때문에 가주어인 it을 주어 자리에 두었다. what ~ acts는 동사 do의 목적어다. '사람들이 죽음을 거스르고, 중력을 거스르고, 균형을 잡는, 어떤 행동들을 할 수 있는지'로 해석할 수 있다.

4. Gruesome Gravity

CHAPTER 5 KEYWORDS

#pressure #Blaise Pascal #vacuum #Isambard Brunel

Under Pressure

Air and water are common enough on Earth but they contain vital chemicals – in fact we couldn't live without them. But if they're under pressure it's hard to live with them. And they can easily prove fatal.

Fatal forces fact file

NAME: Air and water pressure

THE BASIC FACTS: When tiny bits of air and water (molecules) are pushed aside by an object they push back. That's why when you get into a deep bath you can feel the water pushing against your body. It's what is called water pressure.

THE HORRIBLE DETAILS: The deeper you go the more water there is above you. This means more pressure. Divers breathe air that's also under pressure to stop their lungs getting squashed.

THIS SUBMARINE'S AMAZING – IT EVEN HAS A SHOWER IN IT...

ACTUALLY, THAT'S CALLED A LEAK CAPTAIN

One of the first people to study air pressure was French physicist Blaise Pascal.

Hall of fame: Blaise Pascal (1623–1662)
Nationality: French

Blaise Pascal had no sense of humour. Not surprising really, he suffered all his life from violent indigestion so he didn't have the stomach for too many jokes. But that didn't stop brainy Blaise from making some amazing discoveries. At the age of 19 he built a machine to help his tax collector dad count up the loot. And in 1646 he invented a barometer – a machine that measures air pressure. High air pressure pushes a column of mercury upwards.

To test his invention Blaise forced his brother-in-law to walk up a local mountain carrying the barometer. (The scientist's health wasn't up to making the climb himself, of course.) The climber found that the air pressure dropped as he went higher. The higher you go the less air there is pushing down on you. Today the brave brother-in-law is forgotten but pressure is measured in "Pascals". (1 Pascal = 1 Newton per square metre.)

Bet you never knew!

Imagine all those kilometres of air above you pressing down on your head. The air pressure on your body is an incredible 100,000 Pascals. That's the same weight as two elephants. Luckily, the air inside your body is under pressure too. It pushes outwards with the same force so you don't even notice it. Planes that fly at high altitudes have pressurized cabins in which the air is kept at the same pressure as ground level. If a pilot flew without this protection the lower air pressure would cause air bubbles in his or her body to get bigger. The guts and lungs would swell painfully and air bubbles trapped in fillings could make their teeth explode.

Dare you discover... how air pressure helps you drink?

You will need:
Yourself
A bottle of your favourite drink (it's all in the interests of science) - just so long as the bottle's got a narrow neck.

What you do:

1 Try drinking from the bottle. Sit upright and tip the bottle up so it's level with your mouth. You can easily suck the liquid up.

2 Now stick the mouth of the bottle in your mouth. Wrap your lips around the neck of the bottle. Now try to drink.

What do you notice?
a) It's as easy as before.
b) You can't suck any more drink up.
c) You dribble uncontrollably into your drink.

> **Answers:**
>
> b) Liquids flow to areas where the air pressure is less. As you try to suck your drink the air space in the bottle gets bigger. Since no more air gets into the bottle the air pressure drops below the air pressure in your mouth. This keeps the liquid in the bottle. Don't suck too hard — you might swallow the bottle. Mind you, that's not as horrible as a vacuum in your bottle. Here's why...

Bet you never knew!

A vacuum is a completely empty space where there's no air or water pressure. That means that if you absent-mindedly forgot your space suit when you go for a space walk the air pressure pushing out from inside your body would make your guts explode and your eyeballs plop out of their sockets. Erk!

Terrible teacher joke

5. Under Pressure

Under pressure

1. The first man-made vacuum was made by Otto von Guericke (1602–1686) Mayor of Magdeburg, Germany. In his spare time Otto was keen on scientific experiments but in 1631 Magdeburg was destroyed in war and 70,000 people were killed. Von Guericke got away and carried on researching.
2. In 1647 he tried pumping air from a beer cask. But more air got in and made a strange whistling noise.
3. So he put the beer cask in a barrel of water. Water was sucked into the cask with a strange squelching noise.
4. Next he made a hollow copper ball. But when he pumped the air out it was crushed by an unseen force.
5. In 1654 von Guericke made a hollow ball from two stronger copper cups and pumped out the air. He'd made a vacuum. The pressure of the air outside jammed the cups together. It was this pressure that had crushed the earlier ball.
6. Fifty men couldn't pull the cups apart.
7. Two teams of horses didn't stand a chance.
8. But when von Guericke pumped air into the hollow centre the cups fell apart.

Some pressing facts

1. In the 1890s Aimée, a young circus performer, used the power of vacuums to walk upside down. Her shoes had suction caps attached to them and as she walked the air was pushed out of the caps. The pressure of the air outside the caps then glued her feet to a board hung from the ceiling. Very im-press-ive!

❷ Champagne in a bottle is under pressure too. This is due to all the gas bubbles squeezed into the drink. When shaken and heated the cork fires at 12.3 metres a second – as fast as a rock blasted with dynamite. It definitely makes a party go with a bang.

❸ Pressurized liquid or gases are used in hydraulic machines such as the powerful pistons that lift crane jibs. One early hydraulic machine was a nineteenth-century vacuum cleaner. Water was squirted one way and the falling pressure sucked in air and dirt behind it. But when water went the wrong way it flooded your home.

❹ In 1868 American inventor George Westinghouse (1846–1914) made an air brake. It used the cushioning effect of air pressure to halt a train. Rail tycoon Cornelius Vanderbilt called it a "foolish notion". He didn't think air could stop a train. But nowadays air brakes are used on buses and lorries too.

Air pressure can do amazing things but could it also haul a train? It took a genius to see the possibilities in this "train of thought". A hard-driving ruthless workaholic genius in a black top hat.

 **Hall of fame:** Isambard Kingdom Brunel (1806–1859)
Nationality: British

Isambard Kingdom Brunel dedicated his life to engineering. He developed some spectacular engineering projects that used the forces of nature to help make people's lives easier. He built railways, giant iron ships and tunnels on a grand scale. At times he was so wrapped up in his work that he showed little concern for others. He even sent his crippled son to a school where there were daily floggings. When the child complained bossy Brunel snapped at him:

Issie loved to attempt the seemingly impossible. Sometimes he was successful but he also made many fatal mistakes. This story is about one of them… a railway powered by air pressure.

Pipe dreams

Devon, England 1848

Isambard Kingdom Brunel chewed on his giant-sized cigar as he strode angrily along the railway. As usual his mind was jumping with ideas. Fantastic ideas. Mighty plans. Pipe dreams. They had all seemed so easy. Once.

Four years ago Brunel and some other leading engineers visited Ireland to see the world's first "atmospheric railway". A railway where the carriages were pulled quickly and silently. Pulled along by the amazing power of air.

The idea was simple…

How to build your own atmospheric railway.

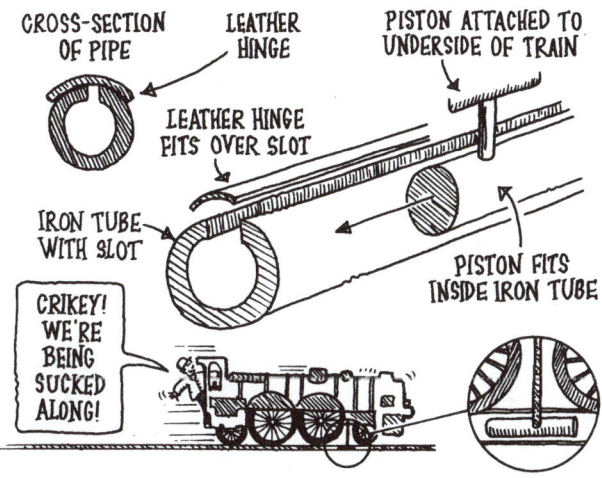

And here's how it worked.

① Powerful steam engines pump the air from the pipe.

② A piston travels along the pipe. It's pushed by air trying to rush back into the vacuum.

③ The piston is linked to passenger carriages and provides the moving power.

5. Under Pressure

The other engineers laughed at the strangely silent railway. They thought it was impractical. But Isambard was quietly impressed. He suggested using atmospheric pressure for the South Devon Railway. But he forgot to mention to anyone that the Irish railway was always breaking down. Little old ladies rushed to sink their savings in a scheme backed by the world's greatest engineer. But the pipe dream soon turned into a pipe nightmare.

Now Brunel had come to see things for himself and young Tom the signalman's boy was showing him around.

"It's the leather hinges, Mr Brunel," said Tom slightly in awe of the great man. "They dry and crack in cold winter weather. And they rot in warm sunshine."

"So I see," said Brunel wrinkling his nose in distaste. "What's that appalling smell?"

"That'll be the fish oil. The railway pays people to walk along the line and paint the leather with soap and fish liver oil to keep it soft. Smells disgusting, it does."

They walked on until they reached one of the massive brick-built pumping sheds.

"Here's the other problem!" cried Tom. He nervously twisted his pale sweaty fingers. "It's the pipes…"

"What do you mean pipes?" bellowed Brunel above the noise of the engines. The huge steam engine snorted foul black smoke like an angry dragon. The gasping pumps sucked the air from the hollow iron pipes. And with the air came a stream of horrible things.

Oily water, rust and dead rats.

Rats. Water.

"How did they get there?" Brunel roared into the boy's ear. But he'd already guessed the terrible truth.

Hungry rats chewed the oily leather flaps until they were no longer air-tight. Water seeped in and rusted the pipes.

The famous engineer strode on furiously with the signalman's boy jogging to keep up. Suddenly Brunel bent down to touch the rat nibbled leather. Tom watched in fascinated horror. "No!" he shouted.

Brunel had his hand on the flap when Tom grabbed his arm.

"Stand aside boy!" ordered Brunel curtly.

"Please don't touch it," gasped Tom.

"Why NOT?"

Then Brunel saw the ghastly danger.

The vacuum inside the pipe wasn't 100 per cent. But it could still pluck his finger bones from their sockets. Scrunch, squelch, plop. No more fingers.

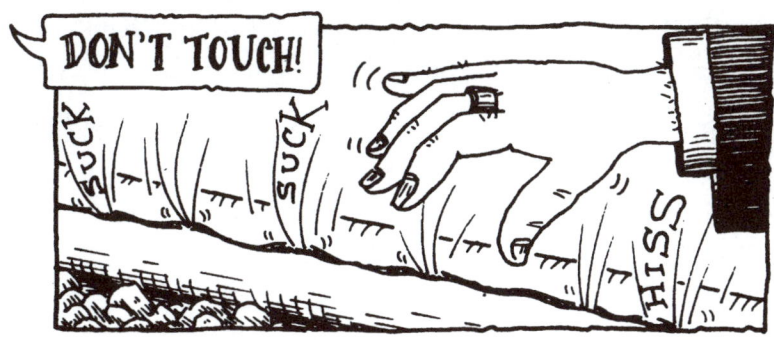

5. Under Pressure

He backed off, muttering. There were some things even the great Brunel dared not do.

In February 1848 Brunel told the Company the problems were almost solved. But seven months later he advised the directors to scrap the entire project. The little old ladies had lost their savings. And they were angry.

So how did Brunel make it up to them?
a) He offered to build a new railway for nothing.
b) He said he wouldn't send his bill for engineering advice.
c) He offered them a lifetime's supply of smelly fish oil.

Answers:
b) Brunel kindly offered not to send his bill. Not just yet. Bet that cheered them up. There was a lot of anger and friction. You get friction in the world of forces too. But this sort of friction can wreck machines and spark fatal fires. That's why the next chapter is RED HOT.

REVIEW

수직으로 미는 힘, 아래로 누르는 힘을 흔히 '압력'이라고 하는데, 사실 압력은 어느 방향에서나 작용할 수 있다. 통조림통을 찌그러뜨릴 수도 있는 공기의 압력, 기압. 콘크리트 댐을 무너뜨릴 수 있는 물의 압력, 수압. 그리고 공부하라고 나를 누르는 엄마의 압력! 모두 종잡을 수 없다는 공통점이 있다. 우리 주변에는 압력을 이용한 발명품들이 많다. 진공청소기, 헤어드라이어, 분수, 샤워기 헤드 등등. 자동차, 기차, 선박, 비행기의 엔진도 압력으로 작동한다. 그런데 압력의 크기를 측정할 수 있을까? 프랑스의 과학자 블레즈 파스칼을 알면 가능하다.

Vocabulary 5

p.118

But if they're under **pressure** it's hard to live with them.
그러나 공기와 물이 압력을 받는 상태라면 그것들과 함께 살기는 힘들다.

pressure '누르는 행동이나 과정'을 표현하는 말이다. 명사로 '누르기, 압력, 압박, 압박감(스트레스)'을 뜻하고, 동사로 '압력을 가하다, 강요하다'를 뜻한다. 동사 **press**의 기본 의미는 '꾹 누르다'이다. 잉크 묻은 판을 종이에 '눌러서' 인쇄했기 때문에 **press**는 '인쇄, 인쇄기, 신문, 출판' 등을 뜻하는 말로도 발전했다. be under **pressure**는 '압력을 받고 있다, 강요받다'를 뜻하는 표현이다.

p.118

When tiny bits of air and water (**molecules**) are pushed aside by an object they push back.
공기와 물의 작은 조각들(분자)이 어떤 물체에 의해 밀려나면 그것을 되밀어 낸다.

molecule '작은 덩어리'인 물질의 '분자(分子)'를 뜻한다. mole은 '덩어리'를 의미하고, cule은 '작은 것'을 의미한다. 핵(nucleus)과 전자(electron)로 구성된 물질의 기본 구성 단위를 원자(atom)라고 한다. 그리고 두 개 이상의 원자가 결합되어 고유한 성질을 나타내는 물질을 '분자'라고 한다. 수소(hydrogen) 원자 두 개와 산소(oxygen) 원자 한 개가 결합해야 분자 H_2O(물)가 된다.

p.119

> Not surprisingly really, he suffered all his life from violent **indigestion** so he didn't have the stomach for too many jokes.
>
> 그다지 놀랍지 않은 것이, 파스칼은 평생 극심한 소화 불량에 시달렸기 때문에 농담을 많이 할 여유가 없었다.

indigestion '소화 불량, 체증, 급체로 인한 복통'을 뜻한다. digest는 '나누어(di) 옮기다(gest)'란 의미를 갖고 있다. 우리가 섭취한 음식은 위에서 소화액과 섞여 잘게 나뉘고 소장으로 보내진다. 이런 소화 작용을 잘 표현한 말이 **digest**다. 동사로 '소화하다, 소화되다, 완전히 이해하다'를 뜻한다. '소화'를 뜻하는 명사형 **digestion** 앞에 부정(not)을 나타내는 in이 붙으면 소화가 안 되는 것을 나타낸다.

p.119

> And in 1646 he invented a **barometer** – a machine that measures air pressure.
>
> 그리고 1646년에 그는 기압계를 발명했다. 기압계는 공기압을 측정하는 기계다.

barometer baro는 '무게, 무거운'을 의미하고, meter는 '측정, 계량기'를 의미한다. 물체의 무게를 재는 기구는 scale(저울)이다. 17세기에 공기의 무게, 대기의 압력을 측정하는 기구가 발명되었는데, scale과는 많이 달랐기 때문에 영국의 과학자 로버트 보일(Robert Boyle)이 이 기구의 영어 이름을 **barometer**라고 새로 지은 것이다. '기압계'를 뜻한다.

p.121

> Mind you, that's not as horrible as a **vacuum** in your bottle.
>
> 기억할 건, 그것이 병 속의 진공 상태만큼 끔찍하지는 않다는 점이다.

vacuum '진공, 진공 상태'를 뜻한다. 라틴어에서 온 어근 vac는 '비어 있는(empty)'을 의미한다. 직장과 학교를 '비우고' 떠나는 '휴가, 방학'이 vacation이다. **vacuum**에서 뒤에 붙은 -um은 '장소, 공간'을 의미한다. 20세기 초에 보급된 '진공청소기'에 **vacuum** cleaner라는 이름이 붙었고, 그때부터 **vacuum**은 '진공청소, 진공청소기로 청소하다'란 뜻도 갖게 되었다.

진공으로는 이런 것도 할 수 있다고!

5. Under Pressure

p.122

> In his spare time, Otto was **keen** on scientific experiments but in 1631 Magdeburg was destroyed in war and 70,000 people were killed.
> 오토는 여가 시간에 과학 실험에 열중했지만, 1631년에 마그데부르크가 전쟁에 파괴되었고 7만 명이 사망했다.

keen 기본 의미는 'a **keen** knife(예리한 칼)'에서처럼 '날카로운, 예리한(sharp)'이다. 감각, 관찰력, 이해력 등이 '예리하고 예민하다'라는 의미를 표현할 수도 있다. a **keen** sense of smell이 '예민한 후각'이다. 자기가 좋아하는 것을 적극적으로 탐색하는 감각이라 keen은 '간절히 원하는, 갈망하는, 매우 관심이 많은'을 뜻한다. [be **keen** on A]는 'A를 무척 좋아하는, A에 관심이 많은'을 뜻하는 표현이다.

p.122

> Her shoes had suction caps **attached** to them and as she walked the air was pushed out of the caps.
> 그녀의 신발에는 흡입 캡이 달려 있어서 그녀가 걸을 때마다 캡에서 공기가 밀려 나왔다.

attach '~에(at, to)'를 뜻하는 at과 '기둥, 말뚝'을 뜻하는 tach가 합쳐진 말이다. 사람들은 기둥이나 말뚝에 많은 것을 붙이고 매단다. 표지판, 안내판, 가로등, 신호등이 기둥에 달리고, 기둥을 세운 후에 벽과 지붕을 붙이고, 소와 말을 말뚝에 매어 놓기도 한다. 이런 모습을 표현한 동사가 **attach**다. '붙이다, 부착하다, 연결하다, 결합하다'를 뜻한다. '떼다, 분리하다'를 뜻하는 반대말은 detach다.

p.123

> Pressurized liquid or gases are used in **hydraulic** machines such as the powerful pistons that lift crane jibs.
> 압력이 가해진 액체나 기체는 크레인 지브를 들어 올리는 강력한 피스톤과 같은 유압 기계에 사용된다.

hydraulic hydr는 '물(water)'을 의미하고, aul은 '튜브(tube), 파이프(pipe)'를 의미한다. 기원전 3세기인 약 2300년 전에 활동한 그리스 수학자 크테시비우스(Ctesibius)가 물의 흐름과 압력을 활용해 연주하는 '물 오르간'을 발명했는데, 악기 이름이 'hydraulikos organon'이었다. 후대 유럽인들이 물의 성질을 이용해 만드는 기계에 같은 이름을 쓰면서 영어 단어로 쓰이기 시작했다. **hydraulic**은 '물(액체)의 압력으로 작동하는'을 뜻하는 형용사다.

p.123

Water was **squirted** one way and the falling pressure sucked in air and dirt behind it.
물이 한쪽으로 분사되면서 떨어지는 압력이 뒤쪽에서 공기와 흙을 빨아들였다.

squirt 물총을 쏴 본 적이 있는가? 물총 안에 물이 가득 들어 있는데 물이 나오는 구멍은 작으니까 방아쇠를 당기면 물줄기가 '가늘고 빠르게 멀리까지' 나간다. 물이 나오는 호스(hose) 끝을 살짝 막으면 물줄기가 세게 멀리 뿌려진다. '액체를 내뿜다, 물줄기를 쏘다, 액체가 찍 나오다, 물이 세게 뿌려지다'를 뜻한다.

p.126

They thought it was **impractical**.
그들은 그것이 실행 불가능하다고 생각했다.

impractical '실제로 해 보다'란 의미를 갖고 있는 **practice**에 '반대, 부정'을 뜻하는 im을 붙여 '실행 불가능한, 비현실적인, 터무니없는'이라는 뜻이 되었다. 배운 것을 실제로 적용해 본다는 의미에서 '연습 문제, 실전 문제'를 **practice**로 표현한다. 그래서 명사로 '연습, 실습, 실행'을 뜻하고, 동사로 '연습하다, 실행하다'를 뜻한다. 형용사형 **practical**은 '실천 가능한, 현실적인'을 뜻하는데, 실행할 수 있는 것은 쓸모가 있기 때문에 '실용적인, 유용한'을 뜻하기도 한다.

p.126

Smells **disgusting**, it does.
냄새 고약하네, 진짜.

disgusting gust는 '맛(taste)'을 뜻하는 라틴어에서 왔다. dis는 '반대'를 의미한다. 그래

5. Under Pressure

서 disgust는 먹지 못할 만큼 맛이 '더럽다'는 뜻으로 쓰다가 '역겨움, 혐오감'을 뜻하는 명사와 '역겹게 하다, 혐오감을 일으키다'를 뜻하는 동사로 발전했다. disgusting은 '역겨운, 구역질 나는, 혐오스러운'을 뜻하는 형용사다.

p.127

Water seeped in and **rusted** the pipes.
물이 스며들어 파이프를 녹슬게 했다.

rust 원래 '붉다, 빨간색(red)'을 뜻하는 말이었는데, 쇠를 공기 중에 오래 두면 붉게 변하기 때문에 '녹, 녹슬다, 부식하다(시키다)'를 뜻하는 말로 쓰게 되었다. 금속이 산소(oxygen)를 만나면 색이 변하고 부식이 발생하는데, 이를 '산화 작용'이라고 한다. 가장 흔한 금속인 '철'은 산화 작용으로 인해 서서히 붉은색으로 변한다.

Sentence 5

p.118

That's why when you get into a deep bath you can feel the water pushing against your body.
그래서 깊은 욕조에 들어가면 물이 몸을 밀어내는 것을 느낄 수 있는 것이다.

[That's why 문장]은 '그것이 ~하는 이유다'라는 뜻이다. why 이하의 문장은 부사절인 when you ~ bath와 주절 you can ~ body로 이루어져 있다.
deep bath는 '물이 가득한 욕조에 몸을 담그고 하는 목욕'이다.

p.119

> The higher you go the less air there is pushing down on you.
> 높이 올라갈수록 당신을 누르는 공기의 양이 계속 줄어든다.

'~할수록 더 ~하다'를 표현하는 [the 비교급, the 비교급] 형태의 문장이다.
'높이 올라갈수록 누르는 공기의 양이 더 적어진다'는 의미다. 뒤의 문장은 'the 비교급' 형태로 만들기 위해 there is less air pushing down on you를 변형한 것이다.

p.119

> Planes that fly at high altitudes have pressurized cabins in which the air is kept at the same pressure as ground level.
> 높은 고도에서 나는 비행기에는 지상과 같은 압력으로 공기가 유지되는 가압 객실이 있다.

문장의 주어는 Planes that fly at high altitudes(높은 고도를 나는 비행기들)이고, in which 이하 문장은 cabins(항공기의 선실)의 상태를 설명하는 내용이다.
[the same A as B]는 'B와 같은 A'를 의미한다. at the same pressure as ground level은 '지상과 같은 압력에'로 해석한다.

p.121

> That means that if you absent-mindedly forgot your space suit when you go for a space walk the air pressure pushing out from inside your body would make your guts explode and your eyeballs plop out of their sockets.
> 우주 유영을 할 때 생각 없이 우주복을 잊어 버린다면 몸 내부에서 밀려나오는 공기 압으로 인해 내장이 터지고 눈알이 눈구멍에서 빠질 수 있다는 의미다.

means의 목적어인 that절은 if로 시작하는 조건절과 주절로 구성되어 있다. 그런데 if절은 또 when you ~ a space walk란 부사절을 포함하고 있다.
결국 that절 전체의 주어는 the air pressure ~ your body다.

5. Under Pressure

p.123

This is due to all the gas bubbles squeezed into the drink.
이것은 음료수에 가스 거품이 압축되어 들어가기 때문이다.

덕분에 이렇게 톡 쏘는 음료수를 마실 수 있는 거지.

[due to A]는 'A 때문에(because of), A 탓에'를 뜻하는 표현이다.
squeezed into the drink(그 술에 압착된)는 앞에 나온 all the gas bubbles(모든 기포들)을 수식하는 분사구문이다.

p.124

It took a genius to see the possibilities in this "train of thought".
이런 "생각의 연속"에서 가능성을 알아차리려면 천재여야 했다.

가주어 It이 진주어 to see the possibilities(가능성들을 이해하는 것)를 대신하고 있다. 동사 took은 '필요로 했다'라는 뜻이다.
"train of thought"는 열차처럼 여러 생각이 꼬리를 무는 상황을 의미한다. 앞에 기압으로 열차를 끌 수 있는지 물었기 때문에 말장난처럼 train을 쓴 것이다.

p.124

At times he was so wrapped up in his work that he showed little concern for others.
때때로 그는 너무 자기 일에 몰두해 있어서 다른 사람들에게는 거의 관심을 보이지 않았다.

이 문장은 '너무 ~해서 …하다'를 뜻하는 [so ~ that …] 형식을 취하고 있다.
at times는 sometimes처럼 '때때로, 가끔'을 뜻하는 표현이다.
[be wrapped up in A]는 'A에 완전히 싸여 있다'는 의미인데, 뭔가에 너무 몰두해서 다른 것은 전혀 신경 쓰지 않는 상태를 표현한다. 'A에 몰두하다, 열중하다'를 뜻한다.

p.126

Little old ladies rushed to sink their savings in a scheme backed by the world's greatest engineer.

체구가 작은 나이 든 여성들이 달려들어 세계 최고의 엔지니어가 후원하는 계획에 자신들의 저축을 쏟아부으려 했다.

sink their savings in a scheme은 '계획에 자신들의 저축을 담그다' 즉, '저축해 둔 돈을 그 계획(사업)에 투자했다'는 의미다. [backed by A]는 'A가 뒷받침하는, 후원하는'을 뜻하는 표현이다.

p.126

Now Brunel had come to see things for himself and young Tom the signalman's boy was showing him around.

이제 브루넬이 직접 보러 왔고, 신호수의 아들인 어린 톰이 그를 안내해 주고 있다.

for oneself는 '스스로, 직접'을 뜻한다.
Young Tom(어린 톰)과 the signalman's boy(신호수의 아들)은 동격, 즉 같은 인물이다.
[show A around]는 'A에게 새로운 곳을 소개하고 구경시켜 준다'는 뜻의 표현이다.

p.128

There were somethings even the great Brunel dared not do.

위대한 브루넬조차도 감히 하지 못한 일이 있었다.

even ~ not do는 앞의 somethings를 수식하는 말이다. even은 '심지어 ~조차도, ~일지라도'를 뜻하는 부사다.
dared not do는 '감히 하려고 하지 않는, 할 용기가 없었던'으로 해석할 수 있다.

5. Under Pressure

CHAPTER 6 KEYWORDS
#friction #perpetual motion
#The Law of Thermodynamics

Facts About Friction

Newton said that a moving object would carry on moving for ever if another force didn't slow it down. That force is called friction. People use the word friction to mean aggro, anger or annoyance. Like a really bad day at school. And in the world of fatal forces friction can also often spoil your whole day.

Fatal forces fact file

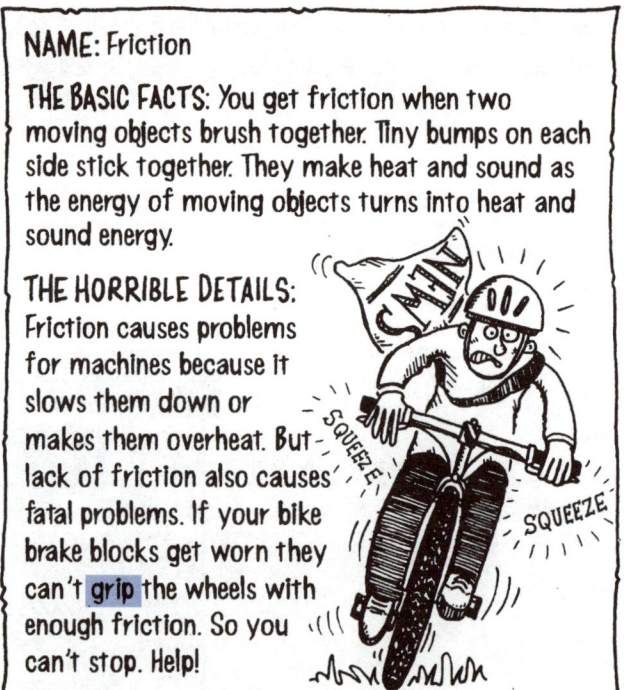

NAME: Friction

THE BASIC FACTS: You get friction when two moving objects brush together. Tiny bumps on each side stick together. They make heat and sound as the energy of moving objects turns into heat and sound energy.

THE HORRIBLE DETAILS: Friction causes problems for machines because it slows them down or makes them overheat. But lack of friction also causes fatal problems. If your bike brake blocks get worn they can't grip the wheels with enough friction. So you can't stop. Help!

Mind you, the man who discovered friction had an amazing life story. He could almost have been a character from friction – er, fiction.

 **Hall of fame:** Benjamin Thompson (Count Rumford of Bavaria)
Nationality: American

Ben Thompson was a teacher who escaped from school. He was born in the United States and besides being a teacher, he was a gymnast and a medical student. Until the war. The American colonists were fighting for their independence from Britain. But which side should Ben choose? The Americans or the British?

Rumour has it that he chose both. He spied for the British and the Americans. He was a sort of a double-agent. But the British never knew this and King George III gave Ben a knighthood when the war was over.

But Ben liked the excitement of being at war. He said he didn't want to "vegetate in England". So what did he do? Simple! He went to Bavaria as a special adviser on War to the government and became Minister for War in 1793.

As Minister of War, Ben devised a cunning plan. The streets were full of beggars and the army was short of uniforms. Ben's idea was to force the beggars to make uniforms. But how should he feed the beggars? After much research Ben found the cheapest food was watery vegetable soup. So he "vegetated" in Bavaria instead of in England – ha, ha. Ben was so keen on his idea he even published a book of recipes. Could this be a new line in school dinners? Then he had a second brainwave.

He put soldiers to work growing potatoes to make the soup to feed the beggars who made their uniforms. Ben's plan was a great success so at least it didn't land him in the soup! Brainy Ben made many other interesting discoveries. A new chimney for houses, a new stove and a coffee percolator to put on the stove.

And then he discovered friction.

One day Ben was watching a cannon being made. The barrel of the cannon was bored by a drill. Ben could feel the heat wafting off the cannon. In those days people thought heat was an invisible liquid. But Ben found you got extra heat if you used a blunt drill. So he figured the heat was produced by the drill. Dead right. The blunt drill had tiny bumps on its surface – and this caused extra friction. And more heat.

Fact or friction?

Often, just like Benjamin Thompson, physicists draw conclusions from things they noticed. Could you do this? Here are some everyday happenings. Which ones are caused by friction?

1. Friction helps you to build a house of cards.
2. Friction explains how you can whip a table cloth off a fully-laid table without breaking anything.

3. Friction makes electrical equipment heat up.
4. The patterns on tyres causes friction with the road. This helps to control the vehicle.
5. People use friction to start fires.
6. Friction helps skiers to ski up hills.

7 Runners use friction to run without slipping.
8 Friction causes people to get burnt by snow.

Answers:

1 **Fact.** Tiny bumps on the surface of the cards help them to stick to the surface of the table. That's friction. It works if the cards are at a steep angle.

2 **Friction.** The inertia of the crockery and the force of gravity pins it to the table. If you pull the table cloth fast enough there isn't enough friction to pull the crockery off the table. However, practising this trick at home may cause fatal friction with your family.

3 **Fact.** As the electrical current runs through the circuits it causes friction which heats up the machine. That's why TV's can burst into flames if you cover their ventilation holes.

4 **Friction.** Smooth tyres provide more friction in dry weather. The treads are better in wet weather. The wheel scoops the water out of the way so the tyres can grip the road.

5 Fact. One of your ancestors hit on a hot method of lighting fires. Rub two sticks together. The heat of the friction can set fire to some dried fungus. Later on people found that partially burnt underwear caught fire again very easily. So it was ideal for getting a blaze going.

6 Fact. Traditional up-hill skis used sealskin for this purpose. Nowadays they have man-made bristles. It's kinder to seals.

7 Fact. Spiked shoes increase friction with the track.

8 Fact. Crazy skiers can suffer serious burns if they go too fast and then fall over. At high speeds, friction causes enough heat to burn the skin before the snow melts.

Messed-up machines

Here's the bad news about friction. It slows machines down. Yes, it's a real spanner in the works for generations of freaky physicists who've tried to devise the ultimate machine. One that keeps on working without power. Perpetual motion.

Between 1617 and 1906 the British Patent Office received ideas for 600 perpetual motion machines. None worked.

Here are four more. Which one was successful?

1 A perpetual bicycle

The power for this bike comes from your bum bouncing on the saddle. This drives the rear wheel using a drive belt. So you could cycle for ever or until you get a sore bum.

2 A self-powered pump

The water-lifting pump is powered by a waterwheel that is powered by water falling from buckets tied to the wheel as it runs around.

3 A perpetual wind machine

Dreamt up by an Italian doctor in 1500. Air from the fan is funnelled down a horn linked to a propeller which in turn powers the fan.

> **Answers:**
> Machine 3 was built in 1765. And it's still ticking! But one day it will stop. Here's why...

A hot halt

Perpetual motion, unfortunately, breaks a law of physics. The Second Law of Thermodynamics to be exact. (Thermodynamics is the branch of physics to do with heat and energy. It's a subject you can really warm to.) The Second Law of Thermodynamics says that energy is lost from a machine as sound, noise, heat and, of course, friction.

So the machine stops because it runs out of energy. By the way, the First Law of Thermodynamics says you can turn energy from motion into heat. And it's true. Try rubbing your hands and friction turns the energy of your moving hands into a nice warm sensation.

A slippery subject

Sometimes we want friction. Brakes, tyres, rubber-soled shoes, sandpaper and driving belts in machines would be useless without it.

But sometimes we don't want friction. We want things to go smoothly. That's why some slippery character invented lubrication. A lubricant such as oil fills out the little bumps that cause friction and allows the surfaces to slide past one another.

Most winter sports depend on lubrication. Sledges, skis and skates move easily because they melt a thin layer of ice beneath them. So they float along on this watery lubricant without too much friction. Until you slip over.

Lubrication also launches ships. That's why in the Middle Ages slipways were coated in revoltingly greasy animal fat. A slave got the risky job of knocking away the props under the ship. At the last minute the slave had to jump clear. If he slipped the ship would crush him – that's why they called it the slip-way. If the slave survived he was given his freedom.

But if lubrication is lethal, friction can be fatal. That was certainly the case in Rome four centuries ago.

Fatal friction

Rome, 1586

It was an ancient obelisk. For 2,000 years it had lain forgotten in the dirt, west of St Peter's Cathedral. But times had changed. The

Pope decided that the stone would look great in front of St Peter's. But how could it be raised? It was quite a problem. The obelisk weighed 327 tonnes.

"They say," murmured old Roberto, "that two engineers turned down the job. Reckoned it couldn't be done."

"I can see why," replied young Marco gazing in awe at the huge stone in its protective cage.

"Well – we'd better give it a try. Gotta earn our pay," grumbled Roberto with a wheezy cough. He and Marco were amongst hundreds of sailors hired to raise the obelisk. They took up their ropes.

The square was ringed by crowds. Thousands of people were cheering and waving handkerchiefs and waiting impatiently for the big event. A smartly dressed young man leapt onto a platform.

Roberto screwed up his creased old face in a scowl. "That's Fontana – he's the engineer who claims he can do it. What a big-head!"

"People of Rome!" proclaimed the young man. "Today we'll raise this great monument from the past. When the trumpet sounds you sailors must pull the ropes. Only stop when you hear the bell. It's vital that these signals are obeyed in silence. There must be no talking on pain of death!" The young man pointed sternly to the

6. Facts About Friction   **147**

nearby gallows.

There was a shocked silence.

The older sailor made the sign of the cross. "That's a bit over the top," he whispered.

The sailors spat on their hands. The moist spit would stop friction with the rope burning the skin off their fingers.

The trumpet blared. The harsh note echoed around the square. Silently the men took the strain. The ropes creaked. Windlasses squealed. Capstans groaned round. Slowly, painfully the great stone began to lift.

Then the bell rang. Everyone rested for a few moments. The trumpet sounded again. Once again the sailors' muscles bunched and knotted until sweat trickled down their backs. Then disaster struck.

The ropes jammed – halted by friction between the ropes and windlasses. The sailors pulled the ropes until their faces screwed up in agony. Nothing moved. The taut ropes groaned and frayed. The stone tottered. Young Marco saw the danger. He shouted instantly: "Water, give water to the ropes!" Then he realized what he'd done. And knew he must die.

"Seize him!" screamed Fontana, his voice cracking with tension and disappointment. "Seize him for breaking the silence!"

Strong arms grabbed Marco. The guards dragged the young sailor towards the scaffold and the waiting executioner. The people gasped in horror but no one dared speak.

"I'm sorry," whispered Marco. But it was too late.

The executioner tightened the harsh hemp rope around Marco's bare throat.

A thin, old priest touched the sailor's arm.

"What's your last request?" the priest mumbled.

"Please, father," croaked Marco. His heart was racing and he couldn't speak clearly. His throat was dry and the rope didn't help. "Please, tell them to pour water on the ropes."

"I don't know if that's possible, my son."

"Please do it!"

The steel-helmeted guards beat their drums. It was the signal for the execution to begin.

The priest hurried over to Fontana. The young engineer nodded his head impatiently. A large water pitcher was found and its contents poured over the straining ropes.

"Come on mate, let's get it over with," said the executioner cheerfully shoving Marco up the ladder of death.

Just then a trumpet blared and the ropes took the strain.

"Why were the people cheering?" thought Marco wildly. Were they pleased to see him die?

No. The ropes were moving easily. The stone was being lifted smoothly and quickly. At the foot of the ladder stood Domenico Fontana. Shamefaced.

"Release that man!" he shouted.

As a sailor Marco was used to hauling wet ropes at sea. He knew that there was less friction on wet ropes because the water acted as a lubricant. You'll be

pleased to know that the brave sailor was pardoned and given his freedom. But what was his reward for saving the obelisk?

a) A golden pitcher of water.
b) Tea with the Pope.
c) His very own ship.

> **Answers:**
> **b)** He met the Pope as a VIP guest. And the sailor's home town of San Remo was given the honour of providing palms for the annual St Peter's Palm Sunday parade.

Well, hopefully you won't slip-up over this easy experiment.

Dare you discover… how to give things the slip?

You will need:

What you do:

1 Flick the bottle top along the first tray. Make sure the top stays on the tray and doesn't fly through the air.

2 Carefully pour a few drops of cooking oil on the first tray. Smear it over the surface with a kitchen towel until the surface is shiny and there is no extra oil on the tray.

3 Now flick the bottle top again as hard as before. Note what happens.

4 Mash up the banana and, using another kitchen towel, smear a little of the mixture over the second tray. Make sure the surface is smooth and shiny and there are no lumps of banana left.

5 (optional) Mash the remaining banana with a little cream and sugar. Eat it. Tell your feeble-minded folks it's all part of the experiment. Who said science was tough?

6 Now flick the bottle top again as hard as before.

What do you notice?
a) Both the oil and the banana make good lubricants. They help the top move faster.
b) The top stuck to the banana and skimmed along over the oil.
c) The top stuck in the oil but skimmed over the banana.

Answers:
a) Lubricating oils are squeezed from peanuts, coconuts or bits of dead fish. In some countries bananas are used because they're slippery too. That's why you slip on a banana skin!

HORRIBLE HEALTH WARNING!

Please do not test your lubricants in any of the following places:

1. School corridors – they're slippery enough already.
2. Your teacher's chair.
3. Stairs. They could prove your downfall!

Any of these things could stretch a grown-up's patience to breaking point. But you ain't seen nothing yet. The next chapter's really taking the strain.

PATIENCE BEING STRETCHED

SCHOOL TIE BEING STRETCHED

REVIEW

운동 에너지를 감소시키는 요소 중 하나는 마찰력이다. 차량의 바퀴는 회전하면서 지면과 마찰을 일으키기 때문에 가속 페달을 계속 밟지 않으면 결국 차는 정지한다. 선풍기의 날개는 공기와 마찰을 일으키기 때문에 바람을 앞으로 보내 땀을 식혀 준다. 그런데 저항은 마찰을 일으키고 마찰로 인해 열이 발생할 수도 있다. 아빠와 내가 엄마의 권위와 명령에 저항하면 엄마의 머리에서 열에너지가 발생한다. 초기 인류는 마찰력을 이용해 불을 피우기도 했다. 결국 마찰력은 우리가 극복하는 동시에 활용해야 하는 힘이다.

6. Facts About Friction

Vocabulary 6

p.138

People use the word friction to mean **aggro**, anger or annoyance.

사람들은 '마찰'이라는 단어를 적대감, 분노, 또는 짜증을 뜻하는 말로 사용한다.

aggro 인터넷에서 상대를 도발해 관심을 끄는 행위를 보고 '어그로(aggro) 끈다'라고 말한다. 약 60년 전부터 영국에서 '분노, 짜증, 악화'를 뜻하는 **aggravation**을 줄인 속어로 **aggro**를 사용하기 시작했다. 원래의 의미에 더해 '폭력, 폭력 행위, 싸움'을 뜻하는 말로도 자주 쓴다.

p.138

If your bike brake blocks get worn they can't **grip** the wheels with enough friction.

자전거 브레이크 블록이 마모되면 충분한 마찰력으로 바퀴를 잡을 수 없다.

> 즉, 멈추기가 아주아주 어려워진다는 말씀!

grip '손에 쥐다'라는 기본 의미가 있다. 책이나 휴대 전화를 손에 쥐어 보고서 '그립감이 좋다' 말할 때의 '그립'이 **grip**이다. '손에 꼭 쥐다, 관심을 끌다, 이해하다'를 뜻하는 동사나 '꼭 붙잡기, 통제, 소유, 이해'를 뜻하는 명사로 쓴다. '움켜쥐다, 잡아채다'라는 비슷한 의미를 가진 **grab**과 사촌지간이다.

p.139

The American **colonists** were fighting for their independence from Britain.

미국 식민지인들은 영국으로부터 독립하기 위해 싸우고 있었다.

colonist 식민지(**colony**)에 사는 사람들을 의미한다. 즉 '식민지 주민'이다. **colony**는 빈 땅을 일궈서 삶의 터전으로 만든다는 의미를 갖고 있다. 원래 살던 곳, 고향을 떠나서 새로운 땅에 정착한다는 의미다. 그래서 '식민지, 집단 이주지'를 뜻한다. 동사 **colonize**는 남의 땅을 빼앗아 '식민지로 만들다'라는 뜻이다. 일제 강점기에 일본인들이 우리나라를 **colony**로 삼았고, 우리나라에 들어와 살던 일본인들이 바로 **colonist**다.

---

p.140

The **barrel** of the cannon was bored by a drill.
대포의 포신은 드릴로 뚫었다.

---

barrel 나무판자나 기둥을 세워 나가지도 들어가지도 못하게 막는 것을 bar라고 한다. **barrel**은 이 bar와 깊은 관련이 있다. 나무판자를 붙여서 곡물이나 액체가 새지 못하게 막는 통을 부르는 말이 **barrel**이다. 원래는 크기가 제각각이었으나 나중에는 둥근 모양의 일정한 규격으로 통일되었다. 석유 한 통을 배럴이라 하고, 1배럴(**barrel**)은 158.987리터다. 총이나 대포의 몸, 즉 총신과 포신은 배럴처럼 원통형이라서 **barrel**이라고 부른다.

---

p.141

Often, just like Benjamin Thompson, physicists draw **conclusions** from things they noticed.
벤저민 톰슨과 마찬가지로 종종 물리학자들은 자신이 관찰한 것에서 결론을 도출한다.

---

conclusion '결론, 결말, 마무리'를 뜻하는 명사다. 동사 **conclude**는 '모두, 함께'를 뜻하는 con과 '닫다(close), 봉하다'를 뜻하는 clude가 합쳐진 말이다. 더 이상 팔 물건도 없고, 보여줄 것도 없고, 얘기할 것도 없으니 문 닫고 집에 간다는 의미다. 모두 끝났다(end)는 얘기다. 그래서 **conclude**는 '끝내다, 마치다, 결론을 내리다'라는 뜻이다.

---

p.142

That's why TVs can burst into flames if you cover their **ventilation** holes.
그래서 TV의 통풍구를 덮으면 불이 붙을 수 있는 것이다.

---

ventilation '(실내의) 환기, 통풍'을 뜻한다. vent는 '바람(wind), 공기를 불다(blow)'를 의미한다. 공기가 정체되거나 차단되지 않고 흐르게 하는 것이 **ventilate**다. '환기하다, 공기를 순환시키다'라는 뜻이다. **ventilator**는 '환기구, 통풍 장치'다.

6. Facts About Friction

p.143

Yes, it's a real spanner in the works for generations of freaky physicists who've tried to devise the **ultimate** machine.

그렇다. 궁극의 기계를 고안하고자 노력한 여러 세대의 괴짜 물리학자들에게는 이것이 정말 큰 난관이었다.

ultimate '마지막, 끝에 이르다'를 뜻하는 말에서 왔다. 그래서 '최후의, 최종의, 궁극적인'이라는 뜻의 형용사로 쓴다. 현재 시점에서 가장 '끝에 있다'는 것은 가장 좋거나 가장 크거나 가장 중요하다는 의미다. 그래서 '최고의, 최상의, 최대의'란 뜻도 갖고 있다. 가장 깊은 것이란 의미에서 '근본적인'의 뜻으로도 쓴다.

p.143

One that keeps on working without power. **Perpetual** motion.

동력 없이도 계속 작동하는 것. 영구적인 운동.

perpetual '앞으로 나아가다'란 의미다. 멈추거나 뒤로 가지 않고 계속 진행된다는 의미에서 '끊임없이 계속되는, 영원한, 빈번한'을 뜻하는 형용사로 쓴다. 비슷한 말로 never-ending, everlasting, permanent 등이 있다.

p.144

Thermodynamics is the branch of physics to do with heat and energy.

열역학은 열과 에너지와 관련된 물리학의 한 분야다.

thermodynamics 열과 힘의 관계, 열의 활용 등을 연구하는 학문인 '열역학'이다. thermo는 '열, 온도'를 뜻하고, dynamic은 '힘, 에너지'를 뜻한다. 그래서 형용사 **thermodynamic**

달리는 자전거의 운동 에너지는 마찰, 소리, 열로 형태가 바뀌고 (열역학 제1법칙) 흩어져서 결국 멈춰. 하지만 반대로 자전거에 소리를 지르고 열을 가해도 다시 움직이지는 않아!(열역학 제2법칙)

은 '열과 힘이 관계된, 열을 에너지로 활용하는'이라는 뜻이다. 이 단어 끝에 s를 붙이면 명사인 '열역학'이다.

That's why some slippery character invented **lubrication**.
그래서 어떤 미끌미끌한 인물이 윤활제를 발명한 것이다.

lubrication '기름칠, 윤활'을 뜻하는 명사다. 동사 **lubricate**는 '미끄러지다, 미끄럽게 만들다'를 뜻하는 말에서 왔다. 뭔가를 미끄럽게 만드는 가장 쉬운 방법은 기름을 바르는 것이다. 그래서 **lubricate**는 '기름칠을 하다, 윤활유를 바르다'를 뜻한다. 미끄럽게 만들기 위해서 바르는 '기름, 윤활유'는 **lubricant**라고 한다.

Lubrication also **launches** ships.
윤활은 선박을 진수시키기도 한다.

launch 찌르거나 던져서 공격하는 무기인 '단창'을 부르는 말에서 유래했다. 창을 앞으로 뻗거나 던지는 동작에 비유해 '밖으로 내보내다'란 뜻으로도 쓰게 되었다. '배를 처음 물에 띄우다(진수하다), 우주선이나 미사일을 발사하다'란 뜻도 갖고 있고, '출시하다, 출간하다, 시작하다, 착수하다'란 뜻도 갖고 있다.

Today we'll raise this great **monument** from the past.
오늘 우리는 과거의 위대한 기념물을 세울 것이다.

monument monu는 '기억하다, 생각해 내다'를 의미한다. 기억하는 것, 생각하게 만드는 것이 바로 **monument**다. 후대의 사람들까지 기억해서 교훈을 얻어야 하는 사건들, 위대하고 고마운 인물, 종교나 정치·사회 면에서 중요한 역사적 일들을 기념해서 세우는 '기념물, 기념비, 건축물' 등을 **monument**라고 부른다. 형용사형 **monumental**은 '역사적으로 중요한, 기념비적인'을 뜻한다.

p.148

The sailors pulled the ropes until their faces screwed up in **agony**.
선원들은 고통으로 얼굴이 일그러질 때까지 밧줄을 잡아당겼다.

agony '레슬링이나 격투에서 승리하기 위해 노력하다'라는 뜻의 고대 그리스어 agon에서 왔다. 거친 경기라서 머리가 깨지고 팔다리가 부러지고 기진맥진하는 게 당연했다. 고통스러울 수밖에 없다. 그래서 **agony**는 '극심한 고통, 참기 힘든 슬픔, 괴로움'을 뜻하는 명사다. 육체적, 정신적 고통 모두 **agony**로 표현할 수 있다.

p.149

"**Seize** him!" screamed Fontana, his voice cracking with tension and disappointment.
"저 자를 붙잡아라!" 하고 폰타나가 소리쳤는데, 그의 목소리는 긴장과 실망감으로 갈라졌다.

seize 재빨리 강하게 뭔가를 잡는 동작을 표현하는 동사다. '꽉 붙잡다, 움켜쥐다'를 뜻하는 말로 grab과 비슷하다. 사람을 '강제로 붙잡다, 체포하다'란 뜻으로도 쓸 수 있다. 또한 자기 것이 아닌 재산, 권력, 기회 등을 '빼앗거나 차지하다'라는 의미로, 또는 손에 쥔 듯 제 '맘대로 움직이고 통제한다'라는 의미로도 자주 쓴다.

p.149

A large water pitcher was found and its contents poured over the **straining** ropes.
커다란 물 주전자가 찾아졌고, 그 안에 있던 내용물이 당겨진 밧줄 위로 부어졌다.

strain 기본 의미는 '잡아당기다(pull), 늘이다(stretch)'이다. 앞에서 잡아 당기면 몸이 앞으로 나간다. 움직일 수밖에 없도록 힘을 강하게 가하는 것이 **strain**이다. 근육이나 인대가 너무 '당겨지면' 통증이 생긴다. **strain**은 '근육, 인대를 다치다, 염좌가 생기다'라는 뜻도 갖고 있다. 신경을 과도하게 쓰거나 정신적 압박이 있으면 '긴장'이 생긴다. '긴장하다, 신경을 집중하다, 압박감을 느끼다'라는 뜻의 명사로도 **strain**을 쓸 수 있다.

p.151

Smear it over the surface with a kitchen towel until the surface is shiny and there is no extra oil on the tray.

표면에 기름을 발라 표면이 윤이 나고 쟁반에 기름이 남지 않을 때까지 주방용 수건으로 문질러야 한다.

smear 인류는 아주 오래 전부터 다양한 목적으로 '기름칠'을 해왔다. 식재료에도 바르고, 목재에도 바르고, 미용과 치료를 위해 몸에도 발랐다. '기름(oil)을 바르다'를 뜻하는 동사 **smear**는 그만큼 오래된 단어다. 기름뿐만 아니라 액체에 가까운 부드러운 물질, 예를 들어 진흙(mud), 잼(jam), 버터(butter) 등을 바르는 행동도 **smear**로 표현할 수 있다.

Sentence 6

p.139

Rumour has it that he chose both.
소문에 의하면 그는 둘 다 골랐다고 한다.

[Rumour has it that ~]은 '소문에 따르면, 들리는 얘기에 의하면'을 뜻하는 표현이다. 이 문장에서 both는 '둘 다'를 뜻하는 대명사로, chose의 목적어다.

p.140

He put soldiers to work growing potatoes to make the soup to feed the beggars who made their uniforms.

그는 병사들을 투입해 감자를 재배하는 일을 시켰고, 그걸로 거지들을 먹여서 군복을 만들게 했다.

to work는 '작업(노동)에'를 뜻한다. potatoes to make the soup는 '수프를 만들 감자'란 의미고, to feed the beggars는 '거지들을 먹이기 위해서'라는 의미다.

6. Facts About Friction

who made their uniforms는 앞에 있는 the beggars를 수식하는 말이다.

> p.142
>
> If you pull the table cloth fast enough there isn't enough friction to pull the crockery off the table.
> 식탁보를 충분히 빠르게 잡아당기면 마찰이 적어 도자기가 테이블에서 떨어지지 않는다.

fast enough는 '충분히 빠르게'란 의미로 부사구 역할을 한다.
도자기 바닥과 식탁보 사이에는 마찰(friction)이 작용한다. 아주 빠르게 식탁보를 당기면 도자기를 쓰러뜨릴 만큼 '마찰력이 크지 않다(there isn't enough friction)'는 내용이다.

> p.142
>
> As the electrical current runs through the circuits it causes friction which heats up the machine.
> 전류가 회로를 통과하면서 마찰이 발생하고 그로 인해 기계가 가열된다.

run through는 '바람, 강물, 전류 등이 빠르게 흘러서 통과하다'란 의미로 쓰는 표현이다.
which heats up the machine은 '그 기계를 뜨겁게 만든다, 가열한다'는 의미로, 앞에 나온 friction(마찰)을 수식하는 말이다.

p.144

The water-lifting pump is powered by a waterwheel that is powered by water falling from buckets tied to the wheel as it runs around.

물을 끌어올리는 펌프는 바퀴에 부착된 양동이에서 떨어지는 물로 구동되는 물레방아에서 힘을 얻는다.

[be powered by A]는 'A의 힘으로 작동하다, 구동하다'를 뜻하는 표현이다. water-lifting pump(물을 퍼 올리는 펌프) ← waterwheel(물레방아) ← water(물)의 순서로 힘이 전달된다는 내용이다.

as it runs around(그것이 돌며 흐를 때)에서 it은 water를 가리키는 대명사다.

p.145

A lubricant such as oil fills out the little bumps that cause friction and allows the surfaces to slide past one another.

오일 같은 윤활제가 마찰을 일으키는 작은 융기를 채워 표면이 서로 미끄러질 수 있게 해 준다.

[A such as B]는 'B 같은 A'란 의미로, B가 A에 속하거나 하나의 예일 때 쓴다. 이 문장의 동사는 fills와 allows다. [allow A to 동사]는 'A가 ~하게 허용(허락)하다, ~할 수 있게 놔두다'를 뜻하는 표현이다.

p.147

He and Marco were amongst hundreds of sailors hired to raise the obelisk.

그와 마르코는 오벨리스크를 세우기 위해 고용된 수백 명의 선원 중 하나였다.

전치사 amongst는 among과 같은 말로, '~ 사이에, ~ 중 하나로'라는 의미로 무리에 속해 있다는 뜻이다.

hired to raise the obelisk는 '오벨리스크를 일으켜 세우도록 고용된'을 뜻하며, 앞에 있는 sailors를 수식하는 말이다.

6. Facts About Friction   161

> **p.148**
>
> Once again the sailors' muscles bunched and knotted until sweat trickled down their backs.
> 다시 한 번 선원들의 근육이 뭉치고 뒤틀렸고 결국 땀이 그들의 등을 타고 흘러내렸다.

once again은 '한 번 더, 이번에도 또, 또 다시'를 뜻하는 부사구다.
until은 '~할 때까지'를 뜻하는 접속사이므로 until sweat trickled down their backs는 '땀이 그들의 등으로 흘러내릴 때까지'로 해석할 수 있다.

> **p.150**
>
> At the foot of the ladder stood Domenico Fontana.
> 사다리 아래에는 도메니코 폰타나가 서 있었다.

문장의 주어 Domenico Fontana가 맨 뒤로 간 도치문이다. 'Domenico Fontana stood at the foot of the ladder.'라고 해야 평범한 문장인데, 서 있는 위치인 '사다리의 발치'를 강조하기 위해 [부사구-동사-주어] 순서로 바꾼 것이다.

> **p.153**
>
> But you ain't seen nothing yet.
> 그러나 당신이 지금까지 본 것은 아무것도 아니다.

이 문장에서 ain't는 haven't로 바꿔 써야 학교 문법에 맞다. ain't는 일종의 속어인데, am not, is not, are not, have not, has not 등을 모두 ain't로 줄여서 표현할 수 있다.
앞으로 더 굉장한 것을 보게 될 거란 의미로 '이제 시작에 불과해. 아직 시작도 안 했어. 이제 맛보기일 뿐이야. 다음을 기대해도 좋다.' 등으로 해석할 수 있다.

> **CHAPTER 7 KEYWORDS**
>
> #stretch #elastic #Robert Hooke #Spring

Stretching And Straining

Hold an elastic band between your fingers. Pull one end ever so carefully. The elastic band is storing the energy you put into pulling it. Let go – the released energy sends the elastic band flying. Oh dear – why does a teacher always get in the way? But just tell him that it's all part of a very technical scientific experiment – he'll understand! One of the first people to experiment with stretching was scientist Robert Hooke.

 **Hall of fame:** Robert Hooke (1635–1703)
Nationality: British

After his bust-ups with Newton (see page 28), Robert must have known all about tension. But this talented scientist was interested in everything from telescopes to making flying machines that didn't fly. Incredibly, he also worked as an architect, an astronomer, a mechanic and a model maker. Yes. Hooke liked working at full-stretch.

According to one story Robert wrote a strange code in his will which deciphered into Latin reads "ut tensio sic vis". Mean anything to you? Thought not. Further translated into English it means "as the extension so the force". And these weird words turned out to be Hooke's Law on stretching. Imagine hanging a weight on a spring – the spring stretches. Double the weight and the spring stretches twice as far. Simple, innit?

Dare you discover 1... what happens when something stretches?

You will need:
Yourself
A 0.5-cm-thick elastic band

What you do:
Suddenly stretch the elastic band.
Put it against your face.
What happens and why?
a) The elastic band feels strangely cold because all the energy has been stretched out of it.
b) The elastic band feels warm. This is due to the energy that you have provided by stretching it.
c) The elastic band feels warm because stretching causes friction with your hot sweaty little fingers.

> **Answers:**
> **b)** The band briefly stores energy from the force that stretches it. The energy tries to escape as heat and that's why the band feels hot.

Dare you discover 2... the power of an elastic band?

Here's a machine that uses stored energy in an elastic band to get moving. Ask an adult to help with some of the cutting.

You will need:

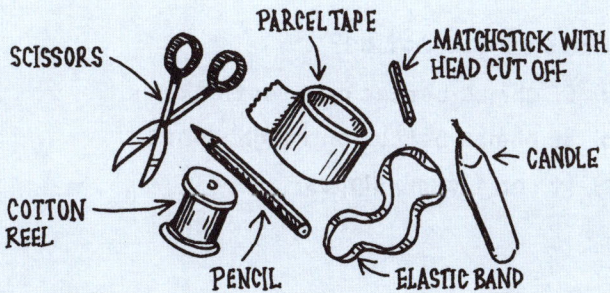

What you do:

1. Cut 2.5 cm off the bottom of the candle.
2. Remove the wick from the wax and make its middle hole large enough for the elastic band.

7. Stretching And Straining

3 Pass the elastic band through the centres of the candle stump and the cotton reel.

4 Pass the matchstick through the elastic band at its cotton reel end. Secure the matchstick with a strip of parcel tape.

5 Pass the pencil through the elastic band at its candle end.

6 Wind the elastic band by turning the pencil. Watch your vehicle creep along as the elastic band unwinds. Compare its performance on rough and smooth slopes.

What do you notice?
a) It climbs better on smooth slopes.
b) It climbs better on rough slopes.
c) It can't climb slopes.

Answers:
b) The machine uses the force you put into turning the elastic band to move. The friction provided by rough slopes helps your machine grip the ground and climb better.

A stretchy subject

Here's some more elastic info to stretch your brain cells. A few hundred years ago you could be sent to prison in England for a long stretch. Stretched out on a timber frame with rollers at each end. This was the rack. The most anyone was ever stretched on a rack was 15 cm. After that their arm and leg joints popped out of their sockets. Rumours that racks were used in schools are just "tall stories". No – teachers just racked children's brains.

In the 1700s rubber thread was used in clothes and underwear. Sadly, the rubber melted in hot weather and cracked in cold.

In 1839 scientists discovered a chemical treatment that stopped this happening and rubber thread known as elastic was used in corsets and knickers from the 1930s. (Corsets are the tight-fitting garments some women wore to squeeze their bulging bodies into shape. Before elastic, corsets were reinforced with bits of whale bone.)

Nowadays man-made elastic is used for much more than just corsets – including the rope bungee jumpers use. Would you want to bungee jump?

If your answer to this question is "ARGGGGGH!" you wouldn't envy Gregory Riffi who in 1992 jumped 249.9 metres from a helicopter over France. With his life hanging by a thread – all right – an elastic rope.

By the way, bungee jumping isn't usually fatal if it's done by experts. But as the jumper falls the blood rushes to their head and this can make their eyeballs bleed a bit. Another sport that depends on stretching is archery.

Big bad bows

1. The bow was invented before 20,000 bc. The idea was that you could store energy by pulling back the string and transfer the force of the energy to fire the arrow.
2. Five seconds later the bow may have claimed its first victim. Ooops!
3. In the 900s the Turks hit upon a better bow. It was made from grisly bits of animal horn and tendons and strengthened with wood. The outward curve of the bow allowed it to be drawn with greater force.
4. Meanwhile the Europeans had invented the crossbow. This deadly weapon could fire a bolt 305 metres
5. But the crossbow string had to be cranked slowly back. And during that time ordinary archers with ordinary bows were so skilled, they could turn the crossbow soldier into a pin-cushion in no time – unless he bolted first.
6. And then a Welsh person invented the long-bow. It could fire an arrow 320 metres. And straight through chain mail. At shorter ranges, the arrows could pierce armour too.
7. Modern bows are really high-tech.

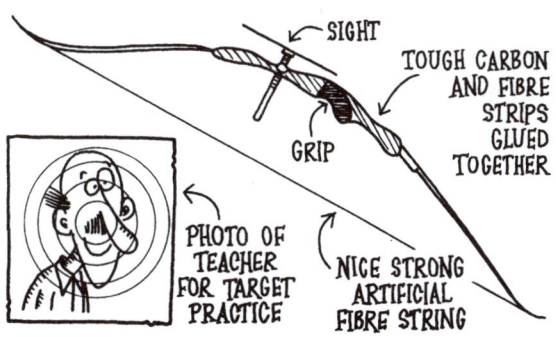

8 In free-style shooting the archers lie on their back, strap the bow to their feet and draw the string with both hands. Of course, it isn't only stretchy things that can store force. Springs can do this too when you push them down and then they pop up again. You'll be surprised to know that the earliest springs were used 600 years ago in mousetraps. And springs can spring real surprises on you. Here are seven more.

Seven springy surprises

1 The first toasters sold in 1919 had powerful springs that shot toast into the air. Bet that surprised a few people.

2 Springs sometimes break. Metal fatigue does for a cheap spring after about 100,000 extensions, but a better spring lasts over 10,000,000 extensions. A surprisingly long stretch.

3 Bed springs are a surprising shape. They're cone shaped – that's wider at their top than at the base. This makes them squeeze easily at first but the harder they're pressed the more difficult they are to squash. A bed that feels comfy and springy to you feels like a rock to a big, sprawling grown-up.

4 You know the circus act where a person is fired from a cannon? You may be surprised to discover that springs rather than explosions are used to provide the necessary force. The bang is a firework let off to make it look like the cannon had really fired.

5 And did you know we've got springs in our legs too? The ligaments that hold your joints together are a bit springy and your "S" shaped backbone jogs up and down as you walk. Together they'll put a spring in your step.

6) In the 1970s two American scientists trained a pair of kangaroos to hop on a treadmill. The scientists found that kangaroos jump using their springy tendons. It's a bit like jumping on a pogo stick.

7) Springy things are important for sport. Traditional tennis rackets were very expensive and strung with springy sheep's guts. Sounds like a bit of a racket. And talking about springy sports equipment, trainers have to be springy too.

Super springy shoes

Do this to your brother's trainers and you better run for it before he takes a swing at you. Funnily enough the next chapter's about swinging and spinning too. Better stand clear.

REVIEW

포동포동한 아기의 볼을 손가락으로 누르면 수축해서 쏙 들어갔다가 손가락을 떼면 다시 팽창해서 원상태로 돌아온다. 자칫 볼을 세게 누르면 심한 옹알이를 들을 수도 있다. 이렇게 팽창하고 수축하는 성질이나 힘을 '탄성, 탄력'이라고 한다. 늘어나는 성질이 있는 물질은 모두 탄성을 갖고 있다. 탄성을 가진 대표적인 물질은 고무줄과 용수철이다. 우리 몸에 걸치는 옷과 신발에도 탄성이 있어서 입고 벗기 편하다. 내 성적표의 숫자에 따라 늘어났다 줄어들었다 하는 엄마의 잔소리에도 탄성이 있다.

Vocabulary 7

p.163

Hold an **elastic** band between your fingers.
손가락 사이에 고무줄을 끼워 잡는다.

elastic '회복, 회복력'을 뜻하는 말에서 왔다. 원래의 상태로 돌아온다는 의미다. 고무줄을 당기면 길어졌다가 놓으면 원래의 길이로 돌아간다. 돼지 엉덩이를 눌렀다가 놓으면 원래대로 통통해진다. 이런 성질을 표현하는 형용사가 **elastic** 이다. '신축성이 있는, 탄력이 있는'을 뜻한다. 이런 성질을 가진 대표적인 물질이 '고무(rubber)' 이기 때문에 '고무, 고무로 만든'을 뜻하는 말로도 쓸 수 있다.

p.163

Let go - the **released** energy sends the elastic band flying.
놓아라. 그러면 풀려난 에너지가 고무줄을 날아가게 한다.

release 잡았던 것을 놓아주고, 막았던 걸 열어서 내보낸다는 의미다. '놓아주다, 내보내다, 방출하다'를 뜻한다. 구속 상태에 있는 사람을 '석방하다 해방하다'란 뜻으로도 쓸 수 있다. 비밀 상태에 있던 것을 공개한다는 의미에서 '영화, 신곡, 신상품 등을 공개(발표)하다'라는 뜻으로도 쓴다. 같은 의미의 명사형도 **release**다.

p.164

And these **weird** words turned out to be Hooke's Law on stretching.
그리고 이 이상한 단어들은 늘어남에 대한 훅의 법칙임이 밝혀졌다.

weird '운명의 장난'이란 말이 있다. 내 의지나 계획과는 상관없이 갑자기 인생을 바꿀 사건들

7. Stretching And Straining

이 일어난다. 건강했던 사람이 갑자기 죽기도 하고 가난한 사람이 갑자기 벼락부자가 되기도 한다. 운명은 이해하기도 예상하기도 힘들다. **weird**는 고대 영어에서는 '운명(fate)'을 뜻했다. 이해할 수 없을 만큼 '너무 이상한, 기이한, 기묘한'을 뜻하고, 소름이 끼칠 정도로 이상해서 '기괴한, 섬뜩한' 느낌을 표현할 때도 쓴다. '이상한 사람, 괴짜, 기인'을 **weirdo**라고 한다.

p.166

Wind the elastic band by turning the pencil. Watch your vehicle creep along as the elastic band **unwinds**.

연필을 돌려서 고무줄을 감는다. 고무줄이 풀리면서 차량이 천천히 나아가는 모습을 지켜보라.

wind '움직이는 공기(moving air)'인 '바람'을 뜻하는 명사다. 바람의 움직임은 종잡을 수가 없다. 한 방향으로 세게 불다가 어느 순간 몸을 휘감기도 하고 굽이치기도 한다. 이런 바람의 움직임을 표현한 동사가 '와인드'로 발음하는 **wind**다. '구불구불하다, 굽이치다, (휘)감다, 감아 돌리다'라는 뜻이다. 반대로 '풀다'는 **unwind**다.

p.167

Rumors that **racks** were used in schools are just "tall stories".

학교에서 고문틀이 사용되었다는 소문은 그냥 '뻥'일 뿐이다.

rack '긴 막대'를 뜻하는 말에서 왔다. 특별한 용도로 쓰기 위해 자른 막대, 막대를 여러 개 이어 놓은 틀을 통칭하는 말이 **rack**이다. '받침대, 선반, 옷걸이' 등등 많은 종류의 **rack**이 있다. 그런데 기독교가 지배한 중세 유럽에는 다양한 형태의 고문용 **rack**이 있었다. 이교도, 범죄자 등을 묶어 놓고 고문하는 틀도 **rack**이라고 부른다.

p.168

Corsets are the tight-fitting **garments** some women wore to squeeze their bulging bodies into shape.

코르셋은 일부 여성들이 불룩한 몸을 조여 체형을 잡기 위해 입던 꼭 끼는 옷이다.

garment 옷을 통칭하는 말로 '의류, 의상'을 뜻한다. 일상에서는 **garment** 대신, clothes

나 clothing을 주로 사용한다. 의류 산업계에 종사하거나 의류 관련 사업을 하는 사람들이 **garment**를 많이 쓴다. '의류 산업'은 **garment** industry, '의류 공장'은 **garment** factory라고 한다.

> Another sport that depends on stretching is **archery**.
> 늘어남에 의존하는 또 다른 스포츠는 활쏘기다.

archery '활쏘기, 궁도, 양궁'을 뜻하는 명사다. **archer**는 '활(bow)'을 뜻하는 라틴어 arcus에서 유래한 말로, '활을 쏘는 사람, 궁수, 활잡이'를 뜻한다. 활처럼 둥글게 휜 모양을 표현하는 단어들도 어원이 같다. arch는 '둥글게 구부러진, 아치형'을, arc는 '곡선의 일부분, 둥근 모양'을 뜻한다.

> At shorter ranges, the arrows could **pierce** armour too.
> 사정거리가 더 짧으면 화살이 갑옷도 뚫을 수 있었다.

pierce '구멍을 뚫다(make a hole in)'란 의미를 갖고 있다. 대충 구멍을 내는 게 아니라, 날카롭고 뾰족한 도구를 사용해 구멍을 뚫는 것이다. '꿰뚫다, 뚫고 통과하다, 관통하다'를 뜻하는 동사다. 장신구를 달기 위해 귀나 입, 신체 부위를 뚫는 행위를 **piercing**(피어싱)이라고 부른다. 갑자기 날카로운 소리가 귀를 뚫을 듯 들릴 때, 갑자기 밝은 빛이 눈부시게 할 때에도 **pierce**를 써서 표현한다.

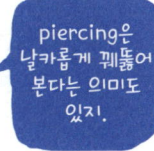

p.170

Metal **fatigue** does for a cheap spring after about 100,000 extensions, but a better spring lasts over 10,000,000 extensions.

금속 피로는 값싼 스프링의 경우 약 10만 번 정도 늘어나면 생기지만, 더 좋은 스프링은 1천만 번 이상 늘어나도 견딘다.

fatigue '부족, 고갈'을 뜻하는 말에서 왔다. 힘이 부족하고 에너지가 다 떨어진 상태를 의미하는 말로 움직이기 힘들 만큼 '극심한 피로, 기진맥진, 파김치 상태'일 때 **fatigue**를 쓴다. 형용사형은 **fatigued**다. 일상에서 자주 쓰는 '피곤한, 지친'을 뜻하는 형용사는 tired와 weary다.

p.171

The **ligaments** that hold your joints together are a bit springy and your "S" shaped backbone jogs up and down as you walk.

관절을 연결하는 인대는 약간 탄력이 있고, 걷는 동안 "S"자 형태의 척추 뼈가 위아래로 약간씩 움직인다.

ligament liga는 '연결하다, 묶다(tie, bind)'를 의미한다. 14세기에 유럽에서 '해부학(anatomy)'이 발달하면서 뼈와 근육을 연결하고 묶어 주는 역할을 하는 끈처럼 생긴 조직인 '인대, 힘줄'을 **ligament**로 부르게 되었다. **tendon**이란 용어도 쓴다.

p.171

In the 1970s two American scientists trained a pair of kangaroos to hop on a **treadmill**.

1970년대에 두 명의 미국 과학자가 캥거루 한 쌍을 러닝머신 위에서 뛰도록 훈련시켰다.

treadmill tread는 '걷다, 발로 밟다'를 뜻하고, mill은 '갈다, 으깨다'를 뜻한다. 사람이나 동물이 걷거나 밟아서 물레나 맷돌을 돌리는 형태의 '방아'나 '쳇바퀴'를 **treadmill**이라고 불렀다. 1960년대에 실내에서도 걷기와 뛰기 운동을 할 수 있는 기구인 소위 '러닝머신'이 개발되었는데, 걷거나 뛰면 벨트가 '돌아가는' 구조가 방아와 비슷해서 **treadmill**로 부르게 되었다.

Sentence 7

p.164

According to one story Robert wrote a strange code in his will which deciphered into Latin reads "ut tensio sic vis".

어떤 이야기에 따르면, 로버트는 자기 유언장에 이상한 암호를 적었는데, 이를 라틴어로 해독하면 "ut tensio sic vis"라고 읽힌다.

[according to A]는 'A에 따르면, A에 의하면'을 뜻하는 표현이다.
which 이하는 his will(그의 유언장)을 수식하는 말이다. deciphered into Latin은 '라틴어로 해석된'을 뜻하는 부사구다.

p.164

Double the weight and the spring stretches twice as far.

무게를 두 배로 늘리면 스프링도 두 배로 늘어난다.

'A하라, 그러면(and) B할 것이다'를 뜻하는 명령문 형태의 문장이다. 여기에서 Double은 '두 배로 늘리다'를 뜻하는 동사로 쓴 것이다.
twice as far는 '길이가 두 배로'를 뜻하는 부사구다.

p.165

Here's a machine that uses stored energy in an elastic band to get moving.

여기 고무줄에 저장된 에너지를 이용해 움직이는 기계가 있다.

Here's a machine은 '여기 기계 하나가 있다'란 뜻이다. 처음 소개하거나 예를 들 때 [Here is/are ~] 표현을 쓴다.
that 이하 구문이 machine을 설명하는 수식어구다. uses의 목적어 stored energy in an elastic band는 '고무 밴드에 축적된 에너지'를 뜻한다.

7. Stretching And Straining

p.167

The most anyone was ever stretched on a rack was 15cm.
사람이 고문대에서 늘어날 수 있었던 최대 길이는 15cm였다.

[A is B] 형식의 문장이다. 이 문장에서 주어인 The most는 '최대치, 최대한'을 뜻한다. 뒤에 that이 생략된 문장 anyone ~ a rack이 The most를 수식한다.
사람의 몸을 묶어서 길이를 늘일 수 있는 최대치가 15cm라는 가학적이고 과학적인 내용의 문장이다.

p.168

NEVER ask your mature female teachers if they still wear whalebone corsets.
절대로 나이 든 여자 선생님께 아직도 고래뼈 코르셋을 착용하는지 묻지 마라.

[Never 동사]는 '절대 ~하지 말라'는 의미의 명령이다.
[동사+간접목적어+직접목적어] 형태의 문장으로, 동사 ask의 목적어(질문의 내용)는 if they still wear whalebone corsets(혹시 아직도 고래뼈 코르셋을 입는지)다.

p.169

The idea was that you could store energy by pulling back the string and transfer the force of the energy to fire the arrow.
그 아이디어는 줄을 뒤로 당겨 에너지를 저장하고 그 에너지의 힘을 전달해서 화살을 발사할 수 있다는 것이었다.

[A is B] 형식의 문장인데, B에 해당하는 보어가 긴 that절로 이루어져 있다.
by pulling back the string은 '줄(활시위)을 뒤로 잡아당김으로써'를 뜻한다. 여기에서 by는 '수단, 방법'을 표현하는 전치사다.

p.169

> And during that time ordinary archers with ordinary bows were so skilled, they could turn the crossbow soldiers into a pincushion in no time - unless he bolted first.
>
> 그리고 그 당시에는 보통 활을 사용하는 평범한 궁수들도 매우 숙련되어 있어서, 석궁 병사들이 먼저 쏘지 않는 한 그들을 순식간에 바늘꽂이로 만들어 버릴 수 있었다.

[turn A into B]는 'A를 B로 변화시키다, 바꾸다'를 뜻하는 표현이다. pin-cushion은 바늘을 꽂아 보관하는 '바늘꽂이'인데, 화살을 많이 맞은 crossbow soldiers의 모습을 은유적으로 표현한 것이다.

in no time은 '순식간에, 당장에'를 뜻하는 부사구다. unless he bolted first는 '석궁 사수가 먼저 쏘지 않는 한'을 뜻한다.

p.170

> This makes them squeeze easily at first but the harder they're pressed the more difficult they are to squash.
>
> 이렇게 하면 처음에는 스프링이 쉽게 눌릴 수 있지만, 더 세게 누를수록 점점 더 납작해지기 어려워진다.

but 뒤의 문장은 '~할수록 더욱 ~하다'를 뜻하는 [the 비교급, the 비교급] 형태다. '침대 스프링이 더 세게 눌릴수록(the harder ~ pressed), 더 납작해지기 힘들어진다(the more ~ to squash)'라는 의미다.

p.170

> The bang is a firework let off to make it look like the cannon had really fired.
>
> 쾅 소리는 대포가 실제로 발사된 것처럼 보이게 하려고 폭죽을 터뜨리는 소리다.

let off는 '터뜨리다, 발사하다'라는 표현이기 때문에 a firework let off는 '터지는 불꽃'으로 해석한다.

look like는 '~처럼 보이다'를 뜻한다. 그래서 to make 이하는 '대포가 진짜로 발사된 것처럼 보이게 만들려고'로 해석한다.

7. Stretching And Straining

> **CHAPTER 8 KEYWORDS**
> #centripetal·centrifugal
> #Foucault's Pendulum #angular

Getting In A Spin

Ever wondered why cars don't have square wheels? No – me neither. Well – round wheels go round better (howls of amazement). Also the force on the outer parts of the wheel produces greater force at the axle. And this is ideal for wheel-based machines such as waterwheels and cars. And there's lots more wheel-life facts to go around (and pathetic jokes too)…

Fatal forces expressions

Stop it! It's conservation of angular momentum!

Who's to blame?

Answers:
No one – his top is rolling away. He's describing how coins and any other spinning objects have a habit of turning until

another force gets in the way. That's why wheels work so well. Best put your foot over the coin and pretend you haven't seen it.

And wheels **are** wonderful. They were invented by some bright spark who lived in the Middle East in about 3500 BC. When a wheel goes around, centripetal force tries to pull it towards its centre – remember that force from page 50? And now let's face a few more facts to get your head spinning ... Oh go on – give it a whirl!

Fatal forces fact file

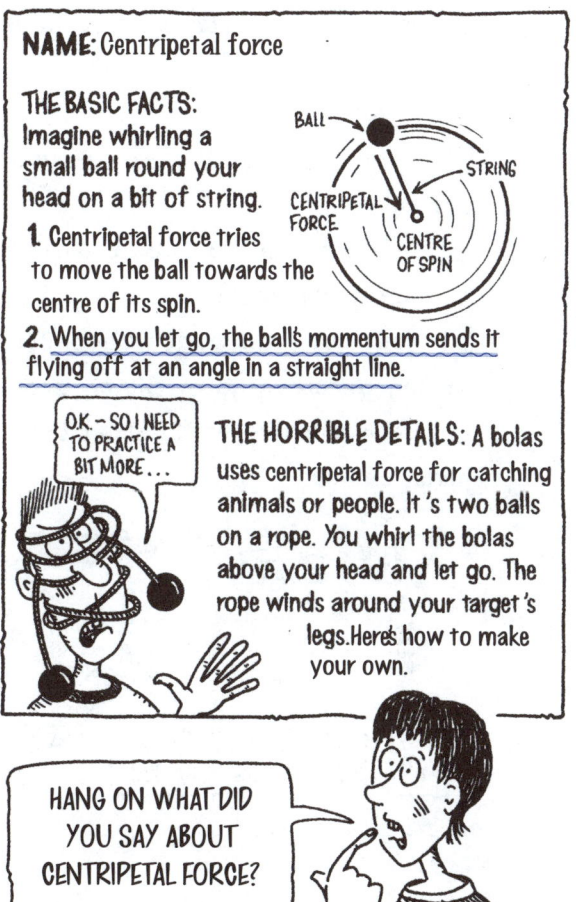

NAME: Centripetal force

THE BASIC FACTS:
Imagine whirling a small ball round your head on a bit of string.
1. Centripetal force tries to move the ball towards the centre of its spin.
2. When you let go, the ball's momentum sends it flying off at an angle in a straight line.

O.K. – SO I NEED TO PRACTICE A BIT MORE...

THE HORRIBLE DETAILS: A bolas uses centripetal force for catching animals or people. It's two balls on a rope. You whirl the bolas above your head and let go. The rope winds around your target's legs. Here's how to make your own.

HANG ON WHAT DID YOU SAY ABOUT CENTRIPETAL FORCE?

8. Getting In A Spin

181

If centripetal force is making you dizzy, this rhyme might help you...

> Centripetal's in a spin
> All the time it's pulling in
> Let go the string – it's worth a try
> In a straight line it will fly

Dare you discover... how a bolas works?

You will need:

Two balls of Blu tak each 2.5 cm across
A piece of strong string or twine 52 cm long

What you do:

1 Wrap a ball of Blu tak around each end of the string.

2 Squeeze the Blu tak to make sure it is holding the string securely.

3 Now you can practise throwing it. Hold the string between your thumb and fingers half-way between the two balls. Whirl the string round your head. Let go.

NOTE: READ HEALTH WARNING FIRST ON PAGE 108

From your observations how does the bolas work?

a) Centripetal force makes the bolas fly straight. When the force stops it wraps round the tree trunk.

b) The bolas flies straight until centripetal force does the wrapping.

c) Centripetal force makes the bolas come back like a boomerang.

Answers:

b) When you release the string, centrifugal force makes the bolas fly off at high speed in a straight line. When the string hits the tree the centripetal force on the string pulls the balls inwards so they wrap round the trunk.

Going round in circles

Between them centripetal force and momentum keep the show on the road and ensure that wheels are an all-round success story. They're useful for cars and trains, and buses and bikes, and tractors and windmills, and capstans that raise anchors. And thousands of other things too. Here are some amazing uses for wheels.

Weird wheels

1. The big Ferris wheels you see in funfairs were first invented in Russia in the 1600s. They were said to be inspired by the custom of giving children rides in the wheels used to scoop water from rivers. If the wheels went round too fast the children would be thrown into the river.

2. The name actually comes from American showman George Ferris who built a 75-metre wheel in 1893. Trouble is it took all of 20 minutes to go round once. Sounds as thrilling as watching porridge cool.

3. Wacky inventor Joseph Merlin gate-crashed a London party to show off the roller skates he'd just invented. The eighteenth-century boffin glided along playing his violin

and feeling dead cool as he swished across the polished floor. Until he found he couldn't stop and crashed into a mirror. Merlin's problem was that his wheels spun easily on the smooth floor. And there wasn't much friction to slow them down. Bet he was really cut up about it.

4. By turning a wheel you can produce a force that can be used to power all kinds of machines. In the nineteenth century prisoners were put on the treadmill. They had to climb a revolting revolving wheel but they never reached the top because the wheel kept turning towards them. In the rotting prison ships the treadmills operated the pumps that stopped the ship sinking!

8. Getting In A Spin

Bet you never knew!

Remember the imaginary force from page 50? As the scientist cycled round the corner she felt as if a force was trying to throw her outwards. Some people wrongly think this is a real force called "centrifugal force". They imagine the force making a lasso fly thorough the air in a cowboy movie. Well, sorry folks – it doesn't really exist!

Test your teacher

The non-existent force is caused by an object's inertia, which opposes centripetal force. So can your teacher tell the difference between this effect a) and b) centripetal force? Or will their head start spinning instead?

1 It's used in labs to separate red blood cells from the rest of the blood.

2 The reason a pendulum swings more slowly in Central Africa than in Europe. (This is true.)

3 It helps your bike go round a corner.

4 The reason that you can whizz upside down on a roller-coaster and not fall out even if you weren't strapped in.

5 The reason why a spacecraft doesn't fall to Earth.

6 You'll find this inside a rotor. That's the theme park ride that whirls you around as the floor drops away leaving you stuck to the wall.

Answers:

1) b The machine is called a centrifuge. It consists of a wheel on which a container is secured. The wheel whirls round hundreds of times a minute and the heavier cells in the blood sink to the bottom. A centrifuge is also used to separate the lighter cream from the rest of the milk. And they don't use the same machine!

2) b There's a special bonus point if your teacher can explain how it works. As the Earth spins round, its middle – otherwise known as the equator – bulges slightly. This is why gravity is a bit weaker than at the poles. – and weaker gravity explains the pendulum puzzle. Our old pal Newton made the pendulum prediction and in 1735 French expeditions to Peru and Lapland swung pendulums and proved him right.

3) a But you remembered that from page 181 – didn't you? In fact the centripetal force is supplied by friction between your tyres and the road.

4) b But it only works as long as you keep moving. Stop and you'll fall out – which is why it's essential to be strapped in.

5) b Imagine you're flying round the Earth. The surface curves away beneath you. This increase in distance cancels out the effects of gravity as you fall. If you weren't moving so fast you would fall to Earth with fatal results!

6) b You spin so fast that you stick to the wall. And if you vomit, your sick sticks to you.

Teacher's tea-break teaser

If you are feeling madly brave, knock on the staffroom door. When it groans, creaks, or scrapes open, smile sweetly at your teacher and say:

Answers:

Incredibly two of the world's greatest scientists puzzled over this for years. That's Nobel prize winners Albert Einstein (1879-1955) and Erwin Schrödinger (1887-1961). In 1926 Mrs S asked Erwin the question but he didn't know the answer. So she asked Einstein. After many calculations Einstein worked out the answer and even wrote an article about it in 1933. According to Einstein centrifugal force does push the tea leaves towards the sides of the cup. But friction between the liquid and the sides slows down the tea leaves at the sides and base of the cup. This weakens the centrifugal force. And as the liquid stops turning the leaves fall towards the centre of the cup. Wow! And you thought it was just a cup of tea! Here's another amazing story to keep things swinging.

8. Getting In A Spin

Getting in the swing

It was 1586 and 17-year-old Galileo (yes, him again) was in Pisa Cathedral listening to a boring sermon. He noticed a chandelier swinging in the breeze. Sometimes it swung in a long arc and sometimes in a shorter swing. But each swing seemed to take the same time.

So Galileo timed the swings using his pulse. He was right. (Could you make a similar discovery during a boring science lesson?)

Galileo used this newly discovered fact to design a new kind of clock. The grandfather clock used a swinging pendulum to keep time. What a time-ly invention.

In 1650 two priests spent a whole day counting the swings of a pendulum in a bid to prove the pendulum really did keep time. It did and they counted 87,998 swings.

But one sickly scientist had even bigger pendulum plans.

Hall of fame: Jean Bernard Léon Foucault (1819–1868)
Nationality: French

Young Jean was a sickly child. And his parents reckoned school would finish him off, so they educated him at home. Why can't all parents be so considerate? Poor Jean was never any good at his lessons. For a time he went nowhere. His bid to become a surgeon failed after he ran away from an operation. One squirt of blood and a bit of suffering and wimpy Jean burst into tears.

But Jean loved writing. So he became a science journalist instead. Then he got interested in experiments. He measured the speed of light and tried to photograph the stars. He then became fascinated by the idea that you could use a pendulum to prove the Earth turned during the day. Although everyone knew this, no one had ever tried to prove it actually happened.

In 1851 Jean devised an amazing test. He hung a huge steel ball 60 cm in diameter and weighing 30.4 kg from the dome of the

Pántheon in Paris, a large building where many famous people were buried.

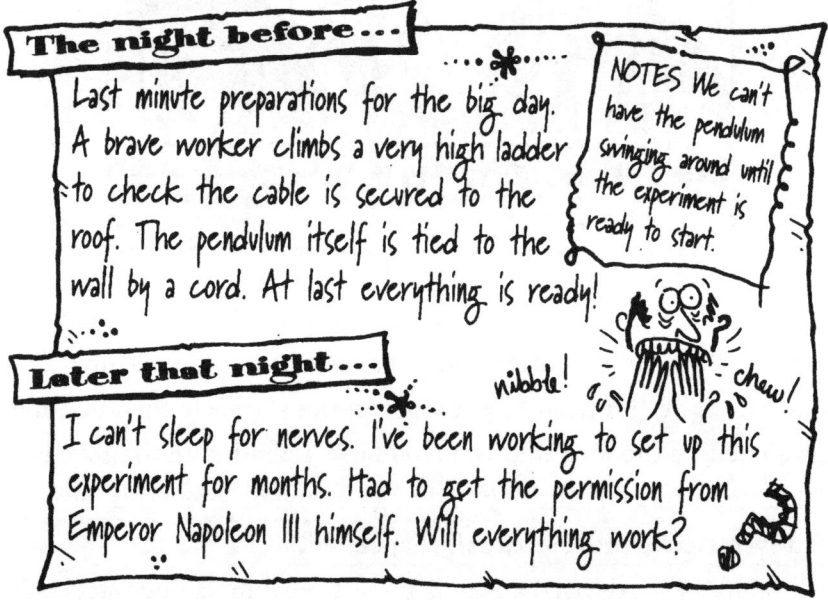

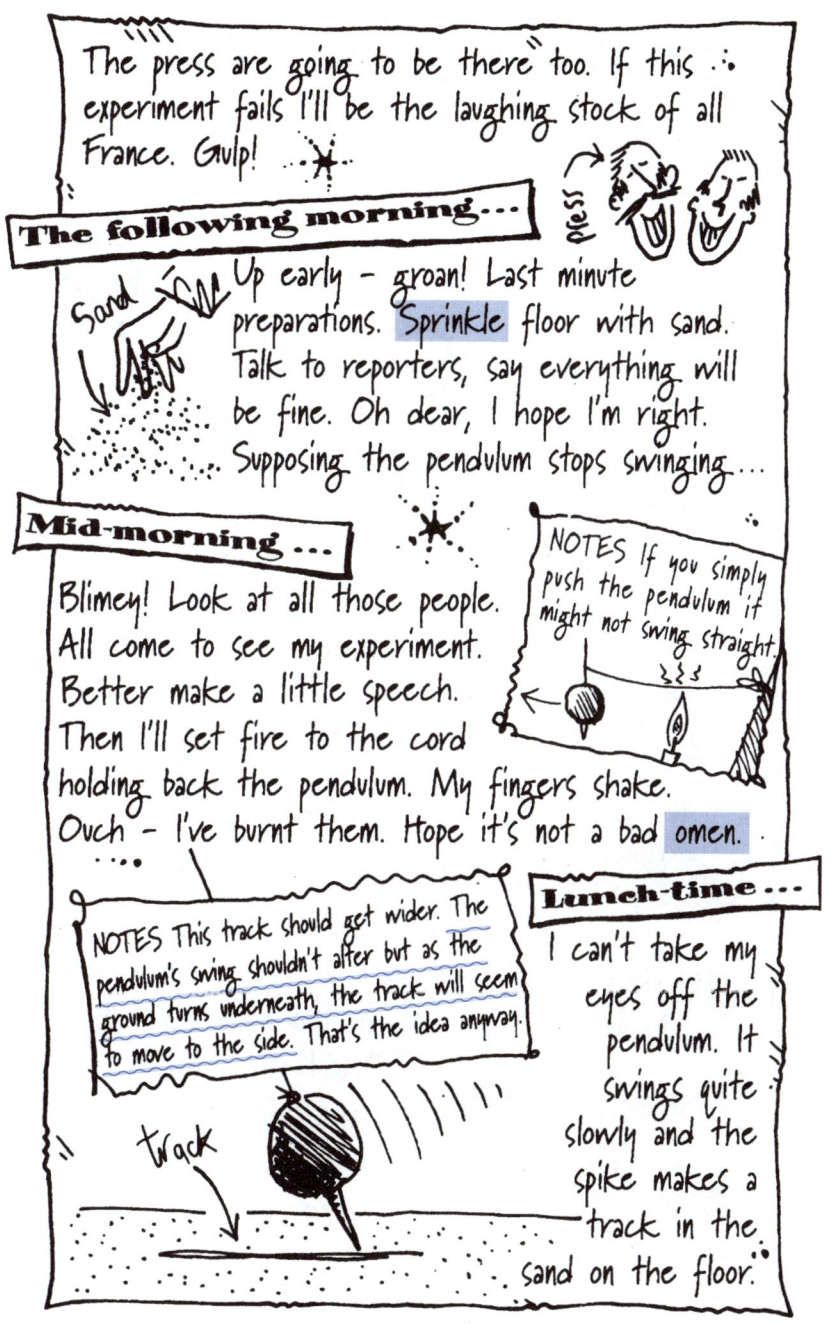

Afternoon...

Still swinging. Time seems to drag. I count the swings. It's like counting sheep.
I'm dozing off. Yawn — should have got more sleep last night. Zzzzzzzzzzz

An hour later...

Still swinging. Nothing happening. I should have known this right from the start. Maybe I could push the pendulum to one side when no one's looking. Help! The Emperor's glaring at me and he's really cross. I'M FINISHED. PANIC STATIONS!!!!

Nap III glaring

← Still sleeping

Just then...
I open my eyes. Phew! It must have been a dream. Everyone's pointing to the sand and talking. THE TRACK HAS GOT WIDER. I'M SAVED!!!

The world really does go round. YIPPEEEEE! I feel like dancing about and kissing everyone.

Foucault found himself a hero. He was awarded the Légion d'Honneur medal. He went on to invent gyroscopes… which work on the same principle as tops as you'll see in a moment. And tops are top toys for freaky physicists.

Top tricks

Physicists like nothing better than playing with their favourite toys. Well, according to them they're investigating forces. Oh, yeah.

There are loads of toys that use the forces of spinning. Toys like, yo-yos, hula-hoops, frisbees. And tops. A top was a favourite toy of Nobel prize winner Wolfgang Pauli (1900–1958) who was trying to work out the physics of inertia. Here's some crucial info to get you "tops" of the class.

Tops balance because angular momentum keeps them going – remember the coin running away from the scientist? Tops keep turning in the same way despite the efforts of gravity to pull them down. Bigger tops need more effort to get going but spin for longer. Tops are popular with kids the world over. Here's a traditional Inuit game you might like to play when it gets really cold.

You will need:

IGLOO   SPINNING TOP

What you do:

Spin the top. Run round your igloo (or house). Try to get back inside before the top falls down. (This could be fatal if you don't wrap up warm first.)

In 1743 English inventor John Smeaton (1724–1794) invented a sort of top that would stay level even on a ship in a storm. This allowed mariners to check where the horizon should be. They could then work out the positions of

YOU ONLY HAVE TO GO ROUND ONCE!

the sun and stars to navigate by. But the new fangled top didn't catch on because seafarers were useless at spinning it.

But Smeaton's brainwave was the ancestor of gyroscopes found on most ships and planes today.

Foucault's invention – the gyroscope – works like a series of tops. They balance on one another and always stay upright. And this is ideal if you want to steer a steady course. Amazingly, your bike wheels work in much the same way. When they spin round the bike is much less likely tip over than when it's stationary. Scientists call this "precession". Something to think about next time you go for a precession on your bike.

Bet you never knew!

The tighter your circle of spin the faster you go. That's why ice-skaters pull in their arms to spin faster. It's the law of conservation of angular momentum again. Because the circle of spin is smaller they go round quicker. This fact also explains why water speeds up near the centre of a whirlpool. You can check this fact by watching the dregs of your washing-up gurgle down the plug hole. And if this isn't your idea of fun you'd better dive into the next chapter. You'll soon get your bounce back.

BAKED BEAN

PEA IS SPINNING FASTER THAN THE BAKED BEAN

REVIEW

세상은 돌고 돈다. 지구는 23.5도 기울어진 자전축을 중심으로 팽이처럼 돌고 있다. 태양계의 행성들은 태양을 중심으로 마치 회전목마의 말과 마차들이 돌듯이 공전한다. 자동차의 바퀴도 돌고 엄마의 훌라후프도 돈다. 벽시계의 초침은 바쁘게 돌고 시침은 느긋하게 돈다. 학교에 돌고 있는 '내가 쟤를 좋아한다'는 소문에도 원심력과 구심력이 작용할까? 오래전부터 볼라(bolas)나 부메랑(boomerang)을 던져 사냥을 했던 사람들에게 회전 운동에 대해 물어보자.

8. Getting In A Spin

Vocabulary 8

p.180

Also the force on the outer parts of the wheel produces greater force at the **axle**.

또한 바퀴의 바깥쪽 부분에 가해지는 힘은 차축에 더 큰 힘을 발생시킨다.

axle '어깨(shoulder)'를 뜻하는 말에서 왔다. 어깨는 몸통과 팔을 연결하는 부위로, 팔의 상하좌우 운동을 가능하게 하는 '축'과 같은 역할을 한다. 그래서 **axle**은 바퀴와 연결해 직선 운동을 원운동으로 바꿔 주는 긴 막대인 '차축, 굴대'를 부르는 말이다. 지구의 '자전축'처럼 원운동을 하는 물체의 중심축을 뜻하는 **axis**도 어원이 같다.

p.181

Best put your foot over the coin and **pretend** you haven't seen it.

동전 위에 발을 올려놓고 그것을 본 적이 없는 척하는 게 가장 좋다.

pretend pre는 '앞으로'를, tend는 '내밀다'를 의미한다. 진짜는 뒤에 감추고 가짜를 '앞으로 내민다'는 의미다. 시치미를 떼고 아닌 척, 안 한 척, 거짓으로 꾸미는 행동이 바로 **pretend**다. '~인 척하다, 가장하다'라는 뜻이다. 실제는 그렇지 않지만 그렇다고 '상상하다, 가정하다'란 뜻으로도 쓸 수 있다.

p.182

Whirl the string round your head.

줄을 머리 위로 빙빙 돌린다.

whirl '돌다(turn)'를 뜻하는 말에서 왔다. 그냥 도는 게 아니라 빠른 회전 운동을 할 때 **whirl**을 쓴다. '빙빙 돌다, 돌리다'를 뜻하는 동사나 '빙빙 돌기, 돌리기'를 뜻하는 명사로 쓴다. 내 몸이 **whirl** 동작을 한다면 반드시 dizzy한 상태가 된다. 비슷한 말로 spin, swirl이 있다.

p.183

Try to resist the **temptation** to throw your bolas at a small brother/sister/cat/dog, even if it is in the interest of science.

과학을 위해서라 할지라도, 어린 형제자매, 고양이, 개에게 볼라를 던지고 싶은 유혹은 참아야 한다.

내 얼굴에 돌돌 감긴 이게 바로 볼라야.

temptation 어근 tempt는 동사로 '유혹하다, 부추기다'를 의미한다. 중세에는 기독교 하나님의 뜻을 거역하라고 악마가 유혹한다는 의미로 tempt를 썼다. 그래서 도덕적으로 나쁜 행동을 하라고, 범죄를 저지르라고, 이기적 욕망을 채우라고 부추기는 '유혹'이나 '유혹적인 대상'을 명사로 **temptation**이라고 한다.

p.183

From your **observations** how does the bolas work?

관찰해 보니, 볼라는 어떻게 작동하는가?

observation 동사 **observe**는 '앞에서(in front of)'를 뜻하는 ob과 '지켜보다(watch)'를 뜻하는 serve가 합쳐진 말이다. 엄마나 선생님이 왜 앞에서 보고 있을까? 잘하나 못하나 '보면서 감시하고' 이러쿵저러쿵 '잔소리하려고' 지켜보는 거다. 바로 이런 모습이 **observe**다. '지켜보다, 관찰하다, 감시하다, 목격하다, 말하다, 평하다, (규칙 등을) 잘 지키다, 준수하다'를 뜻한다. 같은 의미의 명사형은 **observation**이다. 예문에서는 '관찰'을 뜻한다.

p.184

Sounds as **thrilling** as watching porridge cool.

죽이 식는 것을 지켜보는 것만큼이나 짜릿할 것 같다.

thrilling '흥분시키는, 황홀감을 느끼게 하는'을 뜻한다. **thrill**은 '구멍 나다, 꿰뚫다'를 뜻하는 말에서 왔다. 구멍 뚫는 'drill(드릴)'과 어원이 같다. 사냥감이 활이나 창에 몸을 '뚫리면' 충격 때문에 몸을 부르르 떨게 된다. 이렇게 몸이 떨릴 정도의 느낌과 감정이 생기게 한다는 의미로 동사 **thrill**을 쓴다. 형용사형인 **thrilled**는 몸이 떨릴 정도로 격한 감정을 느낀다는 뜻이다. 가슴 졸이고 흥분하게 만드는 범죄, 추리, 스파이 액션 장르의 영화나 소설을 **thriller**라고 한다.

8. Getting In A Spin

p.185

Perhaps on **reflection**, they're not such a brilliant invention.
아마 다시 생각해 보면, 그다지 훌륭한 발명품은 아니었을 것이다.

reflection 동사 **reflect**는 '뒤로, 다시'를 뜻하는 re와 '구부리다(bend)'를 뜻하는 flect가 합쳐진 말이다. 빛이 거울에 부딪히면 구부러지며 돌아온다. 그래서 **reflect**는 '반사하다, 반영하다, 비추다'란 뜻을 갖고 있다. 처음으로 돌아가 다시 생각한다는 의미에서 '숙고하다, 깊이 생각하다'도 갖고 있다. on(upon) **reflection**은 '다시 깊이 생각해 보니, 숙고해 보니'라는 표현이다.

p.186

It's used in labs to **separate** red blood cells from the rest of the blood.
그것은 실험실에서 적혈구를 나머지 혈액으로부터 분리하는 데 사용된다.

separate se-는 '따로, 분리된'을 뜻하고, parate는 '준비하다'를 뜻한다. 따로 분리해서 준비해야 한다는 의미라서 동사로 '분리하다, 갈라놓다, 헤어지다, 이별하다'를 뜻한다. 따로 준비하는 것은 성격이 다르고 가는 방향이 다르기 때문이다. 그래서 **separate**를 형용사로 쓰면 '서로 다른, 별개의, 분리된'이라는 뜻이 된다.

p.188

Our old pal Newton made the pendulum prediction and in 1735 French **expeditions** to Peru and Lapland swung pendulums and proved him right.
우리의 오랜 친구 뉴턴은 진자 예측을 했고, 1735년 페루와 라플란드로 떠난 프랑스 탐험대는 진자를 흔들어 그가 옳았다는 것을 증명했다.

expedition ex-는 '밖으로(out)'를 뜻하고, pedi-는 '발(foot)'을 뜻한다. '밖으로 걸어 나가다, 밖에서 걷다'란 의미다. 이불 밖은 위험하고 집 나가면 고생이다. 먼 옛날, 길거리에는 약자를 노리는 악인들이 많았고, 도시 밖에는 늑대가 우글거렸다. 그래서 **expedition**은 낯설고 위험한 '밖'으로 가는 '탐험, 원정'이나 '탐험대, 원정대'를 뜻하는 명사로 쓴다.

p.189

After many calculations Einstein worked out the answer and even wrote an **article** about it in 1933.

아인슈타인은 많은 계산 끝에 답을 알아냈고, 1933년에는 그에 관한 논문을 쓰기도 했다.

article 전체를 구성하는 요소인 '조각(piece), 부분(part), 구성원(member)'을 뜻하는 말에서 왔다. 기사와 논평들이 모여야 하루치의 신문이 되고 한 권의 잡지가 완성된다. 그래서 '신문이나 잡지에 실린 기사, 논문, 글'을 **article**이라고 한다. 서류의 일부분인 '조항, 계약 조건' 등도 **article**이라고 한다.

p.190

So Galileo timed the swings using his **pulse**.

그래서 갈릴레오는 자신의 맥박을 이용해 흔들림의 주기를 쟀다.

pulse 심장이 펌프질을 하면 혈액이 온몸으로 퍼진다. 그때 심장의 리듬과 피가 혈관 속을 흐르는 것을 '고동(beat)'으로 느낄 수 있는데, 그런 '맥박, 고동'을 **pulse**라고 한다. '맥박 치다, 심장이 두근거리다'를 뜻하는 동사로도 쓸 수 있다.

p.191

Why can't all parents be so **considerate**?

왜 모든 부모가 이렇게 사려 깊을 수 없는 걸까?

considerate con은 '함께, 같이'를 의미하고, sider는 '별들(stars)'을 의미한다. 밤하늘에 펼쳐진 별들의 위치와 움직임을 보고서 운명과 미래를 예측하는 점성술에서 온 말이다. 때문에 동사 **consider**는 정확한 관찰과 판단이 필요한 '숙고하다, 고려하다'란 뜻을 갖게 되었다. 생각이 깊은 사람은 세상을 걱정하고 남을 신경 쓰기 마련이다. 그런 의미에서 형용사 **considerate**는 '남을 배려하는, 사려 깊은'을 뜻한다. 명사형은 **consideration**이다.

8. Getting In A Spin

p.191

> He hung a huge steel ball 60cm in **diameter** and weighing 30.4kg from the dome of the Pantheon in Paris, a large building where many famous people were buried.
>
> 그는 직경 60cm, 무게 30.4kg의 거대한 강철 공을 파리의 판테온 돔에 매달았다. 판테온은 많은 유명인들이 매장되어 있는 큰 건물이다.

diameter dia는 '가로지르는(across), 통과하는(through)'을 의미하고, meter는 '측정, 측량'을 의미한다. 원의 크기, 원통의 부피 등을 측정하려면 반드시 원의 중심을 '가로지르는' 지름의 길이를 알아야 한다. 그래서 '원의 지름, 직경, 지름의 길이'를 **diameter**라고 부른다. '반지름, 반경'은 radius라고 한다.

p.193

> **Sprinkle** floor with sand.
>
> 모래를 바닥에 뿌릴 것.

'Sprinkle=뿌리다' 엄청난 우연이지? 스윽~ 뿌린다는 것 같잖아.

sprinkle '뿌리다, 흩어지다(scatter)'란 의미를 갖고 있다. 액체나 가루 등을 '흩뿌리다, 분무하다'란 뜻으로 쓰고, '비가 보슬보슬 내리다'란 뜻으로도 쓸 수 있다. '흩뿌린 듯 조금 섞여 있는, 조금 묻어 있는' 상태를 표현하려면 형용사형 **sprinkled**를 쓰면 된다.

p.193

> Hope it's not a bad **omen**.
>
> 그게 나쁜 징조가 아니길 바랄 뿐.

omen 소나기가 오려면 먹구름이 몰려오고 할머니 무릎도 쑤신다. 여기서 먹구름과 무릎 통증은 소나기가 올 거라고 '미리 알려 주는' 역할을 하는데, 이런 게 **omen**이다. '징조, 전조, 조짐'을 뜻한다. '좋은 징조'는 a good **omen**, '나쁜 징조'는 a bad **omen**이다. sign도 **omen**과 비슷한 뜻을 갖고 있다.

> This allowed mariners to check where the **horizon** should be.
> 이 발명품으로 선원들은 수평선이 어디에 있는지 확인할 수 있다.

horizon '한계, 경계(limit), 구분'을 뜻하는 말에서 왔다. 그래서 하늘과 땅의 경계인 '지평선', 하늘과 바다의 경계인 '수평선'을 **horizon**이라고 한다. 사람의 '관심, 흥미, 욕구 등의 범위'를 뜻하는 말로도 쓸 수 있다. **horizon**은 수평이기 때문에 형용사 **horizontal**은 '수평(선)의, 가로의'를 뜻한다.

> When they spin round the bike is much less likely tip over than when it's **stationary**.
> 바퀴가 구르고 있을 때가 자전거가 정지해 있을 때보다 넘어질 가능성이 훨씬 적다.

stationary '서는 곳, 서 있는 장소'이란 의미의 station은 bus station(버스정류장), train station(기차역), police station(경찰서), fire station(소방서), gas station(주유소) 등에 쓴다. 형용사형인 **stationary**는 '움직이지 않는, 정지된, 변하지 않는'이라는 뜻이다. 철자가 하나 다른 stationery는 '문구류, 문방구'를 뜻하는 명사다.

> Something to think about next time you go for a **precession** on your bike.
> 다음번에 자전거를 타고 세차 운동을 하러 갈 때 꼭 생각해 볼 거리다.

precession '세차 운동'을 말한다. 회전하고 있는 물체의 회전축이 정지해 있는 어떤 축의 둘레를 도는 운동이나 현상을 지칭하는 과학 용어다. 자전거를 타고 바퀴를 회전시키면 넘어지지 않고 앞으로 나아갈 수 있는 것이 다 **precession** 덕분이다.

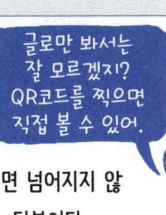

8. Getting In A Spin

Sentence 8

p.180

Ever wondered why cars don't have square wheels?
왜 자동차에 사각형 바퀴가 없는지 궁금했던 적이 있는가?

문장 앞에 조동사와 주어인 Have you가 생략되어 있다. 독자와 저자, 두 사람의 대화라서 굳이 you나 I를 쓰지 않아도 말이 통하기 때문에 생략할 수 있다.
[Have you ever wondered why ~]는 '~ 이유가 무엇인지 궁금했던 적이 있는가?'하고 물을 때 쓰는 표현이다.

p.180

He's describing how coins and any other spinning objects have a habit of turning until another force gets in the way.
그는 어떻게 동전과 다른 회전하는 물체들이 다른 힘이 방해할 때까지 계속 회전하는 습성이 있는지를 설명하고 있다.

[have a habit of ~]는 '~하는 습관(습성, 관성)을 갖고 있다'라는 뜻이다.
get in the way는 '끼어들다, 가로막다, 방해하다'를 뜻한다.

p.181

When you let go, the ball's momentum sends it flying off at an angle in a straight line.
줄을 놓으면 공의 추진력으로 인해 공은 직선상의 일정한 각도로 날아간다.

let go는 잡고 있던 것을 '놓다, 풀어주다'를 뜻한다.

204

at an angle in a straight line은 '직선상의 일정한 각도로'를 말한다. 쉽게 말해 한 방향으로 곧장 날아간다는 의미다.

> Much better to practise outside in a wide open space.
> 야외의 넓게 트인 공간에서 연습하는 게 훨씬 좋다.

문장 앞에 가주어와 be동사 It is가 생략되어 있다. to practise 이하가 진주어다.
much는 good의 비교급인 better을 강조하는 말로, '훨씬'을 뜻한다.
in a wide open space는 '넓고(wide) 탁 트인(open) 공간(space)'을 의미한다.

> They were said to be inspired by the custom of giving children rides in the wheels used to scoop water from rivers.
> 그것들은 강에서 물을 퍼올리는 데 사용된 물레바퀴에 아이들을 태워 주던 풍습에서 영감을 받았다고 한다.

주어 They는 앞 문장에 나온 the big Ferris wheels(대회전 관람차)을 말한다.
were said to be는 '세상 사람들이 그렇게 말한다'는 의미를 수동형으로 표현한 것이다. '~라고 전해진다'로 해석하면 된다. [be inspired by]는 '~에 영감을 받다, ~에 착안하다'를 뜻한다.

p.185

> In the rotting prison ships the treadmills operated the pumps that stopped the ship sinking.
> 썩고 있는 감옥선에서는 쳇바퀴가 펌프를 작동시켜 배가 가라앉는 것을 막았다.

죄수들을 낡은 배 안에 가뒀던 적이 있었는데, 그 감옥선(prison ship)은 나무로 만들어서 '썩고 있는(rotting)' 상태다.
that stopped the ship sinking은 pumps를 수식하는 말이다. [stop A (from) 동사ing]는 'A가 ~하는 것을 막다, 방지하다'라는 뜻이다.

p.187

> The reason that you can whizz upside down on a roller-coaster and not fall out even if you weren't strapped in.
> 벨트에 묶여 있지 않더라도 휙 거꾸로 뒤집힌 롤러코스터에서 떨어지지 않을 수 있는 이유.

문장이 아니라 하나의 긴 구다. that 이하 전체가 앞에 나온 the reason(이유)을 수식하고 있다.
upside down은 위쪽(upside)이 밑으로(down) 내려간다, 즉 '뒤집어진다'라는 말이다. 문장 앞에 접속사 even if가 나오면 '~일지라도, ~하더라도'로 해석한다.

p.189

> Excuse me, I was wondering why when you stir your tea, the tea leaves settle at the centre of the bottom of your tea cup?
> 실례합니다만, 차를 저을 때 찻잎이 찻잔 바닥 가운데에 가라앉는 이유가 궁금한데요?

동사 wonder는 무언가가 알고 싶어서, 궁금해서 곰곰이 생각한다는 의미를 갖고 있다. 이 문장에서 궁금한 것은 '이유(why)'다.
wonder의 목적어는 why로 시작하는 간접 의문문인데, 부사절(when you stir your tea)과 주절(why the tea leaves ~ your tea cup)로 구성되어 있다.

p.191

> Although everyone knew this, no one had ever tried to prove it actually happened.
>
> 비록 누구나 이를 알고 있었지만, 실제로 이런 일이 일어난다는 것을 증명하려고 했던 사람은 없었다.

문장 앞에 나오는 부사절의 접속사 although는 '~이긴 하지만, 비록 ~지만'이라는 뜻이다.
no one had ever tried to prove는 '그 누구도 이제껏(ever) 증명하려고 하지 않았다'는 의미다.

p.193

> The pendulum's swing shouldn't alter but as the ground turns underneath, the track will seem to move to the side.
>
> 진자의 흔들림은 변하지 않지만, 밑의 바닥이 돌면서 궤도가 옆으로 이동하는 듯이 보일 것이다.

The pendulum's ~ alter는 '진자의 흔들림(왕복 운동)은 변하지 않아야 한다'는 의미다. 다른 힘이 작용해서 움직임의 방향과 진폭이 달라져서는 안 된다는 말이다.
이 문장에서 underneath는 '아래에서, 밑에 있는'을 뜻하는 부사다. as the ground turns underneath(지면이 밑에서 회전한다)는 지구의 자전을 표현한 것이다.

p.194

> I should have known this right from the start.
>
> 나는 처음부터 이를 알았어야 했어.

[should have + 동사 완료형]은 '~했어야 했다'는 의미로, 과거에 하지 않은 행동을 '왜 안 했을까' 하고 후회할 때 쓰는 표현이다.
right from the start는 '처음부터 바로(right)'를 뜻하는 부사구다.

8. Getting In A Spin

p.195

> **Physicists like nothing better than playing with their favorite toys.**
> 물리학자들은 자신이 좋아하는 장난감을 가지고 노는 것을 그 무엇보다도 좋아한다.

[like nothing better than A]는 '그 무엇보다 A를 더 좋아하다, A만큼 좋아하는 것도 없다'를 뜻하는 표현이다.

p.197

> **And if this isn't your idea of fun you'd better dive into the next chapter.**
> 이것이 당신이 재미있다 여기는 게 아니라면 다음 장으로 뛰어드는 게 좋을 것이다.

'유머'나 '재미 코드'는 사람마다 다르다. idea of fun이 그런 개인적인 웃음 코드다. 그래서 if this isn't your idea of fun은 '이것이 재미가 없다면, 이게 재미없다고 느낀다면, 이게 네 취향이 아니라면'처럼 해석할 수 있다.

you'd better는 you had better의 줄임말이다. '그렇게 하는 게 더 좋아(better)!'라고 충고하는 말이라서 '꼭 ~해야 해, ~할 필요가 있어'라고 해석한다.

CHAPTER 9 KEYWORDS

#lift #spin #bouncing #juggle

Bouncing Back

What's always "around" for a game and doesn't mind a good kicking? No, not your sports teacher. It's a ball. And oddly enough balls do other forceful things. Like rolling and spinning and bouncing. Here are a few facts to bounce off your friends.

Fatal forces fact file

> NAME: Bouncing
>
> THE BASIC FACTS: When a rubber ball hits the floor the springy coiled rubber molecules that make up the ball are all squashed together. They soak up the energy of the impact and then bounce out again – making the ball bounce.
>
> THE HORRIBLE DETAILS: The first chewing gum was made of chicle, a type of tree sap. American scientists tried to make the chicle into a type of rubber but it wasn't bouncy enough. So they just chewed the problem over, or rather chewed the chicle.

Keep your eye on the ball

When a ball flies through the air, strange things start to happen. Scientists have put loads of effort into working out what these mysterious effects are.

Fatal forces fact file

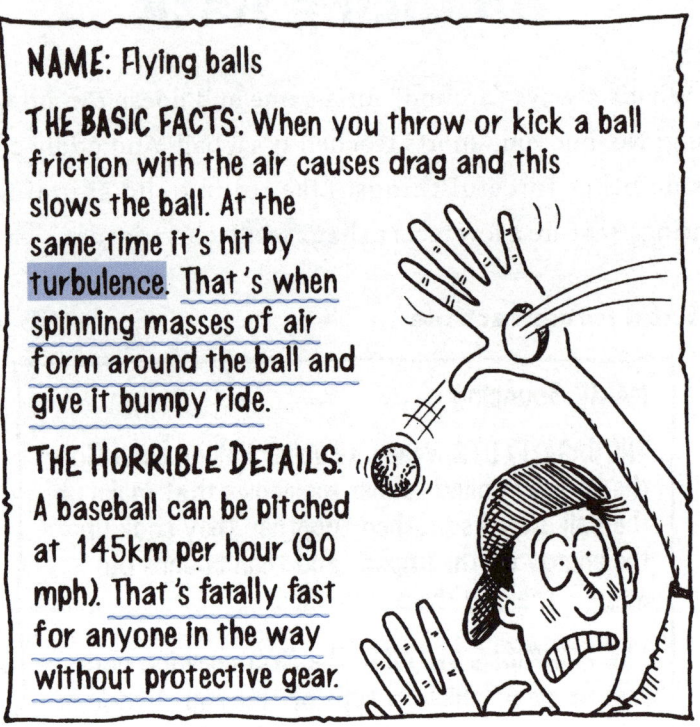

NAME: Flying balls

THE BASIC FACTS: When you throw or kick a ball friction with the air causes drag and this slows the ball. At the same time it's hit by turbulence. That's when spinning masses of air form around the ball and give it bumpy ride.

THE HORRIBLE DETAILS: A baseball can be pitched at 145km per hour (90 mph). That's fatally fast for anyone in the way without protective gear.

Any old scientist will tell you that ball games involve forces. So we invited a tame scientist along to show you how science can help you improve at sports such as tennis. According to the scientist you don't need to work up a sweat. All you need is a few brain cells and a small computer. Oh, yeah?

The scientist's guide to tennis

Tennis ball seams are the same on each side. This means equal amounts of air turbulence. So the ball flies straight.

That's quite a velocity. Slice the racket downwards and you'll get back-spin. The ball tumbles backwards as it flies forwards. This drags air over it. As this air speeds up, the pressure above the ball drops and the greater air pressure under the ball raises it. We call this effect, lift.

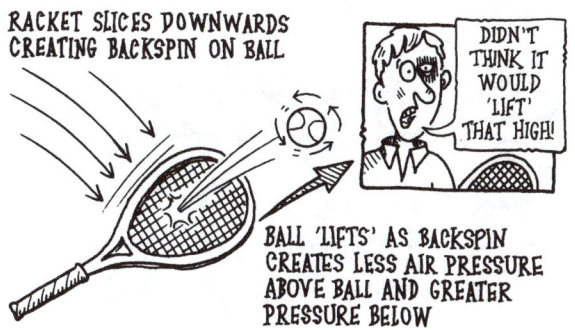

Top spin is the opposite. Strike the ball upwards and the ball tumbles forwards as it flies forwards. This drags air under the ball. And as it speeds up the pressure drops and the ball is pushed lower and it bounces faster.

If you hit the ball a glancing blow it bounces extra slowly when it hits the ground. So it's even easier to whack.

Painless padding

If you find games a pain in the sports bag maybe you need a bit more protection. Here's a few bits and pieces of equipment designed to help you play safe.

- Cushioned shoulder padding and shin pads as worn by American footballers.

- Boxer's gum shield. Stops teeth from being knocked out of their sockets.

- American footballer's helmet. Cage to protect face.

- Dome shape spreads force of blow over whole helmet. Stops head from getting squashed.

- Cricketer's box to protect the vulnerable bits. Very useful – cricket balls travel at 160 km per hour (100 mph).

Here are a few more facts to prove that science really is a ball.

Having a ball

1. The first balls were made by the Romans from bits of dead animal skin stitched together and filled with air. Later on in the Middle Ages balls were made from pigs' bladders filled with air. Yuck – who had to blow them up?

2. The first golf balls were leather bags packed with boiled chicken's feathers. Bet that made the feathers fly. The balls flew very well until it rained when they soon got waterlogged and split. Covering the players in grotty old feathers.

3. In the 1850s someone had the idea of making golf balls out

of rubbery tree sap. But they didn't fly as straight as the old balls until they became scratched and worn. Then they flew really well.

4. So what was going on? Turned out the rough surface of the golf ball trapped tiny pockets of air. The turbulent air flowed around the trapped air and this actually gave a smoother quicker flight. And that's why modern golf balls have little dimples.

5. Cricket balls also do strange things as they fly through the air. Normally the ball just spins horizontally. But at speed, air turbulence makes the ball swerve if the edge of the ball's seam is smooth. That's why some cricketers polish the ball by rubbing it on their trousers.

6. At speeds of 100 km (62 mph) plus, the ball can swerve even more. Especially if the edge of the seam is rough. And that's why some cricketers rub dirt into the ball. But don't do this in your games lesson – it's called cheating.

7. The ball used in rugby and American football has pointed ends. If it's tumbling forward it can bounce oddly. Sometimes it bounces high, sometimes low.

8. This makes it tricky to pick up. And dangerous too unless you enjoy twenty giant people jumping on your head. The good news is that the ball is easier to throw. Pitch it with one end pointing forwards and it'll spin horizontally like an over-sized bullet. This means you can easily get rid of it before you get flattened. It's safer than just standing and juggling the ball…

Dare you discover... how to juggle?

Juggling is a great way to see how forces affect balls in the air. Tell your gullible folks you're doing your homework. Then you can have a bit of fun.

You will need:
Yourself
Something to juggle with. Three balls small enough to fit in your hands would be good. Or you could try rolled up socks
Plenty of space
A mirror
Safety note: When you are learning to juggle try to resist the urge to use your granny's priceless antiques, food (especially at meal-times), and living creatures such as hamsters, goldfish, small brothers and sisters, etc.

1 Stand in front of a mirror with your elbows tucked close to your body and your hands level with your waist. Place your legs apart with your knees slightly bent. Easy, isn't it? Are you ready?

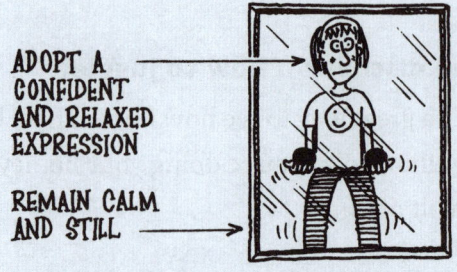

2 Take a deep breath and let it out slowly. That's right – relax. Now without looking at your hands… throw the ball gently up and over your head. Notice how it falls in an arc under the influence of gravity just like the cannonballs Galileo studied – remember? Catch the ball in the palm of your other hand. Keep your eyes in the top part of the ball's flight. OK – that's the easy bit.

3 Now it gets a bit harder. Juggling with two balls takes a bit of practice. Throw one ball up as before. When the ball is just about to drop, throw your second ball up from the other hand. Ideally the second ball should pass just under the first ball.

4 OK, this takes practice. Better practise now to get it right.

5. This is where it gets really hard. Three balls. Sure you want to try? OK. Hold two balls in one hand and one in the other. Repeat Step 3.

6. Now here's the clever bit. When ball 2 is just about to drop throw ball 3 up and try to get it to pass under ball 2. Meanwhile catch ball 1 and throw it up just when ball 3 is about to drop. Easy!

7. Fantastic, keep going!

And while you're doing this, here are some interesting facts to juggle with.

1. It's REALLY difficult to juggle with more than 12 balls. This feat was achieved by several people including American Bruce Sarafian in 1996.

2. Kara, a nineteenth-century German performer used to juggle with his hat, lighted cigar, gloves, newspaper, matches and a coffee cup. Don't try this at home… or at school.

3. It's also possible to juggle with your feet. As long as their back is supported, the performer can juggle quite weighty objects including a small child. And this is something you shouldn't try either!

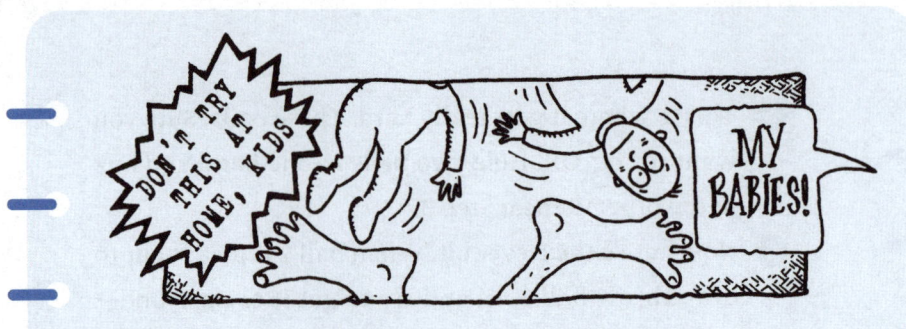

Sooner or later they'll invent a juggling machine. Then people could enjoy the fun of juggling without ever having to learn for themselves. That's typical of us humans. Always inventing machines to get out of hard work. There are loads more mighty machines that use forces to do work. Listen hard and you'll hear them grinding up their gears for the next chapter…

REVIEW

축구, 야구, 배구, 농구, 테니스, 골프 같은 '구기' 종목의 공통점은 말 그대로 둥근 '공(ball)'을 몸으로 다룬다는 것이다. 공은 탄력, 반발력, 회전력이 작용해야 하기 때문에 대개 고무나 가죽으로 만든다. 종목에 따라 공의 크기, 모양, 무게는 다 다르다. 아빠 얼굴처럼 주름이 있거나 심지어 털 달린 공도 있다. 공의 모양, 속도, 회전, 공기의 흐름이 어떻게 다양한 재미를 주는지 알아보자.

Vocabulary 9

p.209

Here are a few facts to **bounce off** your friends.
여기 친구들의 관심을 끌 만한 몇 가지 사실들이 있다.

bounce off 강하게 던지거나 차거나 때려서 그 충격이 내게 돌아오는 것이 **bounce**다. 예를 들어 벽에 대고 공을 차면, 공기 압축으로 인한 탄력과 '작용·반작용의 법칙' 때문에 공이 튀어서 내게 돌아온다. '튀다, 튀어 오르다, 탄력, 반동'을 뜻한다. [**bounce off** A]는 'A를 맞고 돌아온다'라는 의미인데, A가 사람일 경우에는 내 말이나 질문에 대해 그 사람이 반응하고 답을 한다는 의미가 된다. '~에게서 반응을 일으키다, 관심을 끌다'로 이해하면 된다.

p.210

At the same time it's hit by **turbulence**.
그와 동시에 공은 난기류에 맞는다.

turbulence '떠들썩함, 야단법석'을 뜻하는 말에서 왔다. 조용하거나 차분하지 않고 시끄럽다는 의미로, '격동, 격변'을 뜻하는 명사다. 바람이나 물의 흐름이 갑자기 강해지고 소용돌이치는 '난류, 난기류'를 뜻하는 말로도 쓴다. 형용사형 **turbulent**는 '격동의, 요동치는, 난기류의' 등을 뜻한다.

p.211

The ball **tumbles** backwards as it flies forwards.
공은 앞으로 날아가면서 후방으로 구른다.

tumble '우당탕 넘어진다'라는 말이 있는데, 이런 느낌을 잘 표현한 동사가 **tumble**이다. '갑자기 중심을 잃고 넘어지다'를 뜻하는데, '급락하다'라는 뜻으로도 쓸 수 있다. 바닥을 둥글게 만들어 기우뚱거리는 유리잔을 **tumbler**라

9. Bouncing Back

고 불렸는데, 지금의 '텀블러'로 의미가 변했다. tumble 앞에 s를 붙이면, 마치 S자 걸음을 걷듯이 '휘청거리다, 비틀대다, 발을 헛딛다'란 뜻의 동사 stumble이 된다.

p.212

Boxer's gum shield.
권투 선수의 마우스피스.

shield 아주 오래 전부터 전투에 사용하던 '방패'를 뜻한다. 용도는 적의 칼과 창, 화살을 '막아' 자신을 '보호하는' 것이다. 그래서 **shield**를 동사로 쓰면 '위험이나 공격을 막다, 막아서 보호하다, 방패를 치듯이 가리다'를 뜻한다. protect와 의미가 같다.

p.213

Cricketer's box to protect the vulnerable bits.
크리켓 선수의 급소를 보호하는 보호대.

vulnerable 어근인 vulner는 '다치다, 상하다'를 의미하고 able은 '가능성'을 의미한다. '다칠 수 있고 손상될 수 있다'라는 뜻이라서, 형용사로 '상처받기 쉬운, 다치기 쉬운, 취약한, 연약한'을 뜻한다. 명사형은 **vulnerability**로 '취약성'이다. **vulnerable** bits는 다치기 쉽고 연약한 부분인 급소다.

p.214

But at speed, air turbulence makes the ball swerve if the edge of the ball's seam is smooth.
그러나 속도가 빠르면, 공의 봉합선 부분이 매끈한 경우 난기류로 인해 공의 방향이 휘어질 수 있다.

swerve 기본 의미는 '갑자기 방향을 바꾸다'이다. 방향을 바꾸는 이유는 대개 부딪히지 않기 위해서다. 즉 충돌을 피하기 위해 방향을 트는 상황을 묘사하는 동사다. 불이익이나 마찰을 피하기 위해서 '자기 생각을 굽히다, 의견을 바꾸다'라는 의미로도 쓸 수 있다. **swerve**를 명사로 쓰면 '급회전, 회피'를 뜻한다.

p.215

> **Juggling** is a great way to see how forces affect balls in the air.
> 저글링은 힘이 공중에 있는 공에 어떤 영향을 미치는지 볼 수 있는 아주 좋은 방법이다.

juggling 동사 **juggle**은 '웃기다, 즐겁게 하다'를 뜻하는 말에서 왔다. '농담, 우스갯소리'를 뜻하는 joke와 친척사이다. 서커스에서 사람을 '웃기며' 분위기를 잡는 '광대(clown)'들이 흔히 세 개 이상의 물건을 위로 던지고 받는 묘기를 했기 때문에 그런 동작을 **juggle**로 부르게 되었다. '여러 가지 일을 한꺼번에 힘들게 처리하다'란 뜻으로도 자주 쓴다. 명사형은 **juggling**이다.

p.215

> When you are learning to juggle try to resist the **urge** to use your granny's priceless antiques, food (especially at meal-times), and living creatures such as hamsters, goldfish, small brothers and sisters, etc.
> 저글링을 배우는 동안 할머니의 귀중한 골동품, 음식(특히 식사 시간에), 햄스터, 금붕어, 형제, 자매 등과 같은 살아있는 생명체들을 사용하고 싶은 충동을 참아 보자.

urge 어떤 방향으로 '몰다(drive)'나 움직이지 못하게 '누르다(press), 묶다(tie)'를 뜻하는 말에서 왔다. 맘대로 행동하지 못하게 강요한다는 의미다. 그래서 동사 **urge**는 강하게 '촉구하다, 재촉하다, 충고하다'를 뜻한다.

urge는 어떤 행농을 하게 만드는 '강한 충동, 욕구'란 뜻의 명사로도 쓴다. '긴급한, 다급한'을 뜻하는 **urgent**도 **urge**에서 파생된 형용사다.

p.216

> **Notice** how it falls in an arc under the influence of gravity just like the cannonballs Galileo studied – remember?
> 중력의 영향으로 공이 호를 그리며 떨어지는 것에 주목하자. 갈릴레오가 연구했던 포탄처럼. – 기억하고 있나?

notice note와 **notice** 모두 '표시, 표식, 흔적'을 뜻하는 말에서 왔다. 나중에 다시 '보기'

위해서, '알아보기' 위해서 표시를 해 둔다는 의미다. '공책' 필기는 적는 것만큼이나 나중에 다시 보는 것도 무척 중요하다. 그래서 note다. **notice**도 의미가 비슷하다. 특별히 관심을 기울여 보는 것이다. '주목하다, 의식하다, 신경 쓰다'를 뜻하는 동사, '주목, 공고문, 안내문' 등을 뜻하는 명사로 쓴다.

p.217

This **feat** was achieved by several people including American Bruce Sarafian in 1996.

이 업적은 1996년에 미국의 브루스 사라피안을 비롯해 여러 사람들에 의해 달성되었다.

feat '일을 잘하다'를 뜻하는 말에서 왔다. 지식과 실력, 경험이 많아서 일을 잘한다는 의미에서 '뛰어난 성과, 업적, 훌륭한 결과물'을 뜻하는 명사다. 그런데 **feat** 앞에 '반대, 부정'을 뜻하는 de가 붙으면 '실력이 없는' 상태가 된다. 못하면 패할 수밖에 없다. 그래서 **defeat**는 '패배, 패배시키다'를 뜻하는 말이다.

Sentence 9

p.210

That's when spinning masses of air form around the ball and give it bumpy ride.

바로 그때 공 주위에 회전하는 공기 덩어리가 형성돼 공이 흔들흔들 날아가게 만든다.

when 이하의 문장이 보어의 역할을 하고 있다. [That's when ~]은 '그것은 ~하는 때(순간/시간)다'로 해석한다. 앞 문장에 나온 turbulence(난기류)를 설명하는 내용이다.
여기에서 동사 form은 목적어가 없는 자동사로, '생기다, 형성되다'를 뜻한다.

That's fatally fast for anyone in the way without protective gear.
보호 장비 없이 길목에 서 있는 사람에게는 치명적일 만큼 빠른 속도다.

in the way는 '지나가는 길목에 있는, 진로를 막는'을 뜻하고, without protective gear는 '보호 장비 없이'를 뜻한다. 모두 anyone을 꾸며 주고 있다.

아오, 글러브를 낄걸.

And as it speeds up the pressure drops and the ball is pushed lower and it bounces faster.
공기의 속도가 빨라지면서 압력이 떨어지고, 공은 더 낮게 밀리고 더 빨리 튀어 오른다.

as it speeds up(공기의 속도가 빨라지면서)는 문장의 부사절이다. 주절은 and로 연결된 세 개의 문장으로, 시간 순으로 구성되어 있다. the pressure drops(압력이 낮아지고), the ball is pushed lower(공이 더 낮게 밀리고), it bounces faster(더 빠르게 튀어 오른다) 모두 완전한 문장이다.

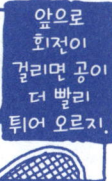

앞으로 회전이 걸리면 공이 더 빨리 튀어 오르지.

p.211

If you hit the ball a glancing blow it bounces extra slowly when it hits the ground.
공을 비스듬히 치면 땅에 닿을 때 매우 느리게 튄다.

a glancing blow는 '살짝 때리기(치기)'를 뜻한다. 일부러 약하게 치거나, 정통으로 맞는 게 아니라 빗맞을 때 쓰는 표현이다.
extra slowly는 '대단히 느리게'로 해석할 수 있다. 부사 extra는 '특별히, 대단히'를 뜻한다.

9. Bouncing Back

p.214

> But they didn't fly as straight as the old balls until they became scratched and worn.
> 하지만 이 공은 긁히고 닳기 전까지는 예전의 공만큼 똑바로 날아가지 못했다.

as straight as the old balls는 '이전의 공만큼 똑바로'를 뜻하는 부사구다. the old balls는 앞 문단에 나오는 '닭털로 속을 채운 가죽 골프공'을 말한다.
until은 '~(할) 때까지'를 의미하는 접속사다.

p.214

> This means you can easily get rid of it before you get flattened.
> 이는 당신이 납작해지기 전에 그 공을 쉽게 제거할 수 있다는 의미다.

[This means ~]는 '이것은 ~라는 의미다'를 뜻한다. 어떤 뜻인지 설명하거나 오해를 풀고자 할 때 '~을 의미하다, ~뜻으로 말하다'를 뜻하는 동사 mean을 쓴다.
[get rid of A]는 'A를 제거하다, A에서 벗어나다'를 뜻하는 표현이다.

p.215

> Stand in front of a mirror with your elbows tucked close to your body and your hands level with your waist.
> 팔꿈치를 몸에 붙이고 양손은 허리와 같은 높이로 맞춘 채 거울 앞에 선다.

in front of는 '~의 앞에, 앞쪽에서'를 뜻하는 전치사로, 공간상의 '앞면, 마주보는 위치'를 표현한다.
your elbows tucked close to your body는 '양 팔꿈치를 몸통 가까이 당기다'를, your hands level with your waist는 '두 손은 허리와 수평이 되게 하다'를 뜻한다. 모두 저글링을 하기 전에 취해야 할 자세를 설명하고 있다.

바로 이런 자세!

As long as their back is supported, the performer can juggle quite weighty objects including a small child.

등이 지지되고 있는 한, 공연자는 작은 아이를 비롯해 상당히 무거운 물체까지도 저글링할 수 있다.

이 문장에서 as long as는 '~가 계속되는 한, ~하는 동안에는(while)'을 뜻하는 접속사 역할을 한다.

quite weighty objects는 '상당히 무거운 물체'를 뜻한다. including은 '~를 포함하여'란 의미로, 뒤에 포함되는 것의 예시가 나온다.

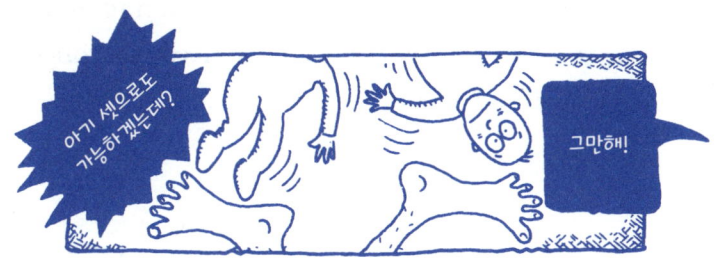

9. Bouncing Back

CHAPTER 10 KEYWORDS

#lever #pulley #torque #gear

Mighty Machines

A machine is a way of using a force in the right place to get a job done with less effort. Good idea. So why, after 10,000 years of science and invention is there no machine for doing homework? Anyway, to make a mighty machine all you need is a collection of effort-saving levers, pulleys and gears.

Fatal expressions

A scientist screws up his face and says:

ARGH! ROTATIONAL INERTIA – I NEED MORE TORQUE!

Should you call a doctor?

Answers:
No – a mechanic. The scientist can't loosen a nut. Torque is the word scientists use to describe the turning force you produce using a spanner. Rotational inertia is the resistance of the nut to being turned. And spanners are good for doing this job because they work like levers, as you'll see.

Lovely levers

A lever is a pole that you use to lever something up or push or pull something around. Either way the lever rests on a point known as the fulcrum. Levers work because the most effective turning force is at right angles to the thing you want to move. So levers help you do more work for less effort. Lovely!

Dare you discover... how a lever works?

You will need:

Yourself

A door

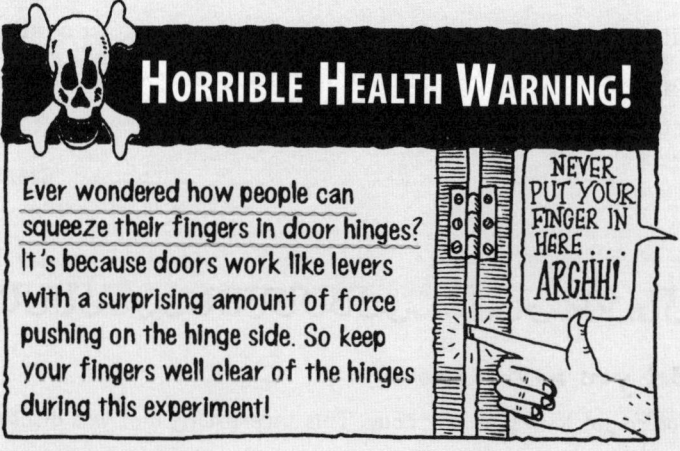

HORRIBLE HEALTH WARNING!

Ever wondered how people can squeeze their fingers in door hinges? It's because doors work like levers with a surprising amount of force pushing on the hinge side. So keep your fingers well clear of the hinges during this experiment!

NEVER PUT YOUR FINGER IN HERE... ARGHH!

What you do:

1 Open the door slightly. Make sure no one charges through the door.

2 Stand outside the door and try to push it by pressing with one finger 2 cm from the hinges.

3 Now press with the same finger 2 cm from opposite side to the hinges.

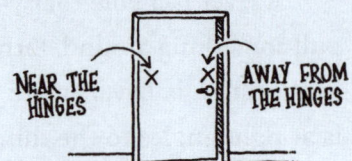

Which is easier?

a) They're both impossible and you got a sore finger.
b) It's easier to push the door near the hinges.
c) It's easier to push the door further away from the hinges.

Answers:

c) The door works like a lever with the hinges as the fulcrum. The further away from the fulcrum you press the more forceful your push is. Nowadays you'll find levers everywhere. From typewriters to tin openers and from scissors to see-saws.

Bet you never knew!

You've got levers in your body. This interesting fact was discovered by the Italian artist and scientist Leonardo da Vinci (1452–1519). Leonardo was cutting up human arms and legs in a bid to find how they worked. He discovered that muscles pulled the bones in much the same way as you pull a lever to move an object. He was so excited by this discovery that he even made a working model leg using copper wires and bits of real human bones. Then he could see it in action.

Teacher's tea-break teaser

This playground puzzle spells break-time bafflement for your teacher. Two children are playing on a see-saw. If the little child jumps off she might get hurt. If the big child gets off he'll get a nasty injury as the see-saw swings up under the weight of the smaller child. What's to be done?

Answers:

The see-saw acts like a lever – that's why it's so good at lifting children off the ground. The problem is caused by the larger child pushing with greater force on his end of the see-saw. If the larger child moved forwards towards the fulcrum this force would be reduced and the smaller child would slowly descend to ground level. Try using your friends to prove this.

Powerful pulleys

Another method of lifting heavy weights off the ground – including large children – is the pulley. Basically it's a wheel hung off the ground with a rope passing over it. This re-directs force. So you can pull on the rope and lift something tied to the other end of the rope.

Add another wheel to the first one and it's even easier. By pulling the rope a longer distance you spread the effort so it seems easier to lift the load. Nowadays you'll find pulleys on cranes and lifts. So whom do we have to thank for this amazing invention? It was a Greek genius – Archimedes (287?–212 BC).

A lovely little mover

Archimedes had a little problem. His relative, Hieron, had asked him to pull a full-sized ship down a beach and out to sea – without help! Now most of us would tell the brother-in-law to jump in a vat of custard and go back to watching the telly. But Archimedes couldn't say that.

Unfortunately, Hieron was the local king – Hieron II of Syracuse to be exact. And you don't refuse royalty even if they are family. Besides, Archimedes was an all-round genius. He was supposed to know these things. He'd already worked out the maths of levers and boasted that with a long enough lever he could lift the world. Hieron thought his brainy relative should be taught a lesson. So he deliberately set him an impossible task.

Archimedes scratched his balding head and chewed his lip. All that night he worked on mathematical plans. And eventually he hit on a solution. An answer so stunningly original, so forceful and amazing that no one had ever thought of it before. A new machine.

Meanwhile, hundreds of grim-faced guards grunted and groaned as they hauled the ship up the beach. Hieron ordered them to load the ship with cargo and told some of them to wait on board.

Archimedes and a few assistants spent the next few hours setting up the machine. History doesn't record what it looked like. But it must have been a series of pulleys standing on wooden frames with the rope tied securely to the ship. When all was ready Archimedes gripped the free end of the rope. He looked rather thin and weedy. Hieron couldn't resist a quiet chuckle as Archimedes rolled up his sleeves and tugged on the rope.

But then the ship slid smoothly down the beach. It moved with eerie ease as if it was sailing on a calm sea. Archimedes' machine was a lovely little mover. The watching crowds gasped in disbelief. The people on the ship looked stunned and Hieron nearly had a heart attack. If he hadn't seen it with his own eyes the king would have accused his brainy relative of pulley-ing his leg.

Grinding gears

No one knows who invented gears but the Romans certainly used them. They're interlocking toothed wheels that pass on force and they have odd sounding names that wouldn't be out of place in an ancient torture chamber. Names such as "bevels", "rack and pinion", "spurs" and "worms". They all work the same way. A smaller wheel that turns quickly and a larger wheel that turns more slowly.

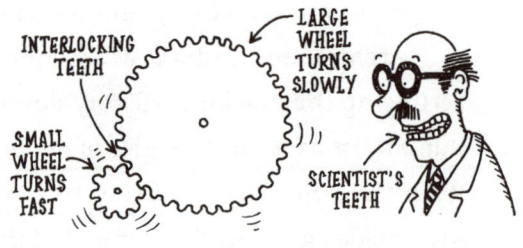

Gears control the speed and direction of the turning force you put in. Take your bicycle gears, for example. The gear wheels on your bike have fewer teeth than the chain wheel. So the gear wheels turn faster and they make your rear bike wheel turn faster than you

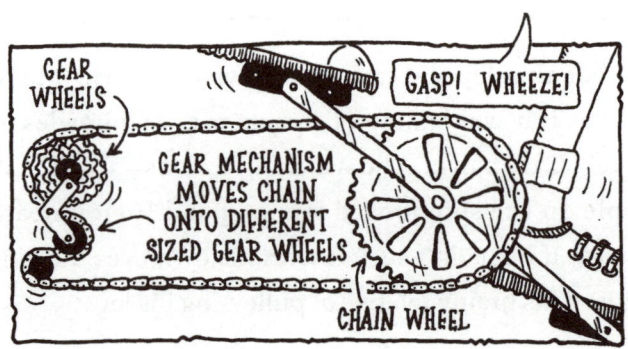

pedal. So it does you a really good turn.

The bicycle was such a good idea that nineteenth-century inventors began to peddle their own pedal-powered machines. Which of these are too silly to be true?

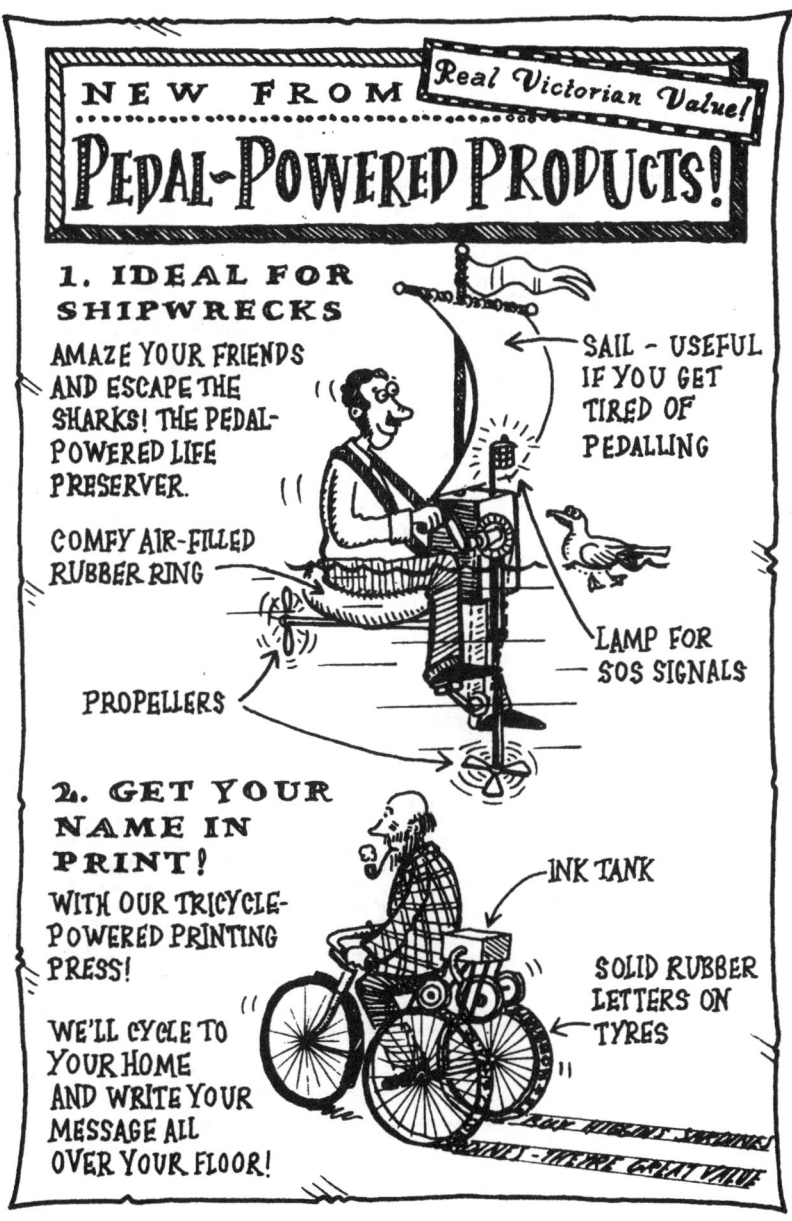

3. DON'T MISS OUR BUS!

NO MORE SCHOOL BUS BREAKDOWNS. TRY THE NEW PEDAL-POWERED SCHOOL BUS. SPECIAL PEDALS UNDER THE SEATS LINKED TO A ROTATING CRANKSHAFT POWER THE BUS AT 35KM PER HOUR (22 MPH).

"GETS THE KIDS TO SCHOOL ON TIME AND KEEPS THEM FIT."
I. FLOGGEM (HEADMASTER)

4. TIRED OUT?

RELAX UNDER OUR DELIGHTFUL PEDAL-POWERED COLD SHOWER!

ALL THE REFRESHING DELIGHTS OF GETTING CAUGHT IN THE RAIN WHILE ON YOUR BIKE!

A NEW AND EXCITING FORM OF EXERCISE THAT LEAVES YOU FEELING FRESH AND FIT.

PEDAL YOUR WAY TO A CLEAN BODY!

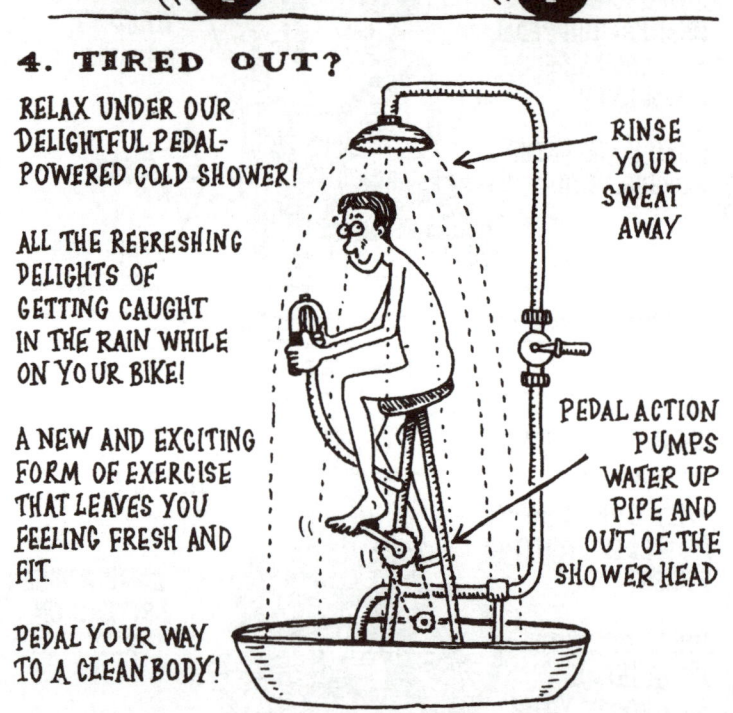

RINSE YOUR SWEAT AWAY

PEDAL ACTION PUMPS WATER UP PIPE AND OUT OF THE SHOWER HEAD

Answers:
1 **TRUE** Invented by Frenchman François Barathon, in Paris, 1895.
2 **TRUE** Another French invention tested in Paris in 1895.
3 **FALSE**
4 **TRUE** Exhibited at a bicycle exhibition in Paris in 1897.

Marvellous mighty machines

A complicated machine is simply lots of simple machines joined together. Easy. Just a load of old screws, pulleys, levers, gears, wheels, axles, chains, transmission shafts and springs that you just happen to find lying about in the garage. Throw them all together and everything should go like clockwork.

From bikes and gears it's a small step to steam engines, petrol engines, trains, buses, cars and planes. Just think. If it wasn't for forces they wouldn't be able to force you to go to school. Terrible. Still, you can relax at home, can't you? No need to worry about forces is there? Safe as houses and all that… er – well, actually, forces can be fatal for buildings, too. The next chapter will really shake you up.

ACTUALLY, THE GARDEN COULD DO WITH A DROP OF RAIN

REVIEW

동네 놀이터는 힘, 운동, 에너지의 법칙들이 쌓여 있는 물리학의 보물 창고 같은 곳이다. 그네를 타면 회전과 진자 운동을 배울 수 있다. 미끄럼틀을 타면 중력, 낙하, 마찰력을 실감할 수 있다. 그리고 시소를 타면 수직운동, 무게, 균형의 개념을 배울 수 있을 뿐만 아니라 다이어트의 필요성도 느낄 수도 있다. 놀이터의 기구들은 비교적 간단한 구조를 갖고 있다. 인류는 중력을 거스르며 에너지와 운동을 적절하게 활용하기 위해서 다양하고 복잡한 기계들을 발명해 왔다. 그리고 그 기계들의 중심에는 지렛대, 도르래, 톱니바퀴 같은 중요한 부품들이 있다. 어떤 원리로 작동하는지 알아보자.

Vocabulary 10

> Either way the lever rests on a point known as the **fulcrum**.
> 어느 방식이든 지렛대는 받침점이라고 알려진 지점 위에 놓인다.

문에서는 이 hinge가 fulcrum 역할을... 아얏!

fulcrum '지탱하다, 지지하다'를 뜻하는 말에서 왔다. 무거운 것을 지탱하는 물체를 부르는 말로 양팔 저울의 받침점, 시소(seesaw)의 중앙 지지대, 지레(lever)의 받침대 등이 바로 **fulcrum**이다. 복수형은 **fulcrums**, 또는 **fulcra**로 쓴다.

> Make sure no one **charges** through the door.
> 아무도 문을 통해 돌진하지 않도록 주의할 것.

charge '바퀴 달린 탈것(wheeled vehicle)'을 뜻하는 말에서 왔다. car(자동차), cart(카트), chariot(전차, 마차) 등도 어원이 같다. **charge**는 주로 짐을 싣고 운반하는 '수레'를 부르는 말이었다. '빨리' 운반할 목적으로 '운임'을 지불하고 운송을 맡기기 때문에, **charge**는 예문처럼 동사로 '빨리, 급히 이동하다, 돌진하다'라는 뜻의 동사로 쓰고, '운임, 요금, 비용'을 뜻하는 명사로도 쓴다.

> This playground puzzle spells break-time **bafflement** for your teacher.
> 이 운동장 퍼즐은 쉬는 시간에 선생님을 당황하게 만들 것이다.

bafflement '어리둥절하게 만들다, 황당함을 느끼게 하다'를 뜻하는 동사가 **baffle**이다. 다른 사람의 언행을 이해하기 힘들거나 어떤 상황이 너무 놀랍고 이상할 때 쓸 수 있다. 수동형 형용사 **baffled**는 '어리둥절한, 황당한, 이해할 수 없는'이라는 뜻이다. 명사형 **bafflement**는 '당혹감, 어리둥절함, 황당함' 등을 뜻한다.

10. Mighty Machines

> **p.229**
> Another method of lifting heavy weights off the ground - including large children - is the **pulley**.
>
> 바닥에서 무거운 물건(덩치 큰 아이들도 포함해서)을 들어 올리는 또 다른 방법은 도르래다.

pulley 직선 운동을 회전 운동으로 바꿔서 손쉽게 무거운 물건을 당기거나 높이 올릴 수 있게 하는 장치, '도르래'가 **pulley**다. 국기를 게양하는 깃대(flagpole), 우물의 두레박 걸이, 낚싯대의 릴(reel), 건축 현장의 크레인(crane), 승강기(elevator) 등등, 도르래는 우리 주변에서 쉽게 찾아볼 수 있다.

> **p.230**
> And you don't refuse **royalty** even if they are family.
>
> 그리고 그들이 가족일지라도, 왕족을 거부할 수는 없다.

royalty 형용사 **royal**은 '왕의, 여왕의'를 뜻한다. '왕(여왕)과 관련된, 왕(여왕)을 위한' 등의 뜻도 갖고 있다. 어원이 같은 regal도 의미가 비슷하다. '왕가, 왕족'을 **royal** family, '왕궁'을 **royal** palace라고 한다. 명사 **royalty**는 '왕족, 여왕의 가족'이다. 거의 모든 것이 왕의 재산이었던 옛날에 일부를 빌려서 사업을 하려면 왕족에게 '임대료'를 내야 했다. 여기에서 유래해 저작권이나 특허 사용료를 **royalty**라고 부르게 되었다.

> **p.231**
> The watching crowds **gasped** in disbelief.
>
> 지켜보던 군중은 믿을 수 없다는 듯이 숨도 제대로 쉬지 못했다.

gasp 원래 몸 안에 산소가 부족할 때 나타나는 생리 현상인 '하품(yawn)'을 뜻하는 말이었다. 비슷하게, 산소가 부족하면 숨이 차고 호흡이 가빠진다. 그래서 **gasp**는 '헐떡이다, 숨을 가쁘게 쉬다'를 뜻한다. 또한 갑자기 놀라거나 통증을 느낄 때 '헉, 흑' 하며 숨이 턱 막히는 느낌이 드는데, 이런 현상도 **gasp**로 표현할 수 있다.

p.232

No one knows who invented **gears**.
누가 기어를 발명했는지는 아무도 모른다.

gear '준비하다, 채비하다'란 의미를 갖고 있다. 어떤 일을 하기 위해 미리 준비해 놓는 '도구, 장치'를 뜻하는 명사로 쓴다. 특별한 기능을 하는 기계의 장치를 흔히 **gear**라고 부르고, 특정 작업에 적합한 '의상, 옷'도 **gear**다. 태권도나 복싱을 할 때 머리에 쓰는 보호 장구가 head**gear**다.

하지만 우리는 기어를 아주 잘 사용하고 있다고!

p.234

Special pedals under the seats linked to a rotating **crankshaft** power the bus at 35km per hour (22MPH).
좌석 아래 특수 페달은 회전하는 크랭크축에 연결되어 버스를 시속 35km(22마일)로 구동한다.

crankshaft crank는 동사로 '축을 따라 돌게 하다, 돌리다'를 뜻하고, 명사로 '돌리는 L자 형태의 막대나 핸들, 크랭크'를 뜻한다. shaft는 '긴 손잡이, 자루'를 말한다. 두 단어를 합친 **crankshaft**는 '크랭크축'이라고 하는데, 대개 '기어(gear)'에 연결되어 직선 운동과 회전 운동을 서로 변환시키는 L자형 축을 말한다.

p.235

A **complicated** machine is simply lots of simple machines joined together.
복잡한 기계는 단순히 여러 개의 간단한 기계가 합쳐진 것이다.

complicated '복잡한, 난해한'을 뜻하는 형용사다. **complicate**에서 com은 '함께(together)'를 의미하고, plicate는 '접다(fold), 엮다(weave)'를 의미한다. 다 모아서 접거나 엮어 놓는다는 의미인데, 이러면 형태가 복잡해진다. 뜨개질해서 만든 스웨터의 털실 구조를 떠올리면 된다. 그래서 동사 **complicate**는 '복잡하게 만들다, 이해하기(해결하기) 힘들게 하다'를 뜻한다.

10. Mighty Machines

Sentence 10

p.226

So why, after 10,000 years of science and invention is there no machine for doing homework?

그렇다면 왜, 1만 년 동안이나 과학과 발명이 이루어졌는데도 숙제를 하기 위한 기계가 없는 걸까?

맨 앞의 So는 '그럼, 그렇다면'으로 해석할 수 있다. 의문사 why로 '이유'를 묻고 있는 의문문이다. 의문사 why와 is there 사이에 있는 after 10,000 years of science and invention(과학과 발명 1만 년 후에도)은 부사구다.

p.227

Ever wondered how people can squeeze their fingers in door hinges?

사람들이 어떻게 문 경첩에 손가락이 끼는지 궁금했던 적이 있는가?

문장 앞에 Have you가 생략되어 있다. '경험'이 있는지 묻고 있는 의문문이다.
wondered의 목적어는 how로 시작하는 간접의문문이다. door hinge는 문을 문틀과 연결해 여닫을 수 있게 하는 금속 '경첩'을 말한다.

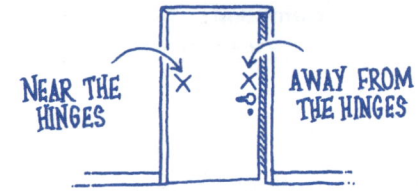

p.228

He was so excited by this discovery that he even made a working model leg using copper wires and bits of human bones.

그는 이 발견에 너무 신이 난 나머지 구리 선과 사람 뼛조각을 활용해 작동하는 다리 모형을 만들기도 했다.

[so ~ that …]은 '너무 ~해서 …하다'를 의미한다.

이 발견으로 너무 신이 나서(so excited by this discovery) 그 결과 작동하는(working) 모형 다리(model leg)까지 만들었다는 내용이다.

> By pulling the rope a longer distance you spread the effort so it seems easier to lift the load.
>
> 로프를 더 멀리 잡아당김으로써 힘을 분산시켜서 짐을 들어 올리기 더 쉬워질 것이다.

By ~ distance는 '로프를 더 멀리 잡아당김으로써'를 뜻하는 부사구다. 여기에서 by는 '방법, 수단'을 의미한다.
spread the effort는 '힘을 분산시키다'를 뜻한다. so는 접속사로 '따라서, 그래서'로 해석할 수 있다.

> An answer so stunningly original, so forceful and amazing that no one had ever thought of it before.
>
> 이전에 아무도 생각해내지 못했던 놀라울 정도로 독창적이고 강력하고 멋진 대답이었다.

문장 앞에 It was를 넣으면 하나의 문장이 된다. [so ~ that …]용법의 문장인데, so가 두 번에 걸쳐서 등장한다. 모두 answer를 수식하고 있다.
that no one had ever thought of it before는 '이전에는 아무도 그것을 생각해 보지 못했다'는 의미다.

> But it must have been a series of pulleys standing on wooden frames with the rope tied securely to the ship.
>
> 그러나 그것은 분명 밧줄이 배에 단단히 묶인 채로, 나무 틀 위에 세워진 여러 개의 연결된 도르래였을 것이다.

[must have 동사완료형]은 '분명 ~했을 것이다'란 의미로, 과거의 일을 확신하며 추측할 때 쓰는 표현이다.
a series of pulleys는 여러 개의 도르래가 연결되어 있다는 의미다.

10. Mighty Machines

p.232

> They're interlocking toothed wheels that pass on force and they have odd sounding names that wouldn't be out of place in an ancient torture chamber.
>
> 기어는 힘을 전달하는 맞물린 톱니바퀴들이며, 옛날 고문실에 있었다 해도 어색하지 않을 만큼 이상하게 들리는 이름을 갖고 있다.

동사 interlock은 '맞물리다, 물려서 연결하다'를 뜻한다. toothed wheels는 '톱니바퀴들'이고, 뒤에서 이를 꾸며 주는 that pass on force는 '힘을 전달하는'을 뜻한다.
odd sounding names는 '이상하게 들리는 이름들'을 뜻한다. out of place는 자리에서 벗어난다는 의미로, '적합하지 않은, 어울리지 않는'을 뜻하는 표현이다.

p.233

> Which of these are too silly to be true?
>
> 이 중에서 너무 어이없어서 사실이 아닐 것 같은 것은?

의문사 which는 여러 개 중에 하나, 또는 일부분을 선택하거나 언급할 때 사용한다.
[too ~ to …]는 '너무 ~해서 … 못하다, … 하기에는 너무 ~하다'로 해석한다.

p.235

> If it wasn't for forces they wouldn't be able to force you to go to school.
>
> 만약 힘이 없다면 당신을 학교에 가도록 강제할 수도 없을 것이다.

가정법 문장으로, [If it wasn't for A]는 'A가 없다면, A가 아니라면'을 뜻하는 표현이다.
[force A to 동사]는 'A가 ~하도록 강요하다, A가 ~하게 강제로 시키다'를 의미한다.

> **CHAPTER 11 KEYWORDS**
>
> #vibration #foundation #arch #demolition

Build Or Bust

Fallen down under the influence of gravity, blown down, blown up or just shaken about. Yep. Forces are fatal for buildings, too.

Bodge-it buildings

Some buildings stand for hundreds of years. Others stand for hundreds of days… or minutes.

Would you be interested in buying any of these structures?

WAT-ER GREAT BRIDGE!

LONDON BRIDGE, Spanning the River Thames in London on 20 narrow arches. (built 1176-1209)

"DON'T DIG THE GRAVE THERE!"

"ARGHH!"

▶ Waterwheels and shops.

▶ Sensational tidal surges through the narrow arches.

▶ All this and the dead body of the architect, Peter Colechurch. He's buried in the chapel on the bridge.

▶ Complete with drawbridge and spikes for traitors' rotting heads.

← ROTTEN TRAITOR

THE SMALL PRINT

The arches were narrow and close together, and this forced the river to surge violently. This damaged the bridge and made life dangerous for boatmen. Up to fifty were killed each year trying to pass under the bridge. Part of the bridge fell down in 1281 and again in 1482. It was finally knocked down in 1832. Peter Colechurch should have designed his bridge with wider arches to allow the water to flow more easily. He should also have banned buildings on the bridge itself because their weight was too great for the bridge to bear.

Go With A Swing!
THE TACOMA NARROWS BRIDGE, Washington State, USA (built 1940)

▶ A graceful lightweight suspension bridge. (That's a bridge supported by cables hung from towers.)

▶ Amazing 853 metre span.

▶ Swings about in the wind for a really exciting crossing.

THE SMALL PRINT
The Tacoma Narrows Bridge swayed so violently in the wind that it earned the nickname "Galloping Gertie". People actually felt seasick crossing it. The bridge had to be reinforced to stop the swaying spreading to the towers that held up the cables. But four months later a strong wind twisted the roadway sideways until it collapsed.

Bet you never knew!

When a building falls down many people can be killed. But when a dam bursts the results can be even more fatal. A dam has to hold back the huge force of water that builds up against it. That's why dams have such thick walls and are often built in a strong arch shape so the water presses the dam into the sides of the valley rather than backwards. But sometimes this isn't enough. In 1975 flooding burst two dams in Henan province in China and 235,000 people were washed away. So you can see how important it is for all architects to be properly trained. If you'd like to be a good architect you'd better pay attention to these simple rules...

Become an architect in six easy lessons
Lesson 1: Understand the effect of forces on your building

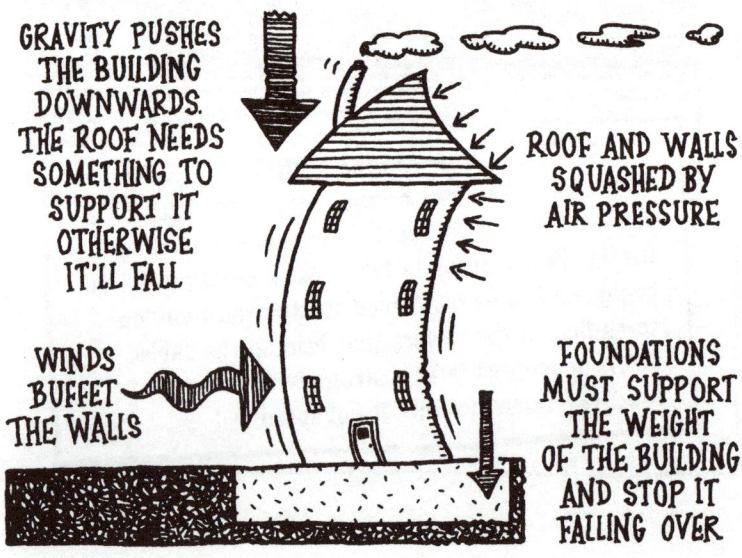

GRAVITY PUSHES THE BUILDING DOWNWARDS. THE ROOF NEEDS SOMETHING TO SUPPORT IT OTHERWISE IT'LL FALL

ROOF AND WALLS SQUASHED BY AIR PRESSURE

WINDS BUFFET THE WALLS

FOUNDATIONS MUST SUPPORT THE WEIGHT OF THE BUILDING AND STOP IT FALLING OVER

Nowadays architects make computer simulations and models of their buildings and even test the models in wind tunnels.

Lesson 2: Develop an eye for forces

A good architect or engineer can look at a building and spot whether the building is well built enough to stand up to the forces on it. Marc Brunel (that's Isambard's dad) once looked at a bridge in Paris and said:

Three days later, the bridge collapsed. Yep, old Marc kept dry and he certainly had a dry sense of humour too.

Lesson 3: Put in proper foundations

If you've ever tried to carry some tall glasses on a tray one-handed like a waiter, you'll know how tricky it is to balance them. It would help if the glasses were partly buried in a really thick tray. That's how foundations work. The taller the building the deeper the foundations you need.

Foundations stop the wind from blowing your building over and they support the weight of your building too. Remember Galileo working at Pisa University? In 1173 Pisa's bell tower was built on soft ground with foundations that weren't broad enough to support its weight. Now Pisa University's famous for its learning and the tower's famous for its leaning.

Lesson 4: Always build your building the right shape

Triangles are a good strong shape. That's why the Egyptian pyramids have lasted 4,700 years. The Eiffel Tower was also made up of a series of triangles and many modern skyscrapers use triangles as the basis of their metal frames.

A column is a good strong shape and ideal for holding up heavy weights. Like the roof, for example. You can use arches to hold up part of the walls. Like columns, arches are great because the harder you push down on them the more they push back. Yes – it's Newton's Third Law again.

Dome shapes are also very strong. But you knew that from finding out about helmets in Chapter 3. An egg shape is also surprisingly strong and can take a weight of 22.7 kg. But don't try leaving an egg on your teacher's chair.

Lesson 5: Make sure your walls don't fall down

If you are designing a very tall stone building you may choose to make your walls very thick like an old cathedral or castle – the walls of the Tower of London are more than 4.6 metres thick. So you want to put in larger windows but you know they will weaken your walls. No problem. Try using buttresses to hold your walls up.

Mind you, disasters do happen. In 1989 the Civic Tower in Pavia, Italy (built 1060) fell with a crash. The cement holding the stones together had slowly crumbled away. Engineers reckoned that the shock waves from years of ringing the bells at the top had brought on the destruction. If this puts you off building in stone you could use a strong steel frame for your tall building and use lighter materials for your walls. This makes them stronger but the building might sway a bit in windy weather.

Lesson 6: Get your roof the right shape

Roofs are usually sloping because the curved shape is more difficult to bend. You can prove this by holding a piece of paper in different ways.

Vicious vibes

One thing that can be very destructive is vibration. Have you ever watched a washing machine shuddering and shaking as it washes and spins the clothes. Perhaps you've bravely laid a finger on the machine and felt the shaking passing up your arms. These are vibrations. And beware. They can be vicious.

Fatal expressions

Should you dial 999? No, her car's shuddering with vibrations. Probably because it's so clapped out. Oscillatory motion is in fact what vibrations are called. Oscillations are regularly repeated movements or shaking. The only way to stop them is to "damp them down". No, this doesn't mean chucking water over the car. Still confused? Well, it means using some soft substance to absorb the vibrations and stop the shuddering.

Vicious vibration facts

Vibrations are particularly vicious in their effects on buildings and bridges. In 1850, 487 soldiers were marching across a suspension bridge in Algiers in Africa. Their heavy boots thudded on the roadway. And soon the whole bridge was shaking with the vibrations. It shook so much that bits fell off it and finally the entire bridge collapsed into the river. Tragically 226 soldiers were killed.

Ever since, soldiers avoid marching in step when they cross a bridge in order not set off the deadly vibrations. That takes a bit of foresight but sometimes it pays to plan the crossing of your bridges before you come to them. Mind you, the most vicious vibrations aren't caused by people – they're caused by the Earth itself.

Every year there are hundreds of earthquakes. Some of them are fatal for people. Movement of vast rocky areas deep under the ground trigger powerful vibrations in the form of shock waves that can destroy entire cities. The damage is done because shock waves make the walls vibrate so violently that the building falls down. Feeling a little shaky?

Dare you discover... how much your body vibrates?

You will need:

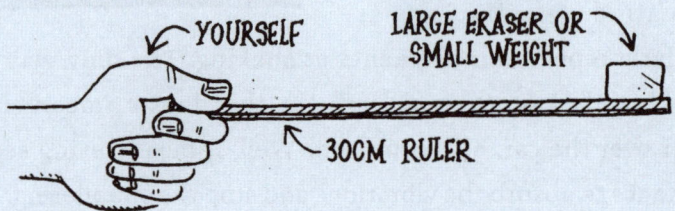

What you do:

1 Place the eraser on the end of ruler.
2 Grip the opposite end of the ruler by your thumb and forefinger. Then hold the ruler as close to its end as you can.
3 Stretch out your hand balancing the eraser on the opposite end of the ruler.

What do you notice?
a) Nothing. I did the test for ten minutes and my hand was steady as a rock.
b) After a few seconds the end of the ruler began to dance around as my arm twitched.
c) I lost my balance and fell over forwards.

> **Answers:**
>
> b) Your body vibrates constantly as your heart beats and the blood squirts around your body. Your muscles also pulse of their own accord. So your body's vibrations pass along the ruler, and make it twitch. If you get answer a) try a heavier weight. If you get answer c) try a lighter one.

A smashing finale

Now you've learnt about how forces affect buildings, let's practise using forces to knock one down. An old school will do. Imagine your school has been condemned as an unsafe building. Perhaps all those hundreds of feet stomping up and down the corridors has triggered vicious vibrations that have fatally weakened the building. Now your school must be flattened. No more science lessons – that's really tough. Oh well – here's how to do the demolition job...

1. Make sure that the school is empty of all pupils and there are no teachers lurking in the corners. You wouldn't want to knock the building down on top of them would you?

11. Build Or Bust

2 Start off by swinging a heavy steel ball against the walls of your school. The ball transfers its momentum to the wall as it crashes into it. Cement is dislodged from the bricks and the wall falls down.

3 If you don't have a steel ball you'll have to smash the walls with a sledge hammer. This has the same effect but it's far slower and much harder work.

4 Some buildings have pre-stressed concrete beams. These are concrete beams with steel wires running through them. The wires are held tight by the weight of the building's upper floors. Be careful if your school has these beams. When you knock down the upper floors the wires in the lower floor's beams aren't held tight any more. So they go ping and the entire building crashes down around your ears.

Alternatively you could try one of these demolition methods.

Method 1. Explosives

In a hurry? Want to knock your school down before science class on Monday? You could blow it up. Place explosive charges around the building and weaken the supporting beams so they collapse easily. Set off the explosives and wait for the dust to clear!

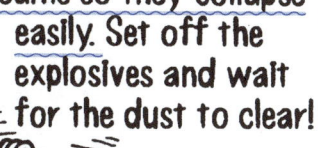

Method 2. Hands

If you can't blow up your school, try using your bare hands instead. A karate blow is forceful enough to break bricks. In 1994 15 karate experts demolished a seven room house in Saskatchewan, Canada using only their bare feet and hands.

REVIEW

창조는 힘들어도 파괴는 쉽다는 말이 있다. 뭔가를 만드는 일은 힘들지만, 이미 만든 것을 부수는 일은 쉽다는 의미다. 도미노 게임을 해 본 적이 있다면 힘들게 세워 놓은 블록들이 순식간에 무너지는 것을 봤을 것이다. 몇 시간 공들여 세워 놓은 수백 개의 도미노 블록들이 친구의 방귀 한 방에 와르르 자빠지고 만다. 힘 중에 가장 무서운 게 파괴력일 것이다. 물리의 세계에는 친구의 뱃속에 잠복해 있는 '풍력'처럼 예상하기 힘든 파괴력이 존재한다. 파괴력은 어떻게 생성되고 어떻게 힘을 발휘할까?

Vocabulary 11

> Winner of an **architectural** award in 1976.
> 1976년 건축상 수상작.

architectural '건축(학)의, 건축 기술의'를 뜻하는 형용사다. **architect**는 '우두머리(chief)'를 뜻하는 archi와 '건설자(builder)'를 뜻하는 tect가 합쳐진 말이다. '건설책임자'로서 건물의 설계와 재료, 시공 등 모든 것을 알고 결정하는 전문가인 '건축가'가 **architect**다. 그런 건축가가 하는 일이나 기술을 의미하는 '건축학, 건축술'을 **architecture**라고 한다.

> Complete with drawbridge and spikes for **traitors'** rotting heads.
> 도개교는 물론 반역자의 부패하고 있는 머리를 위해 필요한 창까지 갖춤.

traitor trait는 '넘겨주다(to hand over)'를 의미한다. '넘겨주는 사람(-or)'이 **traitor**인데, 적에게 우리의 비밀을, 중요한 정보를 넘겨주는 '배신자, 반역자'를 뜻하는 말이다. **trait**는 동사로 쓰지 않는다. '배신하다. 반역하다'를 뜻하는 동사는 **betray**다. 명사 **trait**는 부모가 자식에게 '넘겨준' 성질인 '특성, 개성'을 뜻한다.

11. Build Or Bust

p.245

A graceful light weight **suspension bridge**.

우아하고 무게가 가벼운 현수교.

suspension bridge 명사 **suspension**은 '매달기, 매달리기'를 의미한다. 동사형인 **suspend**의 기본 의미는 '매달다'이다. 대개 줄에 묶어 공중에 매다는 행동을 표현할 때 쓴다. '매달린 다리' 즉, '현수교'가 **suspension bridge**다. 현수교는 다리 상판을 지탱하는 밑기둥이 없고 강철 케이블(cable)로 연결해서 탑에 고정하는 형태의 다리다.

p.247

Foundations stop the wind from blowing your building over and they support the weight of your building too.

토대는 바람에 건물이 쓰러지는 것을 막고 건물의 무게도 지탱한다.

foundation 동사 **found**는 '바닥을 깔다, 기초를 다지다'를 뜻하는 말에서 왔다. 건물을 지을 때 가장 먼저 해야 하는 가장 중요한 일이 기초 공사다. 처음 어떤 조직이나 단체를 '세우다, 창립하다'는 뜻으로 쓰고 도시나 국가를 '건설하다, 건국하다'란 뜻으로도 쓴다. 명사형인 **foundation**은 '건물의 토대, 기초, 설립, 창립' 등을 뜻한다.

p.248

A **column** is a good strong shape and ideal for holding up heavy weights.

기둥은 아주 튼튼한 형태로 무거운 무게를 떠받치는 데에 이상적이다.

column '긴 원통형의 물체, 기둥'을 뜻하는 말에서 왔다. 예문에서처럼 지금도 '기둥, 원통형 물체'를 뜻하는 명사로 쓴다. **column**은 수직으로 세우기 때문에 '세로'라는 의미도 갖고 있다. 여럿이 모여서 정사각형 대형을 이루면 항상 가로줄과 세로줄이 생기는데, 일렬로 늘어선 '가로줄'은 row, '세로줄'은 **column**이라고 한다.

p.249

If you are designing a very tall stone building you may choose to make your walls very thick like an old **cathedral** or castle - the walls of the Tower of London are more than 4.6 metres thick.

매우 높은 석조 건물을 설계하는 경우 오래된 성당이나 성처럼 벽을 아주 두껍게 만드는 방식을 선택할 수 있다. 런던탑의 벽은 두께가 4.6미터가 넘는다.

cathedral '자리(seat), 의자(chair)'를 뜻하는 말에서 왔다. 아무나 앉는 자리가 아니라 높은 지위의 중요한 인물이 앉는 자리를 의미한다. 옛날에 가톨릭교회에서는 큰 도시나 인구가 많은 지역에 교회를 세우고 '주교(bishop)'를 책임 성직자로 파견했다. 그래서 지위가 높은 주교의 자리가 있는 큰 교회를 **cathedral**이라고 부른다. '대성당, 교구의 중심 성당'을 뜻한다.

p.250

They can be **vicious**.

진동은 사악할 수 있다.

vicious 명사 **vice**는 '악행(sin)'을 의미하는 말에서 왔다. '악행, 악한 성향, 범죄 행위' 등을 뜻한다. **vice**의 형용사형인 **vicious**는 악행이나 범죄를 저지를 만큼 '포악한, 잔인한, 사나운' 성향을 표현하는 말이다. 사람뿐만 아니라, 동물이나 자연 현상이 '피해를 미칠 수 있다'면 **vicious**로 표현할 수 있다. 그런 물리적 힘에 의해 희생되는 대상이 **victim**(피해자, 희생자)이다.

p.251

Oscillations are regularly repeated movements or shaking.

진동은 규칙적으로 반복되는 움직임이나 흔들림이다.

oscillation '진동, 오락가락'을 뜻하는 명사다. 동사 **oscillate**는 앞뒤, 좌우, 상하로 '흔들다(swing), 흔들리다'를 뜻하는 말에서 왔다. 그네를 떠올리면 이해하기 쉽다. '계속 흔들리다, 왔다 갔다 하다, 진동하다'를 뜻한다. 조울증에 걸린 듯 '웃었다 울었다' 감정이 급변할 때도 쓸 수 있다.

11. Build Or Bust

> After a few seconds the end of the ruler began to dance around as my arm **twitched**.
>
> 몇 초 후, 내 팔이 경련을 일으키자 자의 끝이 춤을 추기 시작했다.

twitch 입술 가장자리나 눈 밑이 파르르 떨리거나 손이 부들부들 떨리는 경험을 해본 적이 있을 것이다. 몸이 내 명령을 듣지 않고 저절로 움찔거린다. 이렇게 몸의 일부, 근육이 떨리는 움직임을 표현하는 말이 **twitch**다. '경련하다, 씰룩거리다'를 뜻한다. 명사 **twitch**는 '경련, 떨림, 갑작스러운 움직임이나 작은 변화'를 뜻한다.

> Imagine your school has been **condemned** as an unsafe building.
>
> 여러분의 학교가 안전하지 않은 건물로 비난을 받았다고 상상해 보라.

condemn com은 '함께, 강하게'를 의미하고, demn은 '해하다, 손상시키다'를 의미한다. 조직 구성원들이, 사회 전체가 누군가를 심하게 손상시킨다는 의미에서 '심하게 비난하다, 꾸짖다, 규탄하다, 유죄를 선고하다'를 뜻한다. 예문에서는 '나쁘다고(부적합하다고) 판정을 받다'는 의미로 썼다. 명사형 **condemnation**은 '비난, 규탄'을 뜻한다. 철자 n은 동사에서는 묵음이지만, 명사에서는 제대로 발음된다.

> Oh well - here's how to do the **demolition** job…
>
> 아, 그럼, 철거 작업을 하는 방법이 여기 있다….

demolition 동사 **demolish**에서 de는 '반대, 아래(down)'를 의미하고, molish는 '짓다(build)'를 의미한다. 짓는 것의 반대, 지은 것을 밑으로 끌어내린다는 의미라서 **demolish**는 '무너뜨리다, 철거하다'를 뜻한다. **demolition**은 '철거, 파괴'를 뜻하는 명사다.

p.254

Cement is **dislodged** from the bricks and the wall falls down.
시멘트가 벽돌에서 떨어져 나가고 벽이 무너진다.

dislodge 원래 사냥꾼이나 목동들이 잠시 쉴 수 있게 숲이나 들에 만들어 놓은 '막사'를 lodge라고 불렀다. 비바람과 햇빛을 막을 수 있을 정도로만 간단하게 지어놓은 건물이다. 그래서 지금도 명사 lodge는 '원두막, 오두막, 산장'을 뜻하고, 동사 lodge에는 그런 건조물을 짓듯이 '고정시키다, 박히다'라는 의미가 있다. '반대, 거꾸로'를 뜻하는 dis를 붙인 **dislodge**는 고정시킨 것을 '제거하다, 헐다, 뜯어내다'를 뜻하는 동사다.

p.255

Place **explosive** charges around the building and weaken the supporting beams so they collapse easily.
건물을 빙 둘러서 폭발물을 설치하고 지지대를 약화시켜 쉽게 붕괴되게 한다.

explosive 형용사로 '폭발하기 쉬운, 폭발성의'를 뜻한다. 명사로는 '폭약, 폭발물'을 뜻한다. 동사 **explode**에서 ex는 '밖으로(out), 넘침'을 의미하고, plode는 '박수, 박수치다'를 의미한다. 과거에는 밤에 짐승을 쫓거나 밭에서 새를 몰아내기 위해 박수를 세게 쳐서 깜짝 놀라게 하는 행동을 **explode**라고 했다. 지금은 큰 소리로 '터지다, 터뜨리다, 폭발(폭파)하다'를 뜻한다. 명사형인 **explosion**은 '폭발, 폭파'를 뜻한다.

Sentence 11

p.243

Engineers believe rainwater collected on the roof making it sag until its supports couldn't take the weight any longer.

엔지니어들은 지붕에 빗물이 고여 지붕이 내려앉고 결국 지지대가 더 이상 무게를 지탱할 수 없게 된다고 믿는다.

believe의 목적어는 rainwater collected on the roof(지붕에 모아진 빗물)이고 making it sag(지붕이 처지게 만든다고)이 목적 보어다.
[not ~ any longer]는 '더 이상 ~ 않다(못하다)'를 뜻하는 표현이다. take the weight는 '무게를 지탱하다'를 뜻한다.

p.244

He should also have banned buildings on the bridge itself because their weight was too great for the bridge to bear.

그는 또한 다리 위에 건물을 짓는 것을 금지했어야 한다. 왜냐하면 다리가 감당하기에는 그 건물의 무게가 너무 무거웠기 때문이다.

[should have 동사완료형]은 '~했어야 했다'라는 의미로, 과거의 일을 후회하는 표현이다.
[too ~ for A to …]는 'A가 … 하기에는 너무 ~하다, 너무 ~해서 A가 … 못하다'를 뜻하는 표현이다. 그래서 their weight was too great for the bridge to bear는 '그 건물들의 무게는 다리가 지탱하기에는 너무 무거웠다'로 해석할 수 있다.

p.246

So you can see how important it is for all architects to be properly trained.

그러니까 모든 건축가가 똑바로 교육을 받는 것이 얼마나 중요한지 알 수 있을 것이다.

[It is ~ for A to …]는 'A가 … 하는 것은 ~하다'를 의미한다. It is important for all architects to be properly trained(모든 건축가들이 적절하게 교육받는 것이 중요하다)란 문장이 목적절의 원래 형태인데, how important(얼마나 중요한지)를 강조하기 위해 간접 의문문 형태를 취한 것이다.

p.247

If you've ever tried to carry some tall glasses on a tray one-handed like a waiter, you'll know how tricky it is to balance them.

웨이터처럼 쟁반에 긴 잔들을 얹어서 한 손으로 옮겨 본 적이 있다면, 균형을 잡는 것이 얼마나 어려운지 알 것이다.

one handed like a waiter는 '웨이터처럼 한 손으로 (들고)'를 뜻한다.
how tricky it is to balance them은 know의 목적어로, '그것들을 균형을 맞추는 게 얼마나 어려운지'를 뜻한다.

p.248

Like columns, arches are great because the harder you push down on them the more they push back.

기둥처럼 아치도 훌륭한데, 그 이유는 밑으로 세게 누를수록 더 많이 밀어내기 때문이다.

전치사 like는 '~처럼, ~와 비슷하게'를 뜻한다. 이유를 표현하는 because 이하의 문장은 '~할수록 더 …하다'를 뜻하는 [the 비교급, the 비교급] 형태를 취하고 있다. 따라서 the harder ~ push back은 '아치를 누를수록 더 많이 밀어낸다'로 해석할 수 있다.

11. Build Or Bust

p.249

> Engineers reckoned that the shock waves from years of ringing the bells at the top had brought on the destruction.
>
> 엔지니어들은 수년간 꼭대기에서 종을 울리면서 발생한 충격파가 파괴를 일으켰다고 추측했다.

목적절 that 이하의 문장에서 주어는 the shock waves ~ at the top이다. shock waves는 '충격파'고, from years ~ at the top은 '꼭대기에서 오랫동안 종을 치면서 발생한'을 뜻한다.
bring on에는 '~을 초래하다, 야기하다, 발생시키다'는 의미가 있다.

p.251

> That takes a bit of foresight but sometimes it pays to plan the crossing of your bridges before you come to them.
>
> 그러려면 예견이 조금 필요하지만, 때로는 다리에 가기 전에 미리 다리를 건너는 것을 계획해 두면 도움이 된다.

That takes a bit of foresight는 '그건 약간의 예견이 필요하다'로 해석할 수 있다. foresight는 미리 짐작하고 예상하는 것을 말한다.
이 문장에서 동사 pay는 '돈을 지불한다'는 의미가 아니라, '이익(도움)이 되다, 보람이 있다'를 뜻하는 자동사로 쓴 것이다.

p.251

> The damage is done because shock waves make the walls vibrate so violently that the building falls down.
>
> 충격파가 벽을 너무 격렬하게 진동시켰고 그래서 건물이 무너져 피해가 발생한다.

The damage is done은 '피해가 발생했다, 손상이 가해졌다'를 뜻한다.
벽이 너무도 격하게(so violently) 진동한 결과는 that 이하 문장 the building falls down(건물이 무너진다)이다.

p.253

Perhaps all those hundreds of feet stomping up and down the corridors has triggered vicious vibrations that have fatally weakened the building.

아마도 회랑을 쿵쿵거리며 오르내리는 그 많은 발들이 극심한 진동을 일으켰고 그래서 건물을 치명적으로 약화시켰을 것이다.

all those hundreds of feet은 '그 수백 개의 발들 모두'로 해석할 수 있다. stomping up and down the corridors(회랑을 쿵쿵거리며 오르내리는)가 feet을 수식한다.
trigger는 명사로 '방아쇠'를 뜻하는데, 동사로 쓰면 방아쇠를 당겨 총을 쏘듯이 '~을 일으키다, 유발하다, 작동시키다'를 뜻한다.

p.255

Place explosive charges around the building and weaken the supporting beams so they collapse easily.

건물을 빙 둘러서 폭발물을 설치하고 지지대를 약화시켜 쉽게 붕괴되게 한다.

명령문 형태로, 두 개의 동사를 써서 행동을 요구하고 있다. 앞의 place는 '놓다, 두다, 설치하다'를 뜻하고, 뒤의 weaken은 '약화시키다, 약하게 만들다'를 뜻한다.
이 문장에서 so는 결과를 이끄는 접속사다.

CHAPTER 12 KEYWORDS

#gravity #accelerator #graviton #sky-surfing

May The Forces Be With You

Forces were around long before we got here. And although we try to use forces – in the end we can't control them. We can only forecast what forces might do to new buildings or cars. And although designers make fatal mistakes, these embarrassing slip-ups are thankfully rare.

Meanwhile, physicists are making more brain-boggling discoveries about forces. Before Galileo and Newton, no one knew how forces worked. Today we know more about them than ever. And because forces affect so much of our world, they pop up in every area of scientific knowledge.

Take atoms, for example. Scientists are probing how forces hold an atom together. (Atoms are the tiny bits of matter that make up everything in the universe.) The trick is to smash the atoms together in awesome machines called accelerators tens of kilometres long. Then you sift the debris for clues. If you're a scientist it sometimes pays to think small, ha ha.

Forces also come into space travel. To plan a little trip around the solar system you need to know how a planet's gravity will pull your craft. And you need to be sure what happens when you whizz round a planet and zoom off into the depths of space. So you'll be needing an advanced computer to cope with the necessary maths.

Other physicists are looking into how gravity itself works. Are there really tiny things, even smaller than atoms, called gravitons that are somehow involved? And once scientists have found this out, could they perhaps defeat gravity and make planes that hover effortlessly in the air?

And even if we don't crack this one – there's always something new. Like a really wacky new sport. Take sky-surfing, for example. To do this you have to be seriously off your trolley. It involves

jumping from an aeroplane strapped to a board. You enjoy some mid-air acrobatics before your parachute opens – assuming it does.

But one thing is certain – humans will go on pushing forces to their limits and scientists will go on studying how forces work. After all there may be limits to our knowledge, but our curiosity knows no bounds. Yep. You're forced to admit it. Forces are horribly intriguing. Fatally fascinating. But that's Horrible Science for you!

REVIEW

지금까지 물리의 세계에 다양한 형태로 존재하는 힘에 대해 많은 것을 배웠다. 에너지, 힘, 운동, 질량, 무게 등의 개념과 상호 관계, 그리고 그것들이 우리의 삶에 미치는 영향에 대해서도 많이 느꼈을 것이다. 시험을 잘 보려면 공부를 열심히 해야 하고, 공부를 열심히 하려면 힘이 있어야 하고, 힘이 있으려면 에너지가 충만해야 한다. 결국 에너지를 채우는 것이 가장 중요하다. 그러니 엄마한테 충분한 수면과 고기 반찬을 보장해 줄 것을 당당하게 요구하자!

Vocabulary 12

p.266

We can only **forecast** what forces might do to new buildings or cars.

우리는 새 건물이나 자동차에 어떤 힘이 영향을 작용할지 예측할 수 있을 뿐이다.

forecast fore는 '미리, 앞서(before)'를 의미하고, cast는 '준비, 계획'을 의미한다. 어떤 일이나 행사를 계획하고 준비하는 사람은 앞으로 일어날 일에 대해 상당히 많이 알고 있다. 그래서 **forecast**는 '예측하다, 예보하다'를 뜻하는 동사, '예측, 예보'를 뜻하는 명사로 쓴다. '일기 예보'가 weather **forecast**다.

p.266

And although designers make fatal mistakes, these **embarrassing** slip-ups are thankfully rare.

또한 설계자들이 치명적인 실수를 저지르기는 하지만, 감사하게도 이런 창피한 실수는 드물다.

embarrassing 학교 운동장에서 갑자기 우당탕 넘어지거나, 선생님이 학급에서 내 시험 점수(30점)를 큰소리로 외치시거나, 커닝하다가 들키면 얼굴이 벌게지며 식은땀이 나고 어딘가로 숨고 싶다. '부끄럼, 창피, 수치' 등의 감정을 담고 있는 말이 **embarrass**다. 속어인 '쪽팔리다'로 표현하자면, **embarrass**는 '쪽팔리게 만들다'를 뜻하는 동사, **embarrassing**은 '쪽팔리게 만드는', **embarrassed**는 '쪽팔리는'을 뜻하는 형용사, **embarrassment**는 '쪽팔림'을 뜻하는 명사다.

12. May The Forces Be With You

269

p.268

You enjoy some mid-air **acrobatics** before your parachute opens – assuming it does.

낙하산이 펴지기 전에 공중 곡예를 조금 즐긴다. 낙하산이 펴지리라 믿으며.

acrobatics 서커스에서 밧줄을 타거나 공중제비를 넘는 묘기다. 명사 **acrobat**에서 acro는 높은 곳의 '꼭대기, 끝'를 의미하고, bat는 '걷다'를 의미한다. 절벽이나 높은 곳에 매단 밧줄 위를 걸으며 사람들이 가슴 졸이게 하는 '곡예사'가 **acrobat**다. 형용사 **acrobatic**은 '곡예의, 재주 부리는'을 뜻하고, 명사 **acrobatics**는 '곡예, 아슬아슬한 재주, 묘기'를 뜻한다.

p.268

Forces are horribly **intriguing**.

힘은 소름끼칠 정도로 흥미롭다.

intriguing '속임수(trick), 음모'를 뜻하는 말에서 온 단어가 intrigue다. 복잡한 마술, 추리 소설의 스토리 전개 등을 intrigue로 표현할 수 있다. 동사로 '강한 호기심과 흥미를 불러일으키다, 음모를 꾸미다'를 뜻하고 명사로 '흥미진진, 음모' 등을 뜻한다. 형용사 **intriguing**은 '매우 흥미로운, 기묘한'을 뜻한다.

Sentence 11

p.267

The trick is to smash the atoms together in awesome machines called accelerators tens of kilometers long.

비결은 길이가 수십 킬로미터에 달하는 가속기라는 멋진 기계 안에서 원자들을 함께 충돌시키는 것이다.

문장의 보어 역할을 하는 to smash the atoms together는 '원자를 전부 깨뜨리는 것이다'

라는 뜻이다.
accelerator는 '가속기'인데, 전자나 양성자 등의 '입자'를 자기장에서 가속시키는 기계를 '입자 가속기(particle accelerator)'라고 부른다. 충분한 가속도가 필요하기 때문에 '길이가 수십 킬로미터(tens of kilometers long)'에 달한다.

p.267

> And once scientists have found this out, could they perhaps defeat gravity and make planes that hover effortlessly in the air?
> 그리고 일단 과학자들이 이것을 찾아내면, 중력을 거스르고 공중에서 아무런 노력 없이도 떠다니는 비행기를 만들 수 있을까?

문장을 이끄는 접속사 once는 '일단 ~하게 되면, ~하자마자'를 뜻한다.
중력(gravity)을 패배시킨다(defeat)는 것은 중력의 영향에서 벗어난다는 의미다. 따라서 defeat gravity는 '중력을 극복하다'로 해석할 수 있다.

p.268

> After all there may be limits to our knowledge, but our curiosity knows no bounds.
> 결국 우리의 지식에는 한계가 있을 수 있지만, 우리 호기심에는 한계가 없다.

부사구인 after all은 '결국, 어쨌든'을 뜻한다.
limit, bound 모두 '한계, 경계'를 뜻하는 명사다. our curiosity knows no bounds는 '우리의 호기심은 한계를 모른다', 즉 '호기심에 한계가 없다'는 의미다.

우리가 알아낼 수 있는 물리학의 비밀은 백사장의 모래만큼이나 많다고! 설레지 않니?

FATAL FORCES

QUIZ

Now find out if you're a **Fatal Forces** expert!

To be a Horrible Scientist you need more than horrible habits. As every genuine genius knows you need brainpower too. The question is, having read this book have you got what it takes upstairs? (Don't decide until you've got to grips with this queasy quiz!)

Fun forces (these are the basic bits that even a teacher ought to know!)

Before we see if you really can be a Horrible Scientist and test your knowledge of fatal forces, let's see if you've understood the basics. Match the forces below with their mysterious meanings and effects.

1. Mass
2. Velocity
3. Acceleration
4. Friction
5. Energy
6. Momentum
7. Vibrations
8. Work

a. Changing speed or direction
b. The ability to do work

ACTUALLY, THE GARDEN COULD DO WITH A DROP OF RAIN

- **c** Keeps an object in motion
- **d** The amount of matter contained in an object
- **e** When a force causes an object to move a distance
- **f** Speed in a single direction
- **g** Carry force of impact away from an object
- **h** Slows moving objects

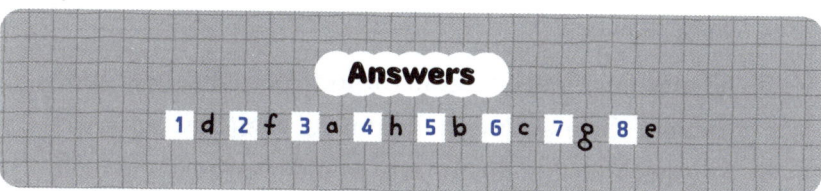

Answers
1 d 2 f 3 a 4 h 5 b 6 c 7 g 8 e

Fantastic forces quiz

So – reckon you've got the measure of forceful forces? Take this quick quiz and find out if you could truly be a freaky physicist…

1 Isaac Newton began investigating the force known as gravity when something fell out of a tree and hit him on the head. What was it?
- **a** An apple
- **b** A pear
- **c** A tomato

2 What would your terminal velocity be if you fell out of an aeroplane?
- **a** 9.8 metres a second
- **b** 50 metres a second
- **c** No one has been brave enough to try this experiment.

FASCINATING!

3 **Why don't smooth golf balls fly as straight as pitted ones?**
   a Smooth things naturally move in curves.
   b The pits create turbulence on the surface so fly better.
   c The pits trap flies rather than allowing the flies to bump the ball off-course.

4 **Why would a perpetual motion machine break the Second Law of Thermodynamics?**
   a All machines lose energy in the form of sound, heat and friction. The machine would run out of energy.
   b Any machine that ran for ever would over-heat and melt.
   c A perpetual motion machine would be bound to run out of spare parts sooner or later.

5 **Which of the following can be defined by gravity?**

   a The force of attraction between two cars
   b The force of attraction between two tennis balls
   c The force of attraction between two people in love.

6 **How heavy is the Moon (to the nearest few kilograms)?**
   a 73,490,000,000,000,000 million kg
   b 1.5 kg
   c 597,420,000,000,000,000,000 million kg

7 **How does living in space affect the size of an astronaut?**
   a He grows several centimeters.
   b He shrinks a few centimeters.
   c He doubles in size.

> **Answers**
> 1 a 2 b 3 b 4 a 5 — all of the above
> (every object with mass has a gravitational pull) 6 a 7 a 8 a

8 What kind of apple did Isaac Newton get hit on the head with?
   a) Flower of Kent
   b) Allington Pippin
   c) Golden Delicious

Force fact or fiction

There are still many misleading myths about fatal forces. Can you figure out which of these silly statements are totally true and which are forcefully false?

1 Archimedes managed to move an entire ship by himself using a pulley system.

2 The longbows used in medieval times were capable of firing an arrow further than a kilometre.

3 In 1996 Bryan Berg built a card tower 13.96 metres high.

4 The furthest a man has been fired out of a cannon using an explosive charge is 87.5 metres.

5 It is possible to create fire by rubbing two sticks together.

6 False. Because the Earth bulges out slightly at the Equator it is further from the centre. This makes the gravitational pull a tiny bit weaker than at the poles.

7 The pressure you would feel at the deepest point of the ocean is equivalent to two men standing on your head.

8 Water can be made to boil at 40° Celsius.

Answers

1 True.

2 False. The arrow could only travel 320 metres — but that was still far enough to injure an enemy before he got to you!

3 False. Bryan's card tower was only 5.85 metres high. Mind you, that's quite a height if you were on top of it.

4 False. To propel a human cannon ball they don't use explosives — they use a very strong spring!

5 True. The friction creates enough heat for it to start to smoke. And where there's smoke there's fire···

6 True. Because the Earth bulges out slightly at the Equator it is further from the centre and this makes the gravitational pull a bit weaker at the poles.

7 False. It's the equivalent of an average person balancing 48 jumbo jets on their head!

8 True. If the pressure is low enough, the water will boil.

Speed, pressure and temperature

You can't escape forces on Earth – or even in space! Speed, pressure and temperature and three of the effects of forceful forces that physicists find fearfully fascinating. But how much do you know about them?

1. How much gravity is there at the centre of the Earth? *(Clue: It's nothing to worry about.)*

2. Why do super-speedy cyclist wear funny-shaped helmets? *(Clue: Oh, what's the point?!)*

3. What happens to your lungs as you diver deep under water *(Clue: Take a deep breath now)*

4. What would happen if you accelerated at a force of 9 g? *(Clue: This one's dead easy)*

5. Why did American cars have cow catchers? *(Clue: think of a flying cow)*

6. Where was the lowest temperature recorded on Earth? *(Clue: Don't go "Russian" into this answer)*

7. Is the acceleration due to gravity on the Moon more or less powerful than it is on Earth? *(Clue: Floating free)*

8. A person standing in high heels on a floor exerts a massive pressure on a small point. How many elephants would pressure be equivalent to? *(Clue: It'd be standing on tiptoe…)*

Answers

1. None. The force of gravity doesn't exist at the Earth's centre — but you don't really want to go there to see if I'm right!
2. The pointed front on the helmet makes the air move around them rather than bumping into them and slowing them down.
3. They get squashed — more and more so as the pressure increases the deeper you go.
4. A force of 4 to 6 g managed for only a few seconds before you'd pass out (or your eyes would start to bleed). At 9 g you'd be dead!
5. They scooped buffalo out of the way of the train.
6. It was recorded in Russia — a bone-chilling -89.4°C.
7. Less. The gravitational pull on the surface of the Moon is 1.62 metres per second squared. This is only about one-sixth of that on Earth.
8. Just one — but it would be standing on one foot!

Freaky physicists

Over the years, strange scientists have conducted many evil experiments and come up with hundreds of ingenious inventions to learn about fatal forces. Can you identify the freaky physicist by what they might have said?

1. "Ow! That will leave a bump!"
2. "Can I have my balls back please?"
3. "Everyone thinks I'm full of hot air!"
4. "I've been under a lot of pressure recently."
5. "I'm in the swing of it"
6. "This invention really sucks!"
7. "Pass me that screw, will you?"
8. "You spin me right round… la la la."

a. Blaise Pascal
b. Otto von Guericke
c. Isaac Newton
d. George Ferris
e. Archimedes
f. Galileo Galilei
g. Jean Foucault
h. Isambard Kingdom Brunel

Answers

1. c) Isaac Newton discovered gravity when an apple fell on his head.
2. f) Galileo used balls to experiment with gravity.
3. a) Pascal invented the barometer – a device to measure air pressure.
4. h) Among other things, Brunel invented a train that was powered by atmospheric pressure.
5. g) Foucault did some amazing experiments with his pendulum.
6. b) Von Guericke invented the vacuum pump.
7. e) Ancient Archimedes invented the machine known as the screw or screwpump.
8. d) Ferris invented the Ferris wheel – well, what did you think he invented the mini-roundabout?

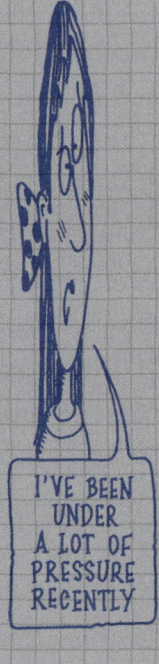

I'VE BEEN UNDER A LOT OF PRESSURE RECENTLY

INDEX

· A ·	
acceleration	50, 57
aerodynamic	66, 79
air pressure	118, 119, 121, 123, 124, 131, 135, 211
airbags	72
aircraft	73
Alexander the Great (king of Macedonia)	45
apple	18, 19, 20, 27, 33, 34
archery	168, 175
arches	248, 263
Archimedes (Greek inventor)	230-1
architects (building designers)	246, 247, 263
Aristotle (Greek philosopher)	44-6, 54-5, 59
atoms	130, 266, 267, 270

· B ·	
back-spin	211

balance 46, 47
balls 109, 209, 213-7, 221, 224
barometers 119, 131
barriers 73-4, 82
bicycles (bikes) 63, 78, 104, 112, 144, 232-3, 235
Blondin, Jean (French tightrope walker) 103-4
bolas (two balls on a rope) 182-3, 199
bouncing 51, 61, 144, 209
bows 169-170, 175, 179
bridges 244-5, 247, 251, 258, 264
Brunel, Isambard Kingdom (English engineer) 125-6, 247
Brunel, Marc (Isambard's dad) 247
buildings 64, 69, 191-2, 202, 235, 243-4, 246-9, 251, 253-5, 258-262, 264-6, 269
bullies 27, 42, 48

INDEX 283

bungee jumpers 168
buttresses 249

· C ·

calculus 18, 29, 42
canals 46, 60
cards 103-4, 111, 141-2, 278
cars 67, 69, 82, 180, 184, 204, 235, 266, 269
cats 91
centrifugal force 57, 183, 186, 189
centrifuges 188
centripetal force 16, 57, 181-4, 186, 188
chemistry 21, 28, 37,
chicle (tree sap) 209
coins 20, 28-9, 42, 103, 180-1, 195, 198, 204
Colechurch, Peter (British architect) 244
columns 248, 258, 263
cornering 50
corsets 168, 174, 178
cow catchers 67, 79
crumple zones 72

· D ·

Da Vinci, Leonardo (Italian artist/scientist) 228
dams 246
demolition jobs 253, 260
domes 191, 202, 213, 248
door hinges 227, 240
drag 15, 38, 50, 61, 66, 91, 149, 211
drink 120-1, 123, 136

· E ·

earthquakes 251
Einstein, Albert (German-born physicist) 189, 201
elastic bands 163-6, 173-4, 177
electrical equipment 141
energy (ability to do work) 24, 39, 52-3, 56, 58, 144-5, 156, 163-5, 169, 173, 177-8
engineers 69, 72, 80, 124-8, 137, 147, 149, 247, 249, 262, 264
equator 188
executions 28, 38, 92
experiments 17, 28, 32, 37, 96-7, 122, 132, 191
explosions 10, 75, 170, 261
eyeballs 51, 61, 121, 135, 168

· F ·

Ferris, George (American showman) 184, 205
fires 67, 92, 98, 123, 128, 141, 143, 169-170, 178-9
First Law of Thermodynamics 145
Foucault, Jean Bernard Léon (French physicist) 191, 195-6
foundations 247, 258
freefall parachuting 90-1
friction 51, 57, 61, 128, 138-143, 145-6, 148, 150, 154, 160-1, 164, 166, 185, 188-9
frisbees 195
fulcrum (turning point) 227-9, 237

· G ·

Galileo Galilei (Italian scientist) 95-8, 101, 109, 111, 117, 190, 201, 216, 221, 247, 266
gears 51, 218, 223, 226, 232, 235, 239
George III (British king) 139
grasshoppers 45, 59
gravitons 267
gravity 9-10, 12, 14, 16, 20, 24-5, 28, 34-5, 41, 47, 49, 60, 75-7, 87, 89-96, 98, 101-2, 105
Guericke, Otto von (German scientist) 122
guillotines 93
gyroscopes 195-6

· H ·

hands 145, 148, 170, 215-6, 224
hanging 92, 107, 164, 168

heat	49, 60, 123, 140-5, 156, 160, 165
heresy	100, 110
Hieron II (king of Syracuse)	230
homework	10-1, 18, 21, 52-3, 215, 226, 240
Hooke, Robert (English scientist)	28, 163-4, 173
horizon	196, 203, 214
hula-hoops	195
hydraulics	123, 132

· I ·

indigestion	45, 59, 119, 131
inertia	47, 50, 55, 67-8, 80, 85, 142, 186, 195, 226
Inquisition	100-1, 110-1

· J ·

juggling	214-6, 218, 221

· K ·

kinetic energy (used when moving)	49, 56
knicker	168

· L ·

labs	186, 200
laws	9-10, 12, 24-7, 35, 42, 50, 67, 119, 144-5, 164, 173, 197, 230, 248
legs	91, 167, 170, 215, 228, 231, 240
Leibniz, Gottfried (German philosopher)	29, 42
levers	226-230, 235, 237
lift	68, 95, 123, 132, 144, 148, 150, 161, 211, 229-230, 238, 241
light	18, 143, 188, 191, 217, 249, 253, 258
Locke, John (English philosopher)	27
lubrication	145-6, 157

· M ·

Mach, Ernst (Austrian physicists)	73
machines	17, 52, 119, 123, 128, 131-2, 142-5, 156, 160, 163, 165-6, 177, 180, 185, 188, 218, 226, 230-1, 233, 235, 239-240, 250, 267, 270
mass	8-9, 48, 76, 95, 222
mathematics	8, 22, 34
mechanics	163, 226
molecules	118, 130
momentum	48, 51, 56, 66-7, 85, 180-1, 184, 195, 197, 254
moon	18, 20, 33, 95
moose	67, 85
motionn	44-5, 52, 143-5, 156, 251
mousetraps	170

· N ·

nails	94, 108
Napoleon III	192, 194
navigate	196
Newton, Isaac (English scientist)	17-8, 20-30, 34-40, 42, 44, 46, 50, 67, 98, 101, 116, 138, 163, 188, 200, 248, 266
Newton's First Law	24, 50, 67
Newton's Second Law	25
Newton's Third Law	26-7, 42, 248
Newtons (units of force)	26, 119

· O ·

obelisks	147-150

· P ·

padding	212
parachutes	75, 77, 83, 90-2, 113, 268, 270
Pascal, Blaise (French physicist)	119
Pascals (units of pressure)	118-9
Pauli, Wolfgang (Austrian-born physicist)	195
pedals	47-8, 51, 233-4, 239
pendulums	16-7, 31, 98, 110, 187-8, 190-1, 200, 207
Philip (king of Macedonia)	45
The Philosophiae Naturalis Principia Mathematica (Newton's book)	23

physicists	52-3, 62, 67, 73, 80, 118, 141, 143, 155-6, 195, 208, 266-7
physics	9, 12, 18, 32, 52, 144, 156, 195
pistons	123, 125, 132
plague	18
planes	73-4, 76, 90, 92, 119, 135, 196, 235, 267, 271
planets	49, 64-5, 98, 101, 110, 117, 267
Plato (Greek philosopher)	44
Poe, Edgar Alan (American author)	16
potential energy	52
precession	196, 203
pressure	105, 118-124, 126, 130-1, 133, 135, 211, 223
pulleys	226, 229, 230-1, 235, 238, 241
pyramids	29

· R ·

racks	100, 167, 174, 178, 232
railways	63, 67, 124-6, 128
relaxing	216, 235
resistance	226
rotors	187

· S ·

safety belts	53, 69-71
Sarafian, Bruce (American juggler)	217, 222
savings	126, 128, 137, 150, 226
Schrödinger, Erwin (Austrian physicist)	189
scientists	9, 16, 21, 27-9, 43-4, 46, 48-52, 56-61, 76, 95, 98, 101, 109, 117, 119, 163, 168, 171, 176, 186, 189, 191, 195-6, 210-1, 226, 228, 266-8, 271
seat belts	72
Second Law of Thermodynamics	144-5
see-saws	228
shape	44, 59, 66-7, 79, 84, 168, 170-1, 174, 176, 213, 246, 248, 250, 258
ships	124, 146, 150, 157, 185, 196, 206, 230-1, 241

shock waves	51, 249, 251, 264
skin	19, 33, 143, 148, 152, 213
skyscrapers	248
slugs (American units of mass)	94-5, 109
Smeaton, John (English inventor)	196
snow	92, 114, 142-3
sound	29, 42, 44, 52-4, 65, 69, 73-4, 82, 85, 145, 147-8, 171, 184, 199, 232, 242
space	20, 34, 46, 60, 64-5, 89, 98, 112, 116, 121, 135, 205, 215, 267
spanners	143, 156, 226
speed	9, 14, 24-5, 35-6, 47-8, 50, 53, 56-7, 63-6, 69, 73-8, 80, 82, 86, 91, 98, 143, 183, 191, 197, 211, 214, 220, 223, 232
spinning	68, 171, 180-1, 186, 195-6, 204, 209, 222
sports	145, 171, 209, 210, 212
springs	51, 164, 170, 176-7, 235
squirrels	91
steam engines	125, 127, 235
strain	75, 148-150, 158
stretching	163-4, 168, 173, 175

· T ·

teachers	10-1, 14, 17, 21, 23, 45, 46, 54, 63, 95, 115, 121, 139, 163, 167, 178, 186, 188-9, 209, 229, 237, 248, 253
teeth	119, 212, 232
telescopes	98-9, 101, 110, 163
tennis	171, 210-1
tension	149, 158, 163
test dummies	69-71
thermodynamics (heat/energy science)	144-5, 156
thermometers	98, 110
Thompson, Benjamin (American scientist/spy)	139, 141, 155
top spin	211
torque (turning force)	226
towers	96, 109, 247-9, 259

toys	21, 93, 195, 208
trainers	171
trains	63, 67, 79, 123-4, 136, 171, 176, 184, 235, 246, 263
treadmills	171, 176, 185, 206
tree sap	214
triangles	248
tricks	19, 67, 142, 195, 267, 270
turbulence	210-1, 214, 219-220

· V ·

vacuums	121-3, 125, 127, 131
Vanderbilt, Cornelius (American tycoon)	123
velocity	48-9, 56, 90-1, 106-7, 211
vibrations	51, 58, 250-1, 253, 265

· W ·

water pressure	118, 121, 244-6
weight	17, 27, 67, 75-6, 87, 93-5, 102, 108-9, 114, 117, 119, 164, 177, 217, 225, 229, 238, 247-8, 253-4, 258, 262
Westinghouse, George (American inventor)	123
wheels	21, 46, 51, 69, 81-2, 86, 104, 112, 142, 144, 154, 161, 180-1, 184-5, 188, 196, 198, 204-5, 229-230, 232, 235, 242
whirlpools	197
wind	47, 50, 61, 77, 83, 144, 166, 174, 247, 258
work (force making objects move)	44, 49, 52-3, 58, 62, 95, 143, 156, 181-3, 188, 195-6, 218, 226-8, 232, 266-8

· Y ·

Yeager, Charles (American pilot)	73
yo-yos	195

지소철

성균관대학교 영어영문학과를 졸업하고 Sungkyunkwan-Gorgetown University의 TESOL 과정을 이수했다. 영어를 보다 재미있게 공부하는 학습법, 영어를 효과적으로 가르치는 교수법 둘 다에 몰두하면서 영어책 저자, 번역가, 도서 기획자로서 영어와 함께하는 삶을 살아왔다. 《플로이드의 오래된 집》《해적과 제왕》《제국의 몰락》《아르마다》 등 100여 권의 책을 번역했고 《행복한 영어 초등학교》《보카 출생의 비밀》《세계 역사 이야기 영어 리딩 훈련》 시리즈, 《영어를 공부하는 이유》《영어 줄임말의 힘》《수능에 가장 많이 나오는 고교 영단어 300》《중학대비 영단어 넥스트레벨》 등 다수의 영어 학습서를 저술했다. 그동안의 영어 학습서 집필 노하우를 살려 이 책의 영단어와 구문을 해설했다. 관심 있는 분야의 원서를 많이 읽는 것, 이것이 그가 제안하는 영어 정복의 지름길이다.

Horrible Science
Fatal Forces

펴낸날 초판 1쇄 2025년 9월 23일
지은이 닉 아놀드, 지소철
그린이 토니 드 솔스
펴낸이 이주애, 홍영완
편집장 최혜리
월북주니어 도건홍, 이은일, 한수정
편집 박효주, 홍은비, 강민우, 안형욱, 김혜원, 송현근, 최서영, 이소연
디자인 기조숙, 김주연, 박정원, 윤소정, 박소현
홍보마케팅 박영채, 김태윤, 김준영, 백지혜
콘텐츠 양혜영, 이태은, 조유진
해외기획 정수림
경영지원 박소현
펴낸곳 (주)윌북 **출판등록** 제2006-000017호
주소 04001 서울특별시 마포구 동교로19길 28
전화 02-323-3777 **팩스** 02-323-3778
홈페이지 willbookspub.com
블로그 blog.naver.com/willbooks
트위터 @onwillbooks **인스타그램** @willbooks_pub | @willbooks_jr
ISBN 979-11-5581-861-9 (73740)

- 책값은 뒤표지에 있습니다.
- 잘못 만들어진 책은 구입하신 서점에서 바꿔드립니다.
- 이 책의 내용은 저작권자의 허가 없이 AI 트레이닝에 사용할 수 없습니다.

 월북주니어는 월북의 어린이책 브랜드입니다